Pensions Under Attack

What's behind the Push to
Privatize Public Pensions

Monica Townson

Co-published by
Canadian Centre for Policy Alternatives and
James Lorimer & Company Ltd., Publishers

James Lorimer & Company Ltd. acknowledges the support of the Ontario Arts Council. We acknowledge the support of the Government of Canada through the Book Publishing Industry Development Program (BPIDP) for our publishing activities. We acknowledge the support of the Canada Council for the Arts for our publishing program.

Canadian Cataloguing in Publication Data

Townson, Monica, 1932-
Pensions under attack: what's behind the push to privatize public pensions

Co-published by the Canadian Centre for Policy Alternatives.
Includes index.
ISBN 1-55028-694-3

1. Canada Pension Plan. I. Canadian Centre for Policy Alternatives. II. Title.

HD7105.35.C3T678 2000   368.4'3'00971   C00-930192-5

Printed and bound in Canada

Canadian Centre for Policy Alternatives
410-75 Albert Street, Ottawa ON K1P 5E7
Tel 613-563-1341   Fax 613-233-1458
www.policyalternatives.ca   ccpa@policyalternatives.ca

James Lorimer & Company Ltd., Publishers
35 Britain Street
Toronto ON M5A 1R7

Table of Contents

Preface and acknowledgements

Everyone is concerned about pensions. Older people worry whether they'll have enough to live on when they retire; younger people wonder when they should start saving for their old age. And everyone wants to know if they can count on public pension programs being there when they need them. It's not surprising that, when the population is aging, people ask if we will be able to afford to look after our older citizens in the way we used to.

Pensions for an aging population were the subject of heated debate throughout the 1990s. Long-established programs like Old Age Security and the Guaranteed Income Supplement were almost sacrificed on the altar of deficit reduction. In the end, they were saved by an improvement in government finances as deficits turned into surpluses. But, after a round of public consultations and discussions, changes were made in the Canada Pension Plan, intended to preserve it as a social insurance program for the foreseeable future. Contribution rates were increased, some benefits were reduced, and an investment fund was established. That fund is now being invested in the stock market for the first time.

But critics of the public pension system say the reforms didn't go far enough. They would like to see the CPP replaced with individual savings accounts—whether as a mandatory replacement for the public plan or as a voluntary arrangement which would allow people to opt out of the CPP and have their contributions directed to their own individual savings accounts instead. Such a move would do away with collective responsibility for and to our older citizens, which has been the fundamental basis for Canada's social programs. Instead, individuals would be expected to provide for themselves: to sink or swim in the maelstrom of "free markets." Other countries have tried it—often with disastrous results.

What's behind the push to get rid of public pension programs in favour of private savings schemes? Why are neoliberal commentators and think-tanks warning of a "demographic time bomb" and a "war between the generations"? Is there a hidden agenda at work here? This book looks at the ongoing attack on public pensions, to see who is promoting it, and why. It considers what happened in countries such as Chile and Britain, where public pensions have been privatized; and in the United States where privatization of Social Security has been on the policy radar for some time and where it figured prominently in the recent presidential election. And we'll see who is still pushing for privatization of the CPP and what might happen if they succeed.

So as not to distract readers with footnotes and other citations, I have listed the sources of quotations and statements in a separate section of Notes at the end of the book. My thanks go to Bruce Campbell of the Canadian Centre for Policy Alternatives for his encouragement and support, to Ed Finn for his valuable editorial input, and to everyone else in the Ottawa office of CCPA who helped in the editing and production of the book.

I am also grateful to Mike McCracken of Informetrica for generously providing economic projections; to Michel Montambeault of the Chief Actuary's office, for calculations and advice on Canada/U.S. comparisons; and to Maarten Cornet, of the Netherlands Bureau for Economic Policy Analysis in The Hague, for arranging my interviews in the Netherlands. Responsibility for the opinions expressed in the book, and for any errors or omissions is mine alone.

Monica Townson
Toronto
November 2000

Chapter 1
Why are public pensions under attack?

Everyone knows we have an aging population. In fact, we've known about it for years. But just lately, cries of alarm and panic have been getting louder. The World Bank warns of an "aging crisis;" the pension industry talks of a "demographic time bomb;" there are even threats of an "age war over pensions" as younger people rise up against the elderly.

The warlike language is enough to strike terror into the hearts of responsible citizens—not to mention anyone who's wondering if they'll have enough to live on when it comes time to settle into old age. Can we afford our aging population? It's no wonder people are feeling increasingly uneasy about their future when that's the kind of question they hear.

Why the panic? Are we really facing chaos and destruction as the "wrinklies" take over our cities and countryside? Maybe it's time to step back and shine the light of reason on some of the hysteria and hyperbole. Who is whipping up the panic, and why? What's behind the attack on pensions? Who stands to gain if governments renege on their commitment to social security and public pensions, leaving the coming generation of seniors to fend for themselves?

This book is an attempt to answer those questions. It will defuse the demographic time bomb and expose the phony crisis of population aging. It will discuss how the "aging crisis" is being used as a cover to implement a political agenda. In particular, it will take a cold, hard look at some of the proposals now being put forward to get rid of social security and public pension programs, replacing them with privatized saving schemes.

We'll see what happened in countries like Chile and Britain that have already taken that step. We'll follow the debate on privatizing Social Security in the United States.

We'll see why people are suggesting we get rid of the Canada Pension Plan, and we'll talk about what they'd like to put in its place. Finally, we'll see why we should resist the attack on public pensions and how we can do it.

The demographic time bomb

Population aging is really nothing new. It's been going on for several decades, and it's something almost all industrialized countries now face. But what exactly is it? It's not just that everyone is getting older and people are living longer than they used to. Population aging simply means that an increasing percentage of a country's population will be senior citizens. For Canada, it's a process that will happen gradually over the next 50 years or so.

At the beginning of the 1990s, the over-65s accounted for just over 11% of Canada's total population. By the middle of this new century, almost one-quarter of our population may be over 65.

Like everything else, population aging is a phenomenon we like to blame on the baby-boomers. That's the generation born between 1947 and 1966 in the days when women typically had three or four children. As this big generation starts to retire, from about 2010 to about 2030, grey power may really come into its own—at least, that's the way some people see it.

Canadians are living longer than ever before. In the 1950s, a woman at age 65 could expect to live another 15 years; a man's life expectancy at that age was just over 13 years. Now, women at age 65 have an average life expectancy of just over 20 years, while men who get to age 65 can expect to live another 16 years, on average.

But living longer is not the reason our population is aging. Blame it on the birth control pill, which made its appearance in 1961 and helped fuel big changes in society. Women stopped having as many children. Of course, the pill wasn't the only reason: society no longer expected married women to stay home when they had children, and women went into the paid work force in record numbers. The women's movement, arguably the most important social movement of the 1960s, was fighting for women's equality.

To use the technical jargon, the fertility rate dropped. From an average of about 3.9 children each in 1959, women now have only one or two children, averaging out to 1.55 each. It's the lowest fertility rate ever recorded in Canada. As one demographer puts it, "population aging is the unplanned byproduct of planned parenthood." Since the baby boom generation had smaller families, the baby boom was followed by the "baby bust"—people born between 1967 and 1979. Fewer children in the generations following the baby boom is the main reason our population is aging.

Some countries are already much further down this road. In many European countries, for instance, the over-60s were well over 20% of the population in 1990. Canada is not expected to reach that stage for quite some time—about 25 years after countries like Greece, Italy, Germany, and the Nordic countries. That's the first thing to remember: population aging hasn't happened overnight, and it's not a surprise.

Between 1950 and 1990, for instance, the number of over-65s in Canada tripled. If the projections are right, it will take another 40 years for the elderly population to triple again. Admittedly, that's a faster rate of aging than in some other countries. For instance, it took a century for the percentage of seniors in France to grow from 10% of the population to 25%. In Canada, that same process will have happened in half a century. But, after 2030, when the over-65s are expected to account for about 23% of Canada's population, demographers expect the aging process will level off and a balance will be reached between mortality and fertility. In other words, Canada will have achieved zero population growth somewhere between 2020 and 2030. And that's another key point in the debate that often gets overlooked: population aging will not go on forever. It will likely continue only for the next 30 years.

All of this assumes women will not start having more children again—probably a reasonable assumption. However, we're talking long-term here. Who could have predicted the increased fertility of the baby boom years, for instance? In effect, we can't say definitively that fertility rates will not increase again. Since the number of children women decide to have is generally determined by social conditions, it's not something that we can forecast with any accuracy. The projections about population aging also ignore the possibility of increases in immigration. Whether or not that's a reasonable assumption is open to debate. Increased immigration could slow down population aging because new immigrants, on average, may be younger than people already in Canada. The latest numbers show immigrants now represent over 17% of Canada's population—the largest share in more than 50 years. Who knows what may happen to immigration—or how policies on immigration might change—over the next 30 or 40 years?

Some demographers argue that, even if fertility rates start going up again or the country is flooded with young immigrants, it won't have much impact on the aging of the population in the short term. But all of these unknown elements underscore the problem of predicting how an aging population will affect our economy, our society, our health care system, and our pension programs 40 or 50 years down the road.

Could our economy be booming forty years from now? What will happen to interest rates? Will inflation remain almost non-existent? Will we find a cure for Alzheimer's? Will healthy lifestyles reduce the incidence of disease and disability in future seniors? No one can project that far ahead with any certainty. But that hasn't stopped the doomsayers in Canada and elsewhere from wringing their hands about the "demographic time bomb" they claim is ticking away, ready to explode in about 30 years from now.

Interestingly enough, the view that aging populations represent a crisis of epic proportions seems to be common in almost all industrialized countries, regardless of what they are now spending on old age benefits or what they expect to spend in the future. Sociologist John Myles, a Canadian who heads the Pepper Institute on Aging and Public Policy at Florida State University, points out that the countries of continental Europe face the highest levels of spending on public pensions now and in the future, in part because of generous pension schemes, but also because of their very high rates of early retirement and labour force withdrawal by those under 65. But the same rhetoric of "crisis" is heard, whether one travels to high-spending Italy or to low-spending Australia, Myles says.

Myles also tells us that, when it was pointed out to a senior official in Australia's Department of Social Security that even the most dire projection for Australia's old age security budget left the country spending only about 4.5% of GDP—less than a third of what Italy spends today—he was told: "That won't cut any ice here."

In Canada, Finance Minister Paul Martin raised the alarm in his 1995 budget, when he kicked off a round of proposed cuts to public pension programs, telling Canadians that, if nothing were done, spending on Old Age Security and the Guaranteed Income Supplement, along with the Canada/Quebec Pension Plan, would jump from 5.3% of GDP in 1993 to more than 8% in 2030. But he neglected to mention that this would still be less than OECD countries were spending for public pensions in 1991, when, according to the World Bank, the cost of public pensions in those countries averaged 9.2% of GDP.

And the finance minister's statement loses a lot of its shock value when you realize that, while the percentage of the population who are seniors is expected to double in that period of time, the cost of supporting them through public pensions, when you measure it as a share of national income, would only increase by 50%. Just what rate of economic growth was assumed as the basis for the finance minister's projections was not stated. Nor did he point out that his spending projections were based on gross spending and did not take into account offsetting tax revenues the government is able to recoup, since both OAS and CPP/QPP benefits are taxable.

The image of the ticking time bomb has now become so integrated into the conventional wisdom about population aging that few dare to challenge it. And, as American economist James Schultz points out, "The calamitous predictions by the prophets of doom have fallen on receptive ears because these people argue that the survival of some of our most important social and economic ideals are at stake." There's nothing like scare tactics to grab headlines.

In Britain, the prophets of demographic doom attacked the state pension program and the National Health Service. Speaking to an American audience in 1984, Prime Minister Margaret Thatcher used the demographic time bomb image to justify cuts she proposed to make in public spending on these programs. In the U.S., the time bomb analogy is being used to support claims that Social Security cannot be sustained and that it is a "bad deal' for younger people. Exactly the same arguments are being made in Canada against the Canada Pension Plan.

Schultz, who is professor of economics at Brandeis University and a specialist in aging policy, castigates the doomsayers for their "voodoo demography." He says the dire predictions should not be taken seriously because "they are based on simplistic and erroneous demographic analyses and—to the extent that economics is considered—the analysis is equally simplistic and seriously deficient."

It's important to emphasize that many of the doom and gloom projections, in fact, fail to take economic growth into account, and they frequently do not incorporate potential improvements in productivity, real wages, or other positive economic variables into their projections. According to

American authors Dean Baker and Mark Weisbrot, opponents of social security and public pensions have used the demographic time bomb scare to threaten these programs. "With a few selected facts dressed up as surprises—such as a rising elderly population or a declining ratio of workers to retirees—and an oversized dose of verbal and accounting trickery," say these authors, "opponents of Social Security have been able to create the impression that the program is demographically unstable. This impression is false," say Dean and Weisbrot, "as would be any economic projections that failed to take into account the other side of the equation, namely, the growth of the economy."

In their 1999 book *Social Security: The Phony Crisis*, these authors also say that many of those who would like to preserve Social Security have abandoned the effort to defend the system on the basis of the facts. Their reasoning is as follows: The public believes that Social Security is headed for a crisis when the baby boomers retire. Therefore, we cannot deny this belief without becoming marginalized in the debate. In a political climate driven by focus groups and polling data, say these authors, it does not take long for the truth to be turned upside down and a consensus to be formed around a whole new "reality."

Much the same developments have taken place in Canada. Relentless pounding from the media—most of it ill-informed and some of it erroneous—seems to have convinced many people that the CPP is "broke" and will not be there when they retire. Financial advisers and financial institutions regularly promote their mutual funds and other investment products by claiming that Canadians would be foolhardy to count on government pension programs to form part of their retirement income in future.

Even the federal Finance Department got into the act when it put out an "Information Paper" in 1996 intended to form the basis for public consultations on CPP reform. Among other things, it stated that "future generations will be asked to pay considerably more than their benefits are worth;" that projected CPP costs were "expected to mount to 14.2% of earnings;" and that "the CPP reserve fund will be exhausted in 2015 if nothing is done now."

The first two of these statements were false; the third was misleading, to say the least, and played on the public's lack of understanding of how the CPP is financed. Contrary to widespread public perception, the "reserve fund" referred to is not the fund from which benefits are paid, but simply a contingency reserve. At the time, it was used to supplement contribution revenue if needed, in the period between each meeting of federal and provincial finance ministers every five years, at which the 25-year schedule of contribution rates was reviewed and adjusted.

The finance department also failed to mention that CPP legislation required that contribution rates be adjusted every five years, if necessary, to maintain an amount in the fund equivalent to two years' worth of benefits. Needless to say, the news was seized upon by the media as "evidence" that the CPP would go bankrupt unless changes were made immediately. Anyone who dared to challenge that view was regarded with considerable skepticism and suspicion.

Dependency ratios

At the heart of the demographic time bomb view of population aging is the argument about "dependency ratios." Because the population is aging, we are told, there will be fewer people of working age to support those who have retired and become "dependent." The Economic Council of Canada produced a study in 1979, at the start of what came to be known in Canada as "the great pension debate," and called its report "One in Three." It was a reference to the assumption that, by the time the baby boom generation has retired—around 2030—the proportion of elderly people among the population aged 20 and over "could jump from one in seven now [1979] to nearly one in three."

Twenty years later, in a January 2000 report claiming Canada's pension system is threatened by the demographic time bomb, the Association of Canadian Pension Management (ACPM), which represents managers of corporate and public sector pension plans, claimed "our current retirement income and health care systems could become unstuck as the workers-to-pensioners ratio falls from 4:1 to 2:1 over the next thirty years."

The ratio of workers to pensioners is known as the "old age dependency ratio." Generally, "workers" are defined as the entire population aged 20 to 64, although sometimes the calculation is based on a working age population defined as those aged 15 to 64. The old, who are assumed to be dependent, include everyone aged 65 or older. The ratio is calculated by dividing the projected population aged 65-plus by the projected population aged 20 to 64. The results may vary, or course, depending on what age is selected as the lower limit for the working age population. Different assumptions about fertility also make a difference to the ratio projections. For example, the assumption of low fertility results in low population growth and hence higher old age dependency ratios, since there would be fewer people of working age compared with those who are aged 65 or older.   Using the definition of 20-64 for working age, calculations made by the Demography Division at Statistics Canada for 1991 resulted in an old age dependency ratio for Canada of 0.19. In other words, since the over-65s represented about 19% of the population aged 20 to 64, there were about four people aged 20 to 64 for each person aged 65 or older. Projections made in 1993 indicated the aged dependency ratio was expected to reach a high of 0.42 in 2036—hence the "one in three" description.

Theoretically, old age dependency ratios are a measure of the economic burden of the old on those of working age and the higher the ratio the bigger the burden. Implicitly, it's assumed that people of working age must support those who have retired. Clearly, it's only a rough approximation. But it's the projected increase in the old age dependency ratio that is being used by the demographic time bomb crowd to predict dire consequences by the year 2030. However, American economists Dean Baker and Mark Weisbrot note that increases in the ratio of seniors to people of working age in the U.S. have actually been much steeper in the past—for example, in the period from 1955 to 1999—without precipitating any economic disaster.

As far as Canada is concerned, studies by the International Monetary Fund (IMF) and the OECD project this country will have the lowest economic burdens for public pensions among G-7 countries at the time when the baby-boom cohort is having its most adverse impact on old age dependency ratios. Observers point out that these two institutions both have "biases towards fiscal prudence." In other words, they are not likely to be exaggerating Canada's favourable position.

There are a few other points that come to mind:

- **The "working" population is not confined to people aged 20 to 64.** Some people under the age of 20 may be in the work force, as may some over age 64. And not everyone aged 20 to 64 is working. Some economists say it would be more appropriate to calculate labour force dependency ratios which would relate those who are actually in the labour force to those who are not. Such ratios are not regularly calculated by demographers. However, one 1998 estimate for Canada suggests the labour force old age dependency ratio would increase from 0.22 in 1991 to 0.57 in 2041.

High labour force participation rates of women may boost the ability of those of working age to "support' the elderly. But, as sociologist Ellen Gee has pointed out, labour-force-based dependency ratios do not take into account the unwaged domestic labour of women (and men) and volunteer activities. An elderly woman who is the primary care-giver for an ill husband, for example, a full-time homemaker, and a volunteer worker at a local arts organization are all considered to be a dependent/non-provider/economic drain. Similarly, a grandmother who looks after her grand-children two or three days a week so her daughter can prof-itably work outside the home is considered a dependent.

- **Seniors pay taxes, too.** Not everyone 65 and over is "dependent." Some seniors continue to work after they turn 65. In fact, raising the age of entitlement for public pension programs has been an option suggested in many countries as a way of encouraging older people to continue working past age 65, easing the problem of dealing with an aging population.

Much more important, however, is the fact that people continue to pay taxes throughout their lives. Seniors pay income taxes, GST, provincial sales taxes, excise taxes, and property taxes—not to mention user fees, which are increas-ingly making an appearance as a way of paying for public services provided by various levels of government. These revenues, flowing to federal, provincial and municipal gov-ernments, are used to finance programs such as the OAS and GIS, as well as services used by seniors, such as health care, home care, and long-term care facilities.

In other words, many of these services are paid for part-ly by taxes collected from seniors themselves. The only taxes seniors do not pay are payroll taxes, such as Unemployment Insurance and CPP contributions. It's worth repeating here that, while retired people no longer contribute to the CPP, they do pay tax on their CPP benefits, and OAS is both taxable and clawed back from higher-income seniors.

As seniors form an increasing percentage of the popula-tion, they will account for an increasing percentage of all taxpayers. They will also contribute an increasing share of amounts collected by various levels of government in dif-ferent kinds of taxes and user fees. Some studies have even suggested that programs such as the OAS and GIS may be largely financed by intra-generational transfers rather than inter-generational transfers. In other words, higher total amounts paid in taxes by seniors themselves will be able to finance these programs through transfers from higher-income seniors to those with more modest incomes, rather than from younger people of working age to older people who have retired. This is also contrary to the conventional wisdom that assumes increased costs of public pensions as the population ages will require a massive transfer from younger generations to the elderly, because they simply translate into an increased burden on future working age generations.

The baby boomers have been described as "the trillion dollar generation"—a reference to the amount they are expected to inherit from their parents, assuming those parents don't have to spend their accumulated wealth on health care in the last few years of their lives. Boomers are also rapidly accumulating savings of their own. In its latest salvo against the demographic time bomb, the Association of Canadian Pension Management (ACPM) added up Statistics Canada's numbers on financial assets currently invested in pension plans and RRSPs and concluded that "an accumulation of $1 trillion would not seem farfetched." It goes on to propose changes to the retirement income system that it says would add another $100 billion a year to private savings in Canada.

Whether its savings come from inheritances or accumulated wealth, or both, the baby boom generation seems set to be much better off in retirement than today's generation of seniors. And, as the boomers draw down their financial assets to support themselves in their golden years, they will pay income taxes on the money they receive from pension plans and RRSPs, as well as from public programs such as

OAS and CPP. They'll also continue to pay sales taxes and GST on their purchases, and property taxes on their mortgage-free homes.

But the role of this big generation as taxpayers is almost never mentioned. Ironically, after highlighting the huge asset build-up it says is happening in Canada, the ACPM claims the demographic time bomb is threatening our pension system and that benefits to current seniors should be drastically cut so that the money saved can be redirected in the form of tax breaks to higher-income younger earners so they can save more for their own retirement.

- **The over-65s are not the only group in society that is not working.** The under-20s are also "dependents." Demographers also calculate a "youth dependency ratio" that shows the percentage of young people in relation to those of working age. And, because Canada's population is aging, the youth dependency ratio has been going down at the same time as the old age dependency ratio has been going up. For example, while the youth dependency ratio at the height of the baby boom in 1961 was 0.83, by 2021, it is projected to have dropped to 0.38.

Adding together both the young and the old populations and relating their numbers to those of working age produces a "total dependency ratio" which can be used to give a rough idea of the economic burden on the working age population of both the old and the young. The total dependency ratio in Canada has actually been declining steadily for the past 120 years. It's expected to drop even further over the next 10 years and will only start to increase again in 2021. By 2031, when the so-called demographic time bomb is supposed to explode, Canada's total dependency ratio will still be lower than it was in 1951.

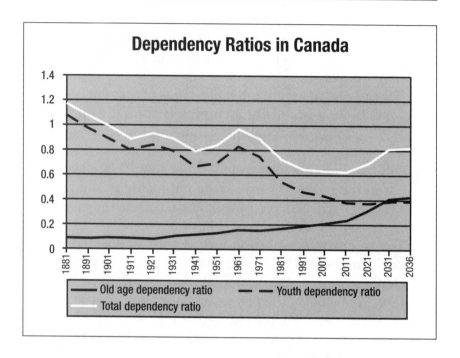

Canada is not alone in this experience. In almost all the industrialized countries, total dependency ratios are much lower than in the past. In other words, the burden of caring for a larger elderly population could be largely offset by reduced spending on child care, education, and other services to dependent children and young people.

Can we afford our aging population?

The scaremongers like to argue that this is not a fair comparison. They claim it costs more to care for the elderly than it does to care for children. As well, they say, the cost of caring for children is largely a private cost: it's parents who pay most of it. On the other hand, the cost of caring for seniors comes out of the public purse through public pensions and health care. That's why they suggest we will not be able to "afford" our aging population. They would like to reduce the public cost of supporting the elderly. The solution they propose is that we abandon our public pension programs and let the elderly fend for themselves.

According to some estimates, per capita *public* expenditures are two to three times greater for the old than for the young. But, if we added in the private costs of supporting the young—in effect, calculating the total *social* cost of a dependent population—the ratio would be smaller than this. In a 1998 paper, demographers Frank Denton, Christine Feaver and Byron Spencer estimated the relative social costs—including both public and private costs—of the young and old. They concluded that total social costs for the elderly would have to be three times higher than for the young in Canada in order for our future overall dependency to exceed what we have already experienced when the baby boom generation were children. As sociologist Ellen Gee points out, no one is suggesting that the total social costs of the elderly would be this much higher than for the young. In other words, it's evident that our aging population will not be any more costly than what Canada has already had to deal with.

With seniors forming an increasing percentage of our population, it is inevitable that more of our economic resources will go to them. As economists like to explain it, the cost of supporting those who have retired is calculated according to the goods and services they consume, because these resources are not available for other uses, such as private investment, collective investment, or consumption by either government or workers. Resources can be allocated to seniors by providing them with public pensions, financed by tax revenues or payroll contributions paid by those of working age, to supplement their own savings and allow them to purchase the goods and services they need. Alternatively, seniors could be expected to rely mainly on their own private resources, such as their private savings, or the support of their families. To the extent that these resources are limited, seniors may consume less of our total output of goods and services, leaving more to the working age population.

Whether we choose to provide for seniors through public programs or private means, the working age population will be affected. For example, adults of working age may increase their contributions to the Canada Pension Plan so that pensions will continue to be paid to an increasing number of retired people. The alternative may be for them to support their own aging parents directly, or to pay increased income taxes to provide a minimal income guarantee (through the OAS or GIS) for an increased number of seniors who have been unable to provide adequately for themselves. Either way, people of working age would have to reduce their own consumption.

Of course, if the economy is expanding in real terms, the total resources available to support the elderly—whether through public or private means—will be increasing. Allocating an increasing percentage of our national output to older people may then be accomplished without the necessity for those of working age to reduce their consumption. But people of working age will have to produce the goods and services needed by seniors and the rest of the population.

However, as British economist Phil Mullan points out, the particular pension system used for distributing part of the national wealth to the elderly does not affect the means of creating that wealth in the first place. In a 2000 book called *The Imaginary Time Bomb: Why an Aging Population is not a Social Problem,* Mullan points out that the emphasis is now on extending private pension provision to reduce even further reliance on "state handouts" and to offload the remaining pressures on statutory pension provision. Aging is advanced as the reason necessitating the reform of the pension system away from universal public pensions towards private provision, he says, with the state merely retaining the residual role of providing a safety net.

This is almost exactly the position taken by the ACPM in its 2000 demographic time bomb report. It even subtitled the report "Dependence or Self-reliance?" and it makes the argument that Canada has been far too generous to seniors.

Benefits such as the OAS and GIS must be cut to the bare minimum, says ACPM, to encourage people to be more "self-reliant" and less "dependent" on the state. Without any apparent awareness of the irony involved, ACPM recommends that the way to achieve "self-reliance" is to direct much bigger tax subsidies to higher-income earners, so they can save for retirement.

Mullan also says the crusade to move from public to private systems cannot be legitimized by even the most extreme of the aging projections. This is because the particular type of pension system employed—private or public, funded or pay-as-you-go—makes no difference to the amount of wealth required at any point in time "to fund elderly, unproductive people to a particular standard of living." Different pension systems are simply different technical means for transferring this wealth to pensioners. When the baby boomers were kids, they posed a challenge that may have been even greater than the prospect of caring for them when they are old, says Richard C. Leone, president of the Century Foundation in New York, a non-profit, non-partisan organization that sponsors analysis of economic policy, foreign affairs, and domestic policy issues. When they were children, there were even more of them, and for 15 or 20 years they produced little. They made complicated demands on the real economy, and society had to respond out of the much smaller economic pie that existed at the time, Leone points out.

As kids, boomers comprised over 40% of the population of the U.S., Leone says. Today they are less than 30%, and in retirement they'll drop below 25%. The cost of raising the boomers was high, he notes. As children, they consumed goods and services from the real economy, just as they will as seniors. School systems routinely were overloaded. And the market for consumer goods was transformed by the special demands of children and teenagers. Odd, isn't it, says Leone, that no one, including the boomers' parents, recalls the 1960s as an era of economic deprivation?

Leone points out that Americans who had lived through the great depression expected the public sector to play a key role in the adjustments caused by the arrival of 80 million boomer children. The government produced vast programs to build schools, train teachers, and, later, to provide college loans and grants. Between 1952 and 1970, he says, elementary and secondary school expenditures increased more than 275% in inflation-adjusted dollars. Between 1964 and 1980, the number of college and university students increased more than 125%, and the number of college instructors more than doubled. The boomers' parents, through their taxes, built these schools and colleges for their own and other people's children, Leone points out.

Public investment in both people and infrastructure in the U.S. was very high during the entire post-war period. The key, of course, is that the economy was booming. But the U.S. economy is still growing, even if more slowly. In fact, economists have pointed out that, compared with 1964, the U.S. will have triple the resources available in constant dollars in the next century—even assuming a relatively modest rate of economic growth.

It has been estimated that parents of the baby boomers in the U.S. registered a per capita GDP of US$12,195 in 1964. Assuming less than 2% annual growth, the retired boomers and their children will enjoy in the year 2030 a per capita income (inflation adjusted) that—at about US$35,659 —is almost three times as large. As Leone says, "the alleged fears of the future by some members of generation X, who will inherit the largest economy in the history of the world, seem somewhat out of proportion."

The same kinds of considerations apply in Canada. Of course, it's difficult to predict future trends in economic growth, productivity improvements, inflation, and so on; but that's no reason to ignore these key variables, which is exactly what many of the doom and gloom predictions have done. Projecting social spending based solely on demographic factors exaggerates the burden of accommodating an aging population and contributes to the view that we are facing an aging "crisis." Such projections are misleading and unrealistic. Taking a broader view of economic growth can make a huge difference to the outcome.

By way of illustration, consider these projections made some years ago by Hans Messinger and Brian J. Powell, formerly of the Economic Council of Canada, but then working at the Department of Health and Welfare. Using Statistics Canada's medium growth population projections, they projected social spending to the year 2031. They assumed that real per capita benefits and program utilization remained unchanged. They also assumed that, in forecasting economic growth, capital/labour ratios are fixed and that there would be no impact on economic growth from changes in the unemployment rate, labour force participation rates, and productivity.

As they point out, zero productivity growth assumes no change in inputs of capital per worker, work-force skills and technology. In other words, the social spending and economic growth forecasts they come up with are affected only by changes in age structure and total size of the population. In their estimates of "social spending," they included education expenditure, child benefits (at that time, these were family allowances and the child tax credit), unemployment insurance payments to the working age population, and social assistance payments provided jointly by the federal government through the Canada Assistance Plan and the provinces. (The Canada Assistance Plan has since been abolished).

The spending estimates under this projection showed that, over the entire period from 1984 to 2031, social spending would increase by 44%, while the total population would grow by less than 19%. They concluded that "This clearly demonstrates that an aging population, holding constant real per capita benefits and program utilization rates, generates a definite upward impact on social spending." It's particularly evident between the years 2011 and 2031, they say, when social spending will increase by 17%, although population will increase by only 1%.

They also said that, while elderly income benefits would increase almost threefold and health costs would rise by 80% between 2011 and 2031, the costs associated with Canada's young population—i.e., child benefits and education—would fall by less than 20%..."and do little to offset the pressures of meeting the needs of the aged."

If that were as far as the projections went, we might indeed have cause to worry. And Messinger and Powell admit that the restrictive assumptions in their projections "do produce results that may generate causes for concern." But are their projections realistic? That, of course, is the point. And, as the authors themselves acknowledge, the answer is clearly No. As these authors tell us, the theory of economic growth is not the clearest aspect of the discipline, but it's safe to say that future changes in gross domestic product will be affected by more than just demographic factors.

They point out that complex economic forecasting models use historic information, as well as established structural relationships and assumptions about external factors, to predict economic growth. Productivity will almost certainly increase; the "quality" of the work force will improve because people will be better educated; technological change will contribute to improved living standards and social conditions; unemployment rates will probably continue to fall; and so on. While it is undoubtedly important, demographics cannot be used as the **sole** independent variable in a reasonable forecast.

Clearly, it is not easy to forecast some of these variables, especially in the longer term. But some attempt must be made if we want to construct a more realistic view of what we might be facing as our population ages. Messigner and Powell do just that, and the result is a significantly different picture from the one they got when they used only demographic factors.

Given no change in social programs— and, by the way, many
of the programs we had in 1987 when they made their forecast
have already been cut back substantially or eliminated—they
found that the "fiscal burden," expressed as the portion of
GDP required to finance social expenditures, will be substantially reduced up to the year 2010 and will only increase over
the following two decades—but to levels that will be far more
manageable than at present.

Here's a comparison of the two projections:

**Social spending as a percentage of
Gross Domestic Product**

Canada, 1985 – 2031
(Using medium growth population projections)

Years	Based only on demographic factors	Using comprehensive economic projections
1984	20.8%	20.8%
1991	21.3	17.0
2001	22.5	15.3
2011	23.4	14.5
2021	25.5	15.1
2031	28.2	16.0

Source: Messinger, Hans and Brian J. Powell (1987) "The Implications of
Canada's Aging Society on Social Expenditures," in *Aging in
Canada: Social Perspectives.* Edited by Victor W, Marshall. Second
Edition. Toronto: Fitzhenry & Whiteside.

More recent forecasts of GDP growth for Canada indicate continued growth in GDP per capita. Projections prepared by Informetrica Limited, an Ottawa-based economic forecasting and analysis company focusing on medium- and long-term issues, indicate that, by the time the peak of the baby boom generation is entering retirement in 2025, GDP per capita will be about $38,000. That compares with $28,518 in 1999 and $17,584 in 1972. These projections assume low fertility rates, fairly high immigration, and slowly improving morbidity rates and they are in constant 1992 dollars. In other words, the "economic pie" when the baby boomers are retiring will be more than double what it was when they were children, after allowing for inflation.

According to the OECD, Canada faces one of the highest projected expenditure growths among OECD countries as a result of population aging. But the demographic time bomb crowd seems to have overlooked the fact that, in its 1998 report *Ageing Populations: The Social Policy Implications*, the OECD also said that, if public spending on the old in Canada is to maintain its share of GDP as the population ages, the average annual growth rate required between 1980 and 2040 is only 1.05%.

The war between the generations

None of this, of course, has been enough to quiet the alarmists who continue to warn of the demographic time bomb. And, pursuing the military metaphor, they predict a war between the generations unless public pensions are immediately reduced or even eliminated. "What is this aging phenomenon going to cost future taxpayers?" asks the ACPM in its latest ticking time bomb missive. Unless we change our retirement income system now, says this organization, "we will be burdening future taxpayers with even significantly higher tax levels than we face today." And even if these future taxpayers choose to pay up, says ACPM, " is it right of us to ask them?" The business press dutifully sounded the alarm under the headline "Study Warns of Age War Over Pensions."

The threat of inter-generational conflict is a familiar one. It is used by the advocates of privatization of public pensions, not only in Canada but also in other countries, including Britain and the United States. As Phil Mullan describes it: "The statistical assumptions are the same as with the dependency ratio demographic time bomb, but the stress on inter-personal conflict seems to give the scare greater impact." The World Bank, for instance, claims that "public old age security programs covering almost the entire population have paid out large pensions over the past three decades of prosperity, as poverty declined faster among the old than the young. But over the next two decades," says the Bank, "payroll taxes are expected to rise by several percentage points and benefits to fall. That will intensify the inter-generational conflict between old retirees (some of them rich) who are getting public pensions and young workers (some of them poor) who are paying high taxes to finance these benefits and may never recoup their contributions."

The basis of the argument is that older people are already taking "more than their fair share" of the national income. And, as the percentage of older people increases, the share of national income going to the elderly will increase even further. Younger people increasingly resent this—or so the argument goes. They will not want to pay taxes to support a larger elderly population, so an "inter-generational war" will break out.

The scaremongers have become quite skilful in promoting their agenda. They claim that poverty among the elderly has been eliminated; that younger people are much worse off than seniors are; and that old people are rich and greedy. In the U.S., Americans for Generational Equity (AGE), founded in 1985 and chaired by Republican Senator David Durenberger, have been promoting their view of the coming inter-generational conflict, with support from Medicare's private competitors: health care providers, insurance companies, banks and military contractors. Financial institutions, of course, have much to gain if public pensions are privatized and mandatory contributions redirected to private savings accounts on which they can earn commissions and fees.

The concept of "greedy geezers" has been promoted in Canada, too. Actuary Malcolm Hamilton, a principal with a major benefits consulting firm that advises the government on pension reform, describes seniors as "the most mercenary of electoral constituencies." He also claims current seniors are "the wealthiest generation in Canadian history." Hamilton, whose views are courted and quoted frequently by the business press, rails against the "generosity" of Canada's public pension programs. "When I look at Canada," he says, "I see a country where the government vacuums up the disposable income of young families and transfers it to senior citizens, and the senior citizens, having no particular use for the money, save it up and give it to their children."

In one presentation, he predicted "the challenge of the next 30 years will not be finding enough money for seniors. It will be persuading seniors to relinquish some of their entitlements, so that their children can live the kind of life that seniors have always wanted their children to live."

The ACPM takes up the theme in its January 2000 time bomb paper. Here's an example:

"Pillar 1 of the system [OAS and GIS] today provides seniors with larger after-tax benefits than working people are allowed to earn before they are subjected to income and payroll taxes. At the same time, seniors collecting CPP/QPP pensions paid only a fraction of their true cost. All seniors' benefits are fully indexed, while working people face automatic tax increases through bracket creep. In short, over-65 Canadians have already become an advantaged class, now better off financially than many of the younger working Canadians who sustain them. Where is the fairness in this? "

Of course, seniors also faced "bracket creep" because both OAS and CPP/QPP benefits are taxable; but the federal government restored full indexing of the tax system in its 2000 budget, so the criticism no longer applies. As well, current seniors include the first generation to receive pensions from the CPP/QPP, which was established only in 1966. As with all newly-established pay-as-you-go pension plans, it is inevitable that the first beneficiaries contribute less in relation to their benefits than subsequent generations will. But the way the ACPM presents its myths and half-truths is guaranteed to fan the flames of inter-generational conflict, which it claims to be so concerned about.

And, while claiming to be so concerned about "fairness," the ACPM proposes changes to the system which are grossly inequitable. It wants to "restrain the future availability" of public pensions "as much as possible." It even suggests making them subject to a means test, which would include assets. It's not clear if it wants to deny the OAS and GIS to seniors with mortgage-free houses; if so, many seniors could be forced to sell their homes if they wanted to qualify for these minimal public programs.

The ACPM wants to redefine poverty, using a much more restrictive definition to determine who would qualify for social benefits. At the same time, however, it claims "there are no viable retirement savings opportunities to maintain pre-retirement living standards for Canadians earning more than twice the average wage, who pay a disproportionately large share of all taxes." It proposes raising the upper limit on RRSP contributions so bigger tax subsidies can be directed to these higher-income earners to help them save for retirement and become "self-reliant."

As for the wealthy seniors, the numbers put the lie to claims by Malcolm Hamilton and the ACPM. Here are just a few examples, taken from Statistics Canada's income data for 1997, the latest information available:

- About 54% of the income of Canadians aged 65 and over comes from OAS, GIS, CPP/QPP, and other government transfers. Older women get 64% of their income from these sources.
- Less than 12% of the income of seniors comes from investment income—most of it interest on bank accounts.
- The median income of people aged 65 and over is just $15,634. In other words, half of all senior individuals have annual incomes below this amount. The median income of individuals aged 45-54 is $29,547—almost double that of seniors; while individuals aged 35-44 have a median income of $28,669, or 83% higher than that of seniors.
- The median income of families headed by someone aged 65 or older is $34,192. The median income of families in the 45-to-54-year age group is $62,034, while families aged 35-44 have a median income of $55,694.
- Almost 19% of Canadians aged 65 and over are considered low income. About 16% of those aged 18 to 64 have low incomes.
- Almost half of unattached women aged 65 and older have incomes below Statistics Canada's low-Income Cut-Off (LICO).
- Only 18% of senior families have incomes above $60,000 a year, and less than 4% have incomes above $100,000.

These statistics clearly do not support the view of Canadian seniors as rich or greedy; nor do they show that seniors are much better off than younger Canadians of working age. In fact, the opposite is true. But the demographic alarmists apparently don't let reality stand in the way of promoting the war between the generations.

We should recognize these threats for what they are. They represent an attempt to justify reducing the role of government and eliminating collective responsibility for our aging population under the guise of preventing inter-generational conflict.

Social cohesion—an idea that policy-makers also pay lip service to—is founded on the concept of interdependence of members of society as one generation follows another. Transfers from one generation to another take place in both directions—from old to young and from young to old. What's more, as sociologist Ellen Gee points out, there's a wealth of social research that shows much of the social exchange that occurs between generations occurs along non-monetary lines.

What is the hidden agenda?

It's quite remarkable how the doomsayers in the debate over population aging seem to use a common language, regardless of what country they speak for. They talk of the demographic time bomb and inter-generational warfare; they focus on old age dependency ratios and imply we cannot afford our aging population. Their doom-and-gloom scenarios have but one goal in mind. It is to eliminate "entitlements" and let the market take over. And that has nothing to do with economics and everything to do with politics and ideology—with a large dose of self-interest.

The World Bank lent its seal of approval to the cause in 1994, when it published a landmark report on aging under the title *Averting the Old Age Crisis,* recommending policies it said would "protect the old and promote growth." Pointing to demographic aging as a worldwide phenomenon, the Bank said that extended families and other traditional ways of supporting the old are weakening. It also claimed that "formal systems, such as government-backed pensions, have proved unsustainable and very difficult to reform."

The conclusion of its study, the Bank said, was that "financial security for the old and economic growth would be better served if governments develop three systems or "pillars" of old age security: a publicly-managed system with mandatory participation and the limited goal of reducing poverty among the old; a privately managed, mandatory savings system; and voluntary savings."

According to the Bank, the first pillar would cover redistribution, the second and third would cover savings, and all three would "co-insure against many of the risks of old age." As well, it claimed, by separating the redistributive function from the savings function, the public pillar—and the size of the payroll tax needed to support it—can be kept relatively small, "thus avoiding many of the growth-inhibiting problems associated with a dominant public pillar."

The World Bank's prescription for dealing with aging populations is intended to apply to all countries, regardless of their stage of economic development. It sets out steps it believes must be taken by young low-income economies; by young but rapidly aging economies; and by older economies with established public pension programs. According to the Bank, older economies with large public pension programs "face imminent problems with their old age systems." The time is now ripe, says the Bank, for these economies to make the transition to a mandatory multi-pillar system—in other words, to get rid of their public pension programs and replace them with mandatory savings schemes.

In advocating that governments replace their public earnings-related pension programs with mandatory savings schemes, the World Bank holds up the example of Chile, which until 1994 was the only country that had fully replaced an existing public pay-as-you-go pension scheme with a mandatory savings scheme. Privatization of public pensions in Chile was implemented in 1981 under the Pinochet dictatorship, with the help of economists from the University of Chicago—known colloquially as "the Chicago boys"—who pushed the Chilean economy down the free enterprise road with deregulation, privatization of public institutions, and pro-market social and economic policies.

Since that time, the Chilean pension system has become the model for many other Latin American countries as they abandoned public pension programs, as well as the goal of other more developed countries where the political climate is one of downsizing the role of the state in favour of a "free market" system. In Canada, for example, the former Reform Party advocated the abolition of the CPP and its replacement with a mandatory savings scheme of "Super-RRSPs" based on the Chilean model. Corporate-funded think tanks and the business press have also supported it.

The World Bank report has been described as "the first attempt to resolve problems of elderly welfare at a global level from a neoliberal perspective." Critics have charged that age transition in developing countries has induced the World Bank "to construct a crisis out of change." In a detailed analysis of the report, Paul Johnson, Reader in Economic History at the London School of Economics, concludes that the "old age crisis" the World Bank is intent on avoiding is not strictly demographic or economic in nature. It is, in fact, "a presumed crisis in the management of public-sector pay-as-you-go pension systems."

The "hidden agenda" in the World Bank report, says Johnson, is that governments should not do what markets can also do, because markets do it better. While he notes that "this anti-state, pro-market ideology is hardly a novelty in World Bank publications," when it is applied to the social sector—and specifically to the issue of aging and pensions —"it has potentially insidious implications."

He suggests that the very strong emphasis on the role of mandatory private pensions, rather than on public pensions, derives from political rather than economic arguments. "Yet the political underpinning to the report is nowhere explicitly stated or discussed: what is, in fact, an intensely political document is presented as an exercise in positive economic analysis."

Collective or individual responsibility?

For many years, there appears to have been a general consensus among international agencies, academics, and most governments about the role of the public sector in providing for the needs of the elderly. The emphasis on collective responsibility has been described as the "traditional welfarist approach," typified by the International Labour Office, which has argued that the economic needs of the elderly should be met primarily through social security programs.

Of these, the ILO considers the two most important to be social insurance, a legal obligation and legal entitlement, financed by contributions from workers, employers and the state; and social assistance, financed by the state alone and generally available, though often means- tested. In the Canadian retirement income system, these programs are represented by the Canada Pension Plan—an earnings-related plan financed by contributions from workers and employers with no government funding and no income test—and by Old Age Security and the Guaranteed Income Supplement, together with the Spouse's Allowance, all of which are financed from general tax revenues and are income tested—including the OAS, which is clawed back from higher-income pensioners.

More recently, however, traditional views about the role of the state in providing for the elderly have been challenged by a number of neoliberal organizations, such as the World Bank. In Canada, strong support for the privatization of public pensions has come from the business press and corporate-funded neoliberal research institutes such as the Fraser Institute and the C.D. Howe Institute. It has also been advocated by the former Reform Party—now transmogrified into the Canadian Reform Conservative Alliance—and others who share that party's views, including the Alberta government.

In the United States, advocates of the privatization of public pensions include neoliberal institutes such as the Heritage Foundation, the American Enterprise Institute, and the Washington-based Cato Institute, where a project on privatization of social security is being led by José Piñera, former Chilean Minister of Finance under the Pinochet regime, who spearheaded the privatization of Chile's public pension plan. Observers say that the Cato Institute and the Heritage Foundation, with funding from investment firms that would gain from privatization, have worked hard and effectively to undermine the loyalty of the U.S. public and politicians to Social Security.

It is perhaps significant that the International Labour Organization says the Chilean model, espoused by the World Bank, has come to be seen as "the epitome of the 'private' approach as opposed to 'public' systems" in the ideological battle for and against privatization of public pension systems.

The attack on social security

Since the publication of the World Bank report in 1994, the right-wing attack on social security has been gathering steam in the United States. Perhaps inevitably, the same arguments and strategies used against public pension programs in that country have found their way to Canada. In a 1998 paper on funding public pension plans, Bob Baldwin of the Canadian Labour Congress quotes a passage from *Challenge* —a U.S. magazine of economic affairs—which he says illustrates the long-term nature of the attack and the points of political vulnerability of public pensions.

"Those calling for radical restructuring of social security (i.e. Chilean type schemes) have been very successful in their efforts to shift the terms of the debate. They understand well the role of crises—real and artificially constructed—in fostering political change. Writing in 1983 in the journal of the libertarian Cato Institute, Stuart Butler, vice president for domestic policy at the Heritage Foundation, and Peter Germanis, then an analyst with the Heritage Foundation, discussed what they mischievously called a "Leninist strategy" to deconstruct social security. Butler and Germanis mapped out a strategy for "guerrilla warfare against the current social security system and the coalition that supports it." The advocates of radical change must: 1) calm existing beneficiaries and older workers by assuring them proposals such as privatizing or means-testing will not affect them; 2) take every opportunity to demonstrate weaknesses in the current program; 3) develop a fully privatized alternative; 4) work to sell this privatized alternative to the young, the majority of whom question the future of social security; and 5) activate powerful private interests, including the banks, insurance companies, and other institutions that will gain from privatization."

Anyone who followed the recent debate about reform of the Canada Pension Plan cannot help but be struck by how closely those very same tactics were pursued by the advocates of privatization of public pensions in Canada, including the Fraser Institute, the C.D. Howe Institute, the Reform Party, and the business press. It is clear that the same strategies are now being used to undermine support for the CPP.

The direction of pension policy in Canada

Governments in Canada have not yet been willing to go as far as the advocates of privatization of public pensions would like. For the time being, privatization of the CPP has been rejected—although it could be argued that the recent move to partial funding of the CPP is the first step along the road to privatization.

Polls show there is still strong support for the CPP among Canadians. A poll conducted for the federal Finance Department in December 1996, for example, found "a massive majority of Canadians which wants the CPP to continue," and that "this desire cuts across all age groups and all income levels." Nevertheless, the direction of pension policy in Canada is clearly to transfer more of the risk and responsibility for providing for retirement onto individuals. Reducing the role of public pensions in the retirement income system is part of that trend.

Scaling back the CPP, for instance, along with the proposed income-tested Seniors' Benefit—since abandoned—

and increasing pressure to raise the limits for RRSP contributions, are clear indications of the direction public policy on pensions in this country is taking. The approach also fits with trends evident in most other areas of current economic and social policy, which emphasize smaller government, privatization, individual initiative, and market-driven solutions.

The current approach to retirement income policies in Canada is in marked contrast with what the government saw as a priority when pensions were last at the top of the public policy agenda almost 20 years ago at the beginning of the 1980s, when the country was engaged in what came to be known as the "Great Pension Debate." The framework for that debate was set out in the introduction to the 1979 report of the federal Task Force on Retirement Income Policy, commonly known as the Lazar Report after Harvey Lazar, an official from the federal Department of Finance, who chaired it.

The report was described as "a response to a growing concern among many groups about the current and future well-being of Canada's elderly." The well-being of the elderly—and particularly of older women—was in fact the focus of a national conference on pensions held in Ottawa in 1981. The implication was clearly that the public sector has an important role to play in providing for the elderly.

So far, federal and provincial governments in Canada, which are responsible for administering the CPP—the social insurance tier of the retirement income system in this country—have resisted pressure for privatization. In his 1996 budget speech, for example, Finance Minister Paul Martin said the government did not share the view that the Canada Pension Plan should be abandoned. But the pressure is mounting. At the conclusion of the first triennial review of the CPP in December 1999, then Alberta Treasurer Stockwell Day threatened to take Alberta out of the CPP and set up a provincial plan instead unless the other finance ministers agreed to a number of changes, including allowing people to opt out of the CPP and have their contributions directed to private savings accounts. The finance ministers apparently agreed to study Alberta's proposals, although there was no indication they would act on them. But the growing influence of the Canadian Alliance party, now led by Stockwell Day himself, and sympathetic right-wing governments in Ontario and Alberta make it a virtual certainty that the pressure for privatization of the CPP will continue.

There has certainly been a marked change in the emphasis of pension policy in Canada over the two decades since the Lazar Task Force reported. The transition is evident in the finance minister's public statements about pension policy since the Chrétien government was first elected. In his first budget speech on February 22, 1994, the federal finance minister expressed some concern about the aging population. "As Canadians live longer and healthier lives," he said, "the roles and needs of seniors will change." He promised to release a paper that would look at "what an aging society will need in terms of services; and what changes are required to the public pension system to ensure it is affordable."

The paper on the aging society has never materialized. But more recent policy pronouncements from federal and provincial governments have placed much greater emphasis on the cost of public pensions. In the 1995 federal budget, for example, references to Canada's aging population seemed to take on more urgency. This was the budget when the finance minister warned about steadily rising costs of public pensions as a percentage of Gross Domestic Product (GDP).

The World Bank's prescription on how to reduce the cost of public pensions appears to be for governments to get out of the business completely. Its model fits within the broader neoliberal philosophy of the World Bank, which advocates the primacy of free market forces, the deregulation of labour markets, and reducing the scope of the public sector in all areas of the economy.

Chapter 2
The push for privatization as the answer to an aging population

If there really is a demographic time bomb waiting to explode, and if the countries of the western world face a crisis of population aging, how would it help to get rid of public pension plans? How would replacing social insurance pension programs with mandatory savings schemes help societies deal with the needs of an aging population? The answer—at least in the minds of the privatization advocates—seems to be that, by getting rid of public pensions, society would no longer have to face the problem. That challenge would be placed squarely on the shoulders of individuals, who would then be expected to sink or swim. Society would only pick up the pieces for the very poorest, through a minimal anti-poverty or social assistance program.

If Canada were to go this route, of course, there would still be the problem of who would pay for the pensions already promised to everyone who has been contributing to the CPP up to now. The huge transition cost associated with switching from a pay-as-you-go plan to a private savings scheme with individual retirement accounts is something the advocates of privatization often conveniently overlook. It's a crucial issue and we'll return to it later.

The problem as the World Bank sees it

Population aging may result from declining fertility, improved life expectancy, or a combination of both. Either way, the World Bank sees population aging as having adverse economic consequences because countries with aging populations will experience more years of old age dependency supported by relatively few years of productive work. The Bank sees the real problem occurring when these necessary transfers occur through a public pay-as-you-go pension system. Working-age people will suffer a reduction in their current consumption as payroll taxes increase to provide transfers to a growing population of elderly people. But, as Paul Johnson of the London School of Economics explains, two important points must be noted here. First, if the transfers are mediated through private pension systems instead of through public social security pensions, working age people may experience an equally large reduction in current consumption as private pension premiums have to rise in response to an increased number of retirement years. For example, if the CPP were to be replaced with a system of mandatory savings accounts—perhaps Super-RRSPs, as the Reform Party once recommended—younger people of working age would still have to reduce their current consumption because they would be required to make mandatory contributions to their personal savings accounts.

Secondly, says Johnson, such reductions in consumption during working life will occur only because most people will survive to take out more during a longer retirement. Such reductions in consumption should be accepted gladly, not resented, he says. "They are, after all, simply the price we have to pay for a longer life."

Johnson also points out that, if the number of years worked does not change but the number of years lived increases, then everyone has to transfer more resources from their working to their non-working years. Whether this is done publicly or privately has little bearing on the total cost, but the cost is high—much higher than most people think. He notes that the World Bank report implies that these pension costs can be reduced without adversely affecting the welfare of pensioners, simply by shifting from public pay-as-you-go pensions to private funded pension schemes. This is most unlikely to be true, Johnson says. In fact, given the high administrative costs evident in many private pension systems, he suggests pension costs might even be increased.

Other observers make similar arguments. For example, in a 1987 book on *The Economics of the Welfare State*, author Nicholas Barr says:

> The widely held (but false) view that funded schemes are inherently 'safer' than PAYGO is an example of the fallacy of composition. For *individuals* the economic function of a pension scheme is to transfer consumption over time. But (ruling out the case where current output is stored in holes in people's gardens) this is not possible for society as a whole; the consumption of pensioners as a group is produced by the next generation of workers. From an *aggregate viewpoint*, the economic function of pension schemes is to divide total production between workers and pensioners, *i.e.* to reduce the consumption of workers so that sufficient output remains for pensioners. Once this point is understood it becomes clear why PAYGO and funded schemes, which are both simply ways of dividing output between workers and pensioners, should not fare very differently in the face of demographic change.

The World Bank's critique of collective responsibility

Peter Lloyd-Sherlock, lecturer in Latin American Studies at the University of Glasgow, in a paper presented at a one-day workshop on Aging and Social Policy, held at the London School of Economics in early 1995, offered a detailed comparison of the neoliberal alternative proposed by the World Bank and the "welfarist" approach of the ILO. He lists a number of key features of the World Bank's argument:

- The value of benefits provided by public schemes are reduced because publicly-managed pension reserves are invested unproductively, earning low or even negative rates of return.
- The failure to index benefits means that pensioners in many countries have not been protected from inflation.

- High payroll taxes associated with public schemes stifle growth by reducing savings, discouraging employment and denying the private sector financial resources—perhaps even pushing some workers into the informal economy.
- Public social security is inherently regressive because large income transfers go to upper-income old people, while many of the lower-income old are not helped.
- Public transfers tend to undermine informal systems of support: for example, children may provide less support for elderly parents if the public sector provides more.
- Public sector schemes are vulnerable to political manipulation and a short-term focus.

Similar arguments were made by neoliberal commentators in Canada during the recent debate about CPP reform. But Canadian actuary Bruce MacDonald, in a detailed analysis of the CPP, points out that many of the Bank's criticisms of pay-as-you-go public pensions do not apply to Canada's public pension system; for instance, Canada's public pensions are fully indexed for inflation.

And Lloyd-Sherlock says that some of the World Bank's criticisms of public pension programs had already been countered by the ILO. For example, the ILO says that unproductive investment of pension funds and failure to index benefits are not inherent problems with public programs; they simply reflect the inefficiency of management.

The ILO also argues that payroll taxes would be just as large in a privatized system. And while both the World Bank and the ILO agree that informal support of the elderly is becoming less significant, the reasons they put forward are diametrically opposed. The ILO argues that public welfare systems are required to compensate for the impact of modernization in rapidly changing societies, while the World Bank blames such interventions for the decline of informal support.

LLoyd-Sherlock outlines a number of guiding principles that inform the World Bank model. They include:

- An assumption that the private sector is better suited to meeting the economic needs of the elderly and does not suffer the shortcomings listed above. Consequently, the private sector should be given primacy over the public one—a view which fits within the broader neoliberal philosophy of the World Bank.
- The assumption that the great majority of the population is in a position to save or defer consumption for later life. If this does not occur, it is due to market failure or individuals' irresponsibility. Lloyd-Sherlock points out that, in its list of factors that account for gaps in insurance coverage, the World Bank leaves the impact of long-term poverty until last.

The Bank argues that the key determinant of the economic welfare of the elderly is the performance of the economy as a whole. In this respect, it agrees with the ILO. It also argues that its own model is universally applicable —a position the ILO also takes for its welfarist approach. But critics of the World Bank approach—including Joseph Stiglitz, a former World Bank senior vice-president and chief economist—point out that optimal pension policy is so complex that we should be wary about believing that "a similar set of recommendations would be appropriate in countries ranging from Argentina to Azerbaijan, from China to Costa Rica, from Sierra Leone to Sweden."

The mantle of economic respectability for privatization

The advocates of privatization of public pensions have tried to dress up their case in a mantle of economic respectability. They have argued that the public costs of an aging population just cannot be sustained. When the population is aging, they say, pay-as-you-go public pension plans require unacceptable transfers from younger generations to the old. They claim such plans are unfair to young people, who would get a much better return if they contributed to an individual savings account for themselves rather than to the public pension program. And, in an attempt to give their arguments some economic credibility, they argue—along with the World Bank—that replacing the public earnings-related plan with mandatory individual savings accounts would increase national savings, bringing a variety of other economic benefits with it. Of course, this begs the question of whether the objective of public pension programs is to promote economic growth or to provide for the well-being of future seniors.

It is perhaps significant that the demographic time bomb crowd don't spend much time talking about whether people would be able to generate an adequate retirement income from individual savings accounts. Of course, in a market-driven, individualized system, whether or not you got enough to live on in retirement would be entirely up to you. The privatizers characterize this as "putting pension provision under individual control." Evidently, it's also what the Association of Canadian Pension Management (ACPM) had in mind in its January 2000 report on the retirement income system when it called for people to become more "self-reliant"—with the help of generous tax-breaks, of course.

In keeping with their neoliberal approach, the advocates of privatization apparently see no virtue in the pooling of risks and acceptance of collective responsibility which is the hallmark of public pension programs based on social insurance principles, such as the Canada Pension Plan or U.S. Social Security. The role of government, according to this neoliberal vision, should be to provide a very minimal safety net through the first pillar of the retirement income system, with a limited goal of alleviating poverty among the old—in much the same way as Canada's income-tested Guaranteed Income Supplement does. Everything else should be left to the market. In other words, individuals should be expected to provide for themselves.

Ironically, of course, the Canadian proponents of the World Bank vision still expect the government to assist those individuals through generous tax subsidies, paid for by all taxpayers—including those lower-income earners who can't take advantage of the system themselves. And in Canada's system of RRSPs, the higher a person's income, the higher the subsidy. Not only are higher-income earners allowed to contribute more to an RRSP in dollar terms, but, because our tax system is progressive, higher-income earners receive a bigger tax refund for any given contribution than lower-income earners would receive for the same dollar amount contributed to an RRSP.

The impact on retirement incomes

Notably absent from the World Bank analysis is any assessment of whether individuals acting on their own—subject to some government regulation of their mandatory private savings arrangements—would be able to provide adequately for their retirement years. And what would be the consequences if they failed to do so? The World Bank model envisages a minimal flat-rate or means-tested basic benefit to alleviate poverty, but its emphasis is very much on "affordability" and the "limited goal of reducing poverty among the old." This first pillar of its proposed retirement income system should be "modest in size," the Bank says. It admits that reducing demands on its proposed first pillar will depend on the success of the second pillar: the mandatory savings scheme.

The question that seems to go unanswered is how well can a mandatory savings scheme provide adequate retirement income for future retirees? Failure of the second pillar could lead to unanticipated demands on the first pillar, which governments might be unable to meet. The World Bank does not consider this possibility, which could potentially lead to significant increases in poverty among the elderly.

It's worth repeating that the very essence of a social insurance program is that members of society agree to come together and pool the risks of providing for the loss of income that all face when they retire or become disabled. In doing so, they create citizenship rights or entitlements that reflect a collective responsibility for and to future seniors. Those entitlements are now under attack by the advocates of privatization.

The World Bank, however, does not accept the rationale for pay-as-you-go public pension programs that "workers who pay the taxes to support the program view it as an implicit, ongoing inter-generational contract," where "current workers pay for the pensions of current retirees and expect to receive pensions that others will pay for in the future—very much like an extension of the informal system." It believes that "The complexity of a dominant public pillar enables influential groups to exert political pressures for design features that are neither equitable nor efficient—from which they benefit while passing the hidden costs on to others in their own or future generations."

A multipillar old age security system reduces these adverse political pressures, the Bank claims. The social insurance part of public pension systems, says the Bank, "can be turned over to a mandatory, funded, privately managed competitive scheme in which benefits are directly tied to contributions, so reducing the incentives for evasion and the opportunities for manipulation. This scheme is likely to have a more positive effect on national saving, labour productivity, and growth," according to the Bank's analysis.

It should be noted that the claim that "benefits are directly tied to contributions" in a mandatory savings scheme is misleading at best. Typically, mandatory savings schemes are "money purchase" or defined contribution arrangements where no particular benefit is guaranteed. Unlike an earnings-related social insurance program, where the retirement pension is a defined benefit, related to earnings and years of service or years of contributions to the plan, a mandatory savings scheme accumulates contributions in a fund, which is eventually used to purchase a pension. The amount of the pension depends on the size of the fund, which in turn depends on investment returns, administrative costs, the cost of commissions and fees, and so on, as well as the level of interest rates at the time the pension is purchased.

Just how would a system of mandatory individual savings accounts address the avowed concerns of the demographic doomsayers? Let's take a look at their key arguments and see.

The public costs of an aging population

The attack on public pensions has been bolstered by calculations that purport to show the public cost of our aging population just cannot be sustained. Getting rid of public pensions would presumably relieve taxpayers of the burden of contributing to programs to support the elderly through contributions to Social Security or the CPP. According to conventional wisdom, elderly people consume more health care. When you add in the cost of their public pensions and maybe also the cost of paying down government debt, the dollar total may be enough to scare even the most dedicated supporter of public pensions.

This is the kind of ammunition the demographic doomsayers have used to make their case for the privatization of public pensions. In effect, they have added together a variety of public expenditures and concluded that public pensions, which are only one element of the total, are no longer "affordable." In both Canada and the United States, this kind of calculation is being used to undermine "entitlements" for the elderly.

In the United States, according to Dean Baker and Mark Weisbrot, even well-respected and progressive economists have fallen for the "entitlements trick." Proponents of Social Security privatization lump together Social Security and

Medicare, branding them as "entitlements for the elderly." Then, on the basis of the last 30 years of health care inflation in the U.S., it's easy to project explosive growth in Medicare spending. The federal budget therefore also explodes, and the whole economy goes down the tubes. The conclusion is that Social Security must be privatized: converted to a system of individual savings accounts along the lines recommended by the World Bank.

But Baker and Weisbrot point out that Social Security and Medicare are two separate programs funded by separate taxes. As well, they note that, while it's true the elderly consume more health care than the young, overall health care spending does not necessarily have to increase with the average age of the population. In most developed countries, they say, there seems to be no correlation between health care spending and the percentage of the population that is over 65. For instance, as a percentage of GDP, the U.S. spends almost twice as much on health care as does Sweden, yet 17.3% of Sweden's population is over 65—a proportion the U.S. will not reach for another 25 years.

Such scare tactics are not unknown in Canada, either. A 1995 report from the Canadian Institute of Actuaries (CIA), called *Troubled Tomorrows*, added together the cost of the OAS, GIS, the CPP, Medicare, and the national debt, and concluded government spending could approach 60% of GDP by 2030. According to the CIA, this could mean a GST of 35% (instead of the current 7%) or social security contributions totalling 30% of payroll (instead of the proposed 10%).

It would appear the CIA's nightmare prognosis assumes that, over the next 35 years, the economy will grow at an average annual rate of about 2%, or half the growth rate of the past 35 years. There's no indication of any assumption about productivity, which of course is a key element in the equation. But here's a reality check. In its 2000 budget, the federal government said its program spending in the fiscal year 2001-02 would be roughly 11.6% of GDP—the lowest ratio in half a century. When public debt charges were added in, total government spending was expected to be 15.6% of GDP. Yet the demographic doomsayers are suggesting it will leap to 60% of GDP in a period of less than 30 years. By the accounting standards used in most other G-7 countries, the federal government said it would post a financial surplus for the fourth consecutive year in 1999-2000— the only G-7 country to do so.

Real GDP growth in 1999 was estimated at 3.8%, and private sector forecasters expect continued robust economic growth in 2000 and 2001. A 1999 survey conducted by consulting firm KPMG of 27 of the country's foremost economists and financial market prognosticators in organizations such as chartered banks, investment management firms, and other corporations showed projections for real economic growth in the period from 2005 to 2014 as high as 3.5% a year. The median growth projection for this period was 2.5% a year.

Credible Canadian projections are also available from private sector sources. A thorough and detailed analysis of the Canadian situation, published in 1999 by respected economists Frank Denton and Byron Spencer of McMaster University, concluded that government expenditures necessary to maintain social security and health care at current per capita levels will rise in the coming decades (albeit slowly) as a consequence of population aging, as is widely anticipated. Rates of increase will exceed both the rate of growth of the population and the rate of growth of GDP. But these economists say the evidence indicates also that those increases will be offset elsewhere in the budgetary framework, especially in education, but in other categories as well. The overall increase for all budgetary items combined will be at about the rate of growth of the population, and below the rate of growth of GDP. Total expenditure for all budgetary categories combined is projected to fall rather than rise over the 40-year period from 1991 to 2031.

Interestingly enough, the CIA's *Troubled Tomorrows* report comes to the conclusion that Canada should not abandon its pay-as-you-go approach. "Any attempt to fund or replace Canada's public pension plans will be expensive in the short term, with no guarantee of a commensurate reduction in long-term cost," says the report. "Today's environment favours funded retirement savings plans, but tomorrow's environment, like the environment of the 1960s might not." That's an interesting admission, given the current pressure for privatization. But it's one that was made in 1995. By 2000, the CIA was joining with the ACPM to sponsor a National Symposium on Aging at which views supporting privatization of the CPP by way of individual accounts were featured prominently.

And the ACPM, in its "demographic time bomb" report of January 2000, claims to believe that "Canadians, if they understood the financial implications 20-30 years hence of today's rules, would prefer the path of self-reliance to financing their retirements over the path of entitlement and state dependence, which is the orientation of much of today's retirement income system." This is a view in which pooling of the risks of providing for retirement through a contributory earnings-related public pension plan, and acceptance of collective responsibility for elderly citizens are seen as "state dependence." Our senior citizens should not be "entitled" to financial support in their old age, according to this view—we just can't afford it any more. Let them fend for themselves. Let them strengthen their moral fibre and be "self-reliant."

What is left unsaid in this approach is the fact that a system where everyone is expected to be "self-reliant" is one where there will be considerable inequality of results. In contrast, recent studies have shown that Canada's public pension system—and particularly the CPP—has made a significant contribution to reducing poverty and inequality among seniors. As the Lazar Task Force pointed out in its landmark 1979 report, individuals and private institutions are ill-placed to offer insurance against certain economy-wide developments. The reason we set up the CPP, it said, was to assure for all Canadians an earnings-related pension that they could not otherwise guarantee through the private market. If that plan were abandoned, many people would be unable to provide adequately for their retirement though private savings. That could actually increase the cost of publicly-funded programs, because more people than expected might then have to claim the basic anti-poverty guarantee from the first pillar of the system.

Among other things, the Lazar Task Force said, "A person who saves and insures himself adequately can find that unanticipated inflation, depression, or a poor investment climate seriously erodes the value of his private savings and insurance." When governments require individuals to participate in public pension programs, some of these difficulties are eliminated and others are reduced. Public pension programs pool the risks inherent in unforeseen future events, lessening the risk faced by any single individual.

Abandoning public pension programs in favour of mandatory private savings would eliminate the public cost of an earnings-related pension such as the CPP. It would shift the cost of the aging population into the private realm instead. However, this "solution" does not address the fact that, no matter how pensions are financed—whether through pay-as-you-go public pension plans, general tax revenues, or fully funded private savings arrangements—they must be paid out of current incomes.

Those who have saved for retirement through private investments in RRSPs, for example, must eventually sell their investments to someone to provide an income for themselves. Younger people, who may be saving for their own future retirement, may buy the investments, thus reducing their own current consumption.

When the baby boom generation retires and the elderly form a much higher percentage of the Canadian population, it is inevitable that they will have a larger claim on the total economy because of their numbers. Claims on national income by the elderly can only be reduced if their numbers are reduced—perhaps through later retirement—or their relative incomes can be reduced. But if the economy is growing and productivity is improving, increased claims on the national income by retirees should not result in a reduction of the claims of younger Canadians.

Increasing the age of entitlement

Of course, we could try to address the problem by increasing the size of the work force, which we might do if we required people to work longer before claiming their pensions. Raising the age of entitlement to public pensions is, in fact, an approach suggested by a number of people in the current debate on pension reform. In the U.S., for example, the age of eligibility for a full Social Security pension is being raised to 67 from 65. Other countries have also raised the age of entitlement. But it should be noted that some of these countries are simply bringing their retirement ages into line with what Canada already has. In New Zealand, for instance, the age of eligibility for public pensions was set at 60 and is being gradually increased to reach age 65 in 2001. Other countries, such as Britain, allowed women to claim benefits at age 60, while men were not eligible until age 65. These countries are now increasing the age of eligibility for women to make it the same as men's.

Getting your pension at age 65 is said to be something that was established by Bismarck, who was Chancellor of Germany at the end of the 19th century. Given that life expectancy has increased quite a bit since then, we might reasonably expect people to work longer before they are pensioned off. But most people now want to retire **before** age 65. In fact, the latest information from the CPP shows that almost 60% of new retirees claim their CPP retirement pension prior to age 65.

Pay-as-you-go plans and inter-generational equity

Canada's public pension plans are based on pay-as-you-go financing. Current taxpayers fund the cost of these programs through their taxes or social security contributions. Essentially, this represents a transfer of resources from younger to older generations. And, when the population is aging, the size of the transfer must increase, because there are more older people in relation to the number of younger people.

Advocates of pension privatization say that, when the population is aging, pay-as-you-go public pension plans require unacceptably large transfers from younger generations to the old. . A switch to private individual accounts would relieve working age people of the "burden" of paying for the pensions of retirees. Instead, their mandatory contributions would be directed to saving for their own pensions and this would eliminate the intergenerational inequity of a pay-as-you-go pension plan, according to the advocates of privatization. Of course, unlike the CPP which is effectively a defined benefit pension plan, there would be no promise of any particular pension under a system of mandatory individual accounts. The amount of the eventual pension would depend on the circumstances of each individual throughout their working life and in retirement.

In Canada, the first pillar programs of Old Age Security (OAS), Guaranteed Income Supplement (GIS) and Spouses' Allowance (SPA) are financed through general tax revenues collected by the federal government. No fund is accumulated to pay the benefits, which are paid from current taxes. Benefits under the CPP are paid for by contributions from the current work force and their employers. The government does not contribute to the cost of the CPP.

A key feature of the recent CPP reforms, however, was a rapid increase in the contribution rate so that contribution revenue would be enough both to pay the benefits and establish an investment fund to be invested in the stock market.

In the future, earnings on the fund will be used to supplement contribution revenues from which benefits are paid. However, even with the new investment fund, the CPP will remain largely a pay-as-you-go plan. Under the new funding formula, the assets of the fund are expected eventually to reach 20% of liabilities. The balance of the plan's liabilities—the benefits that are promised to contributors—will still be financed by contribution revenues. By mid-2000, the assets of the CPP Investment Fund had reached only 8% of liabilities.

By definition, pay-as-you-go pension plans, such as Canada's CPP or U.S. Social Security, require a transfer from younger workers to older people because mandatory contributions from workers and their employers are used to pay the pensions of those who have retired. The system represents an implicit contract between generations. Each generation contributes to the plan in the expectation that, when they retire, the succeeding generation will maintain contributions to pay for the pensions of its predecessors.

Public pension programs as a Ponzi scheme

For the demographic doomsayers, the idea that one generation should pay for the pensions of another through a pay-as-you-go plan is unfair. It is especially "unfair," they say, if the younger generation of working age people must pay relatively more than their predecessors did for the same benefits because the population is aging. Social Security or the Canada Pension Plan is a Ponzi scheme, they claim. Just like a chain letter or a pyramid scheme, it's a state-sponsored scam that draws in ever-increasing numbers of younger contributors, who pay more and more into the plan and get less and less out of it

The concept is named after Charles Ponzi, a notorious swindler who was born in Italy at the end of the 19th century. He emigrated to Canada, then went to the United States, where he operated an audacious pyramid scheme in the 1920s. Contributions paid in by new members were used to finance dividends to existing members, and of course Ponzi skimmed off funds for himself. Such plans are not based on any real investment, so, if the number of contributors fails to grow, the dividends dry up and the scheme collapses. After serving time in jail, Ponzi was deported back to Italy, where he died penniless in 1949.

It's difficult to see how a pay-as-you-go social insurance program, established through the collective will of citizens and backed by the taxing powers and the regulatory authority of federal and provincial governments, can be compared to Ponzi's scheme. But the colourful and exaggerated rhetoric, piled on top of the demographic scare tactics, seems to be a sure-fire way for the advocates of privatization to destroy confidence in public pension programs and build a constituency for replacing them with individual savings accounts. William Robson, for instance, a senior policy analyst at the corporate-sponsored C.D.Howe Institute, claims the CPP is a Ponzi Scheme. Canada should "send Ponzi packing," he says and start preparing for a future without the CPP. Robson has advocated phasing out the CPP in favour of expanded private retirement saving.

Exactly the same rhetoric is being used in the United States, where Social Security is also being attacked as a Ponzi scheme in which the first participants benefit at the expense of those who join in after them, with the whole structure collapsing underneath the hapless Generation X or perhaps their progeny.

The contract between generations

People who think the CPP is not fair, because it involves a transfer from the younger generation to the older, must be reminded that inter-generational transfers occur throughout society, and not just in the pension system. Transfers are made from old to young as well as from young to old. And they take place in the private as well as in the public sphere. This point was raised frequently during the public consultations held prior to the recent CPP reforms. Older participants pointed out that, while younger Canadians might be asked to contribute more to the CPP to pay the pensions of the elderly, older Canadians paid—and continue to pay—taxes to finance the building of infrastructure, such as schools, hospitals, transportation, and so on, and to fund the education of the young. They supported and actively participated in the war effort during the Second World War. They also bore the private costs of raising the baby boom generation.

Generational accounting

Some researchers have tried to quantify the inter-generational contract by using "generational accounting," first popularized by U.S. economist Lawrence Kotlikoff of Boston University in the early 1990s. This is an approach that tries to measure the lifetime tax burden on different age groups. The general idea is that generational equity is achieved if it can be ensured that each generation carries the same tax burden— no more and no less than other generations do. It's also another way in which the opponents of public pensions have tried to lay a veneer of economic credibility over their views on the inter-generational inequity of these public programs.

Generational accounting has been used in the U.S. ostensibly to demonstrate that successive age cohorts will face higher and higher lifetime tax burdens, to the point where 80%, 90% or even 100% of their incomes will be eaten up by taxes. Needless to say, such calculations do much to fan the flames of inter-generational conflict over public pensions.

To compare income and tax payments at different points in time, analysts use a discount rate: in effect, an interest rate which takes into account the possibility that money can be lent out and earn interest through time. The discount rate selected for a particular analysis can make a big difference to the outcome, especially over long periods of time. In the standard version of generational accounts, U.S. analysts generally use a 6% real discount rate, although the conventional rate used in analyses of Social Security is only 2%. Using a much higher discount rate has the effect of raising the net tax burden for future generations enormously, because it lowers the value of Social Security and Medicare benefits that future generations are projected to receive throughout their long retirements. That's why critics charge that generational accounting is being used to cook the books. Canadian sociologist Ellen Gee agrees. This is clearly linked to apocalyptic demography, she says, in that it is "a mechanism to attempt to deal with the perceived crushing tax burden of the elderly." And it is being used to justify cuts in government transfer programs.

Here's evidence of the sleight-of-hand involved. Economists Dean Baker and Mark Weisbrot say that simply changing the discount rate from 6% to 3% lowers the lifetime tax burden for future generations by 29-39 percentage points. Using the standard 2% rate lowers the net tax burden an additional 11.6 percentage points, to less than 40%. As these authors point out, the lower discount rate goes a long way toward eliminating the horror story the generational accountants have constructed.

Generational accounting has also been criticized on the grounds that it only takes into account the costs of social programs and not their benefits. And it doesn't consider family-based transfers across generations. There is a wealth of social research that shows much of the social exchange that occurs between generations occurs along non-monetary lines, but these private transfers have been unrecognized by the media and by policy-makers.

Just the same, the generational accounting approach seems to have gained some credibility in Ottawa policy circles, with Statistics Canada and Human Resources Development Canada holding a joint conference on the issue at the beginning of 1997 at which Kotlikoff himself made a presentation. The editor of the published proceedings of the conference referred to growing interest in the issue of generational equity, of which he said reform of public pension programs was "the most obvious example."

But critics of the approach who attended the conference pointed out the difficulty of measuring inter-generational equity. One asked if it was even relevant to try and measure it as far as the tax/transfer system is concerned. "The primary goal of the tax/transfer system," he said, "is not to ensure inter-generational equity." Others said, "The very idea of framing the issue of the sustainability of government tax/transfer arrangements, including public pensions, in terms of generational equity may be seriously misleading." In principle, they said, it is necessary to go beyond the arithmetic, "since inter-generational fairness ultimately depends on future working age generations' "ability to pay" for transfers to the then elderly. This in turn depends on society's future productive capacity: the wealth or "capital stock" current generations will have bequeathed to future generations."

They pointed out that society's capital stock should be very broadly defined for this kind of analysis. For instance, it should include the state of the environment and accumulated knowledge, as well as more conventional productive assets like roads and factories. The processes determining future inheritances therefore include the myriad inter-generational transfers occurring within families, the evolving state of the natural and built environment, private sector investments, and public sector revenues and expenditures.

It is almost impossible, however, to measure most of these transfers in money terms. That's why judgements of inter-generational fairness based only on money flows are necessarily partial, these authors pointed out. It is even more restrictive to focus only on those monetary flows associated with the public sector, because that leaves out financial flows within families, as well as the accumulation of private assets by businesses.

As economist Lars Osberg of Dalhousie University pointed out in a paper also included in the conference proceedings, in the private sector most accountants would think it odd to focus on only half the balance sheet and consider only liabilities. One could easily reduce the tax liabilities of future generations, he said, by closing public schools and by selling off the road network, but it is worth asking if future generations would be better off paying tuition fees and highway tolls. Said Osberg, "Such questions cannot be considered by a theoretical framework that recognizes only the costs of government, while assuming the benefits of government activity to be non-existent." Important aspects of our inter-generational bequest are difficult to measure, he said, but it may be dysfunctional to ignore issues just because of this difficulty. And in the entire volume of papers from the conference, he said, there is not one word of discussion about the legacy of productive capacity that this generation of Canadians will leave to the future.

Declining rates of return

When it comes to inter-generational equity in public pension plans, there are two main points at issue. One is the fact that, in countries where the population is aging, succeeding generations must pay relatively more into the plan than their predecessors did. The other is the question of what younger contributors to the plan will get out of the plan compared with those who were the original plan members. Associated with these concerns is the perception that, for younger generations, the return on their "investment" in the public pension plan will be unacceptably low.

Critics say a pay-as-you-go pension may have been a great deal for the first generation of beneficiaries. They paid relatively low contributions into the plan, compared with what they'll get out of it. What's more, critics say, today's seniors only paid in for a small part of their working lives, yet they are entitled to a full pension. Younger people who'll come up to retirement in the future won't do nearly as well as today's seniors, so the argument goes. In effect, current seniors are getting a much higher rate of return on their contributions than today's working-age generation will. According to this argument, this will create inter-generational conflict because younger generations will see the CPP as a "bad deal" and will refuse to support it.

Critics of the public pension system say the high rates of return that stock market investors have been earning recently are much more attractive—especially to younger workers—than the kind of return they can expect to get by investing in a social security plan like the CPP. Younger workers, so the argument goes, would be much better off investing their own money in an RRSP or some other private investment plan than paying into a public pension plan.

Of course, it's usually the case when a pay-as-you-go pension plan like the CPP is first established that the early generations who benefit from the plan receive more in benefits per dollar contributed than those who receive benefits once the plan has matured. Such an outcome is almost inevitable because new plans like this have to start somewhere. When the CPP was set up in 1966, it was decided to phase in benefits quickly over a ten-year period. During the transition years from 1967 to 1975, the pension was 10% of the potential maximum retirement benefit for each year between 1966 and the year of retirement. Full retirement benefits were paid in 1976, just ten years after the plan was set up. So people who retired only ten years after the plan was established were entitled to a full pension.

Generations who benefit from the CPP

In a paper on inter-generational equity, Bob Baldwin of the Canadian Labour Congress estimates that the generation that received the most in CPP benefits per dollar contributed is the generation born before 1922. They paid the initial 3.6% contribution rate, which was maintained until 1987, and many of them received pensions equivalent to 25% of their pre-retirement earnings, up to the maximum permitted. Baldwin says all generations in the labour force between about 1986 and 2034—that is, people who were born between 1922 and 2015—can expect to receive declining net intergenerational transfers from earlier generations. But the relatively stable contribution rates predicted after 2035 indicate that net inter-generational transfers within the CPP will have been virtually eliminated by that time.

Claims that young people will pay "more than their benefits are worth," or that they will pay more into the CPP than they will ever receive in benefits, are certainly not true. For instance, one Canadian actuary estimates that, for people who reach age 65 in 2013, the ratio of the benefits to the contributions they made will be 10.7. In other words, their benefits will be worth 10.7 times what they contributed to the plan. For those reaching age 65 in 2033, this ratio is estimated at 5.9; for those reaching age 65 in 2053, it is 5.0; and for those reaching age 65 in 2073, it is expected to be 5.1. According to this expert, "This means that all future generations are expected to receive in current dollar benefits over five times what they and their employer contributed, contrary to the belief that they will receive less in benefits than the amount contributed."

The real rate of return from social security

Experts have also calculated the real rate of return (after allowing for inflation) for different age groups. In effect, these calculations indicate the implicit rate of return on the contributions of participants in the plan by determining the present value of the streams of contributions that a person makes over their lifetime, related to the benefits they might be expected to receive. For the U.S., it's been estimated that an average-income, single male employee, born in 1920, would have received an expected real rate of return of 2.73% on his contributions to Social Security, compared with 1.37%

for someone born in 1943.

In Canada, it has been estimated that individuals born in 1929 and reaching age 65 in 1994 would have received a real rate of return on their CPP contributions of 10.2%. Those born in 1968 and reaching age 65 in 2033 will receive a real rate of return of 2.9%, while the average real rate of return for those born in 1988 and reaching age 65 in 2053 will be 1.6%, and 1.5% for those who turn 65 in 2073

World-renowned economic Paul Samuleson showed more than 40 years ago that the real rate of return on a mature pay-as-you-go system is equal to the sum of the rate of growth in the labour force and the rate of growth in productivity. Looked at another way, implicit rates of return on a mature pay-as-you-go pension plan such as the CPP over the longer term will be equal to the rate of growth in the earnings base on which CPP contributions are assessed. And the Chief Actuary's Seventeenth Actuarial report on the CPP, as at December 31, 1997, estimated long-term growth in real earnings at 1.5% a year.

How does it compare with the stock market?

These rates may seem paltry compared with the kind of returns stock market investors have been getting recently. But is it even relevant to make this kind of comparison? Experts have called such comparisons "fundamentally misleading." And, according to a landmark paper from the World Bank's former senior vice-president and chief economist, Joseph Stiglitz, "The comparison of rates of return is misguided fundamentally because higher returns in the long run can be obtained only at the expense of reduced consumption and returns for intervening generations."

The CPP is not a personal savings plan like a mutual fund or an investment portfolio. It is a social insurance program that pools the risks of providing for the loss of income that individuals face when they retire or become disabled. An investment portfolio or mutual fund can't provide the

additional benefits available through the CPP, such as infla-
tion-indexed pensions, disability coverage, survivor benefits,
and benefits for the dependent children of disabled or
deceased contributors.
The CPP guarantees a retirement pension related to lifetime earnings and years of contributions to the plan. An
RRSP or mutual fund investment does not guarantee any
particular benefit. The amount of any pension generated
under a system of individual savings accounts will depend
on a variety of personal circumstances. Individuals would
end up with lower pensions if they had periods out of the
work force because they were ill or unemployed; if they had
extended periods of further education and training; or if they
took time out of the paid work force to raise children. Most
of these situations are accommodated in the CPP without
penalizing the individual.
Under a system of individual accounts, the amount of
any pension will also depend on financial markets and individual investment expertise. Lower pensions would also
result for individuals who made poor investment decisions:
if the stock market dropped so that the rate of return on their
investments was much lower than they had anticipated, or if
interest rates were low when they retired and used their
funds to buy an annuity. Fees and commissions also
reduce the proportion of the individual's contribution that
will actually generate a pension.
The pooling of risk is a central characteristic of a pension
plan. It does not even exist in a system of individual
accounts, which—by definition—are based on the individual
investor bearing the entire risk. Critics suggest that the line of
argument about the CPP representing a bad rate of return on
investment for younger generations is based on a poor
appreciation of this fundamental principle of pension plans,
as well as reflecting a very limited historical perspective on
what constitutes reasonable rates of return.
High stock market returns cannot be expected to contin-

ue indefinitely, nor can they be predicted with any accuracy 30 or 40 years into the future. The 1.5% wage growth assumption which forms the basis for the long-term implicit rate of return in the CPP exceeds real returns on Treasury Bills from the mid-1930s through the mid-1970s, and even real returns on long-term Government of Canada bonds from the mid-1940s through the mid-1970s. However, in each of the five-year periods starting in 1981 and running through 1995, real returns on long-term Government of Canada bonds were 9.57%. 4.70%, and 12.20%. This compares with average real returns of 1.29% and 2.49% over the 50 and 70-year periods up to and including 1992. The returns on common stocks were not extraordinary over the period since 1980. Although they were strong in the 1990-to-1995 period, they have been quite irregular from decade to decade.

The high cost of individual accounts

The advocates of privatization like to talk about the spectacular returns investors could get by directing their pension contributions to individual accounts instead of to the public pension plan. But they conveniently overlook how charges and commissions eat into those returns. A British government task force, appointed to look into what had happened to retirement incomes since the Thatcher government allowed people to opt out of the public pension plan in favour of individual savings accounts, observed that the costs of running personal pensions are significantly higher than those for most occupational pension schemes.

Individual accounts also involve much higher costs than pay-as-you-go pension plans. Investors have to pay fees and commissions to financial institutions to manage their money. They must pay commissions to brokers who trade the securities in their accounts, and commissions to the insurance companies that sell them a pension at retirement. There are also underlying costs, such as sales and marketing costs of the financial institutions selling the plans, which are passed on to investors.

High costs reduce amount of savings available to provide a retirement income. According to the World Bank report, where investors are relatively uneducated and uninformed about financial matters, they are susceptible to intensive marketing campaigns which increase costs. Inevitably, the British task force said, administration costs reduce the share of contributions that result in pension rights. In the United States, the Advisory Council on Social Security estimated that administrative costs under a decentralized system of individual accounts in which workers held their accounts with various financial firms and were allowed a broad array of investment options—like Canada's RRSP system, for instance—could consume about 20% of the value of the account accumulated over a 40-year work career.

Rates of return for individuals under a system of individual accounts may actually be negative because of fees and commissions. According to one estimate, under the Chilean system, despite double-digit rates of return for the privatized funds over most of the first decade, the cumulative rate of return for account holders was negative. High management fees account for the difference between what a fund earns on investments and what the account holder receives. In most privatized schemes in Latin American countries, management fees are in the region of 15% to 20% of the annual contribution. Final benefits at retirement are 15% to 20% lower than they would have been in the absence of the fees.

The World Bank estimated that promotional costs account for as much as 30% of the operating costs of the Chilean system. These costs are eventually passed on to consumers in the form of higher fees. Other estimates suggest that, for an average worker in the Chilean system, the costs of their personal pension plan, plus the costs associated with purchasing an annuity pension on retirement, would be well over one-third of their contributions. In contrast, the administrative cost of operating the CPP, prior to the recent establishment of the CPP Investment fund, was less than 2% of contribution revenue.

Even if privatization is limited to allowing people to opt out of a public pay-as-you-go plan rather than converting the plan to a system of individual accounts, there are significant cost increases. One recent study of the British system of opting-out found that between 40% and 45% of the value of individual accounts in the U.K. is consumed by various fees and costs.

High transition costs of privatized schemes.

Whether privatization takes the form of replacing a pay-as-you-go plan with a system of individual savings accounts, or simply of allowing opting-out from the pay-as-you-go plan, policy-makers have to address the problem of who will pay for the benefits accumulated under the public system up to the point of privatization. Converting to either form of privatization involves high transition costs. A major reason why studies show the British system is so costly is that transition costs have been included in the estimates.

Advocates of privatization have suggested various ways in which these transition costs might be dealt with. The Reform/Alliance Party's latest proposal to allow opting-out from the CPP seems to recognize this problem. But it would almost certainly land in political hot water with its proposed solutions. Its 1998 booklet raises the issue of what to do with the CPP benefits already accumulated by those who might choose to opt out. People might be asked to give up their accumulated CPP benefits if they want to opt out, Reform suggested.

Even more important is how to finance the benefits for those who choose to stay in the CPP. On this one, Reform said, "Changes to premium levels, benefit levels and/or general tax levels may be necessary to keep it solvent." Several possibilities are suggested: the age of eligibility could be increased; disability coverage could be handled separately, possibly by the provinces; future benefits could be income-tested; people who choose to stay in the plan could be asked to pay more for their benefits.

Increasing national savings

The World Bank provided a blueprint for the privatization of public pensions in its 1994 report on *Averting the Old Age Crisis*. Significantly, the subtitle of the report was *Policies to Protect the Old and Promote Growth*. Essentially, "growth" was to be promoted by getting rid of public earnings-related pensions and replacing them with mandatory individual savings accounts. Not only would this reduce the size of the public sector by reducing the role of the state and eliminating the need for payroll taxes (otherwise known as social security contributions), but the system of individual accounts would increase national savings—according to the World Bank—which would lead to stronger investment and economic growth. However, there appears to be little or no evidence that this would be the case.

It seems the World Bank took a giant leap of faith here. In its report, it admitted that "The impact of pension financing —pay-as-you-go or full funding—on saving has been a subject of considerable controversy on both theoretical and empirical grounds." The Bank said that studies in a number of countries yielded conflicting results. In fact, it was also forced to admit that a balanced review of available evidence is inconclusive on whether the way in which public pension arrangements are financed actually does affect saving, investment and growth. While claiming that "it seems likely that a mandatory savings scheme will increase household saving relative to the situation without a scheme (and even more so relative to a pay-as-you-go system)," the Bank conceded that "empirical evidence on the savings effect of mandatory saving schemes is ambiguous." For instance, it noted that in Chile private saving went up sharply in the decade after the mandatory saving scheme was introduced. But so many other factors were at work, the Bank said, that "it is difficult to pin down how much of the high saving, if any, was due to the mandatory saving scheme." Despite the lack of evidence to support their position, advocates of replacing public pensions with a system of individual accounts have continued to claim such systems increase national savings and promote economic growth. But the World Bank's "leap of faith" has been challenged by no less a person than its own former senior vice president and chief economist, Joseph Stiglitz. While he was still employed at the Bank, Stiglitz made a joint presentation with Peter Orszag, president of Sebago Associates Inc. and a lecturer in macroeconomics at the University of California, Berkeley, to a World Bank conference on "New Ideas About Old Age Security" held in Washington in September 1999. The paper they presented, titled *Rethinking Pension Reform; Ten Myths About Social Security Systems*, tackles the mythology about social security systems and suggests the World Bank's report has, in fact, created new myths about privatization—in particular, that privatization of social security is always a good idea. The arguments most frequently used to promote individual retirement accounts, say these authors, are often not substantiated in either theory or practice.

The very first myth tackled in the paper was the view that private defined contribution plans raise national saving. Stiglitz and Orszag point out that "It is common to assert that moving toward a system of "pre-funded" individual accounts would raise national saving." But, while there is a large academic literature on whether the introduction of a pay-as-you-go social security system reduces national saving, these economists say, that is a fundamentally different issue from whether shifting an existing pay-as-you-go system to one of individual accounts would raise national saving. It is entirely possible, they say, that the introduction of a pay-as-you-go system reduces national saving (as some studies suggest), but that a shift to individual accounts would not raise national saving.

If pre-funding is the issue, they note, this can be achieved without privatization or switching to individual accounts. The government could simply accumulate assets in anticipation of future benefit payments due under the public defined benefit plan. In effect, the pay-as-you-go plan would become a funded plan, with the government holding assets from which benefits would eventually be paid. Ironically, a key reason why countries with public pension plans established them as pay-as-you-go plans in the first place was because of public apprehension about such huge funds being under government control and the potential for misuse of the funds or diversion of the money for other purposes. The diversion of Canada's unemployment insurance fund to reduce the federal government deficit is a good example of what can happen to such "dedicated" funds.

In fact, Canada has already moved to a partially funded system by establishing the CPP Investment Fund—a move which retains the CPP as a defined benefit, earnings-related public pension plan. Canada has in fact also chosen to invest the fund in the market, so to this extent the creation of the CPP Investment Fund might be seen as a limited form of privatization. But, as Stiglitz and Orszag point out, pre-funding does not necessarily have to take the form of private market investments.

A key reason for the establishment of the CPP Investment Fund was to provide investment earnings to supplement contribution revenue, which federal and provincial finance ministers believe will allow the contribution rate to be held steady for the foreseeable future without any further increases. To this extent, then, this step might be seen as an attempt to minimize the inter-generational pressures that arise for pay-as-you-go pension plans when the population is aging and contribution rates must increase. And, clearly, the introduction of some form of private market investment of contribution revenues can be achieved without abandoning social insurance principles or the pooling of risk in favour of individual defined contribution savings accounts.

Other myths about privatization through individual accounts

There are plenty of other myths about the benefits of privatization of public pensions. In the paper they presented to the World Bank conference, referred to earlier, Orszag and Stiglitz chose just ten of them. In the course of debunking these myths, these high-profile economists demonstrated that the arguments most frequently used to promote individual retirement accounts are often not substantiated, either in theory or in practice.

These economists divided the myths into three groups:

Macroeconomic myths:
1. Individual accounts raise national saving.
2. Rates of return are higher under individual accounts.
3. Declining rates of return on pay-as-you-go systems reflect fundamental problems.
4. Investment of public trust funds in equities has no macroeconomic effects.

Microeconomic myths
5. Labour market incentives are better under individual accounts.
6. Defined benefit plans necessarily provide more of an incentive to retire early.
7. Competition ensures low administrative costs under individual accounts.

Political economy myths
8. Corrupt and inefficient governments provide a rationale for individual accounts.
9. Bailout policies are worse under public defined benefit plans.
10. Investment of public trust funds is always squandered and mismanaged.

We have already looked at some of these myths in detail. We'll get to some of the others later in this book. But, in the course of their analysis, Orszag and Stiglitz make several general points that are worth repeating here.

- In looking at the effect of pension reform, one must be careful not to confuse the issue of whether a shift to individual accounts would be socially beneficial with the separate issue of whether an individual account system would have been preferable the first place. The social effects of transforming a mature pension system into a system of individual accounts may be substantially different than the social effects of the initial choice between a public defined benefit system and individual accounts. Very few nations face that initial choice: almost all have some form of old age insurance program. It is of little practical import at this point to re-examine those initial choices.
- Politicians are known for focusing exclusively on the short run, ignoring the long-run costs (or even viability) of public programs. In analyzing transitions, however, we have to be careful not to make the opposite mistake: focusing exclusively on the long run and ignoring short-run costs.
- We need to keep in mind our ultimate objective. Savings and growth are not ends in themselves, but means to an end: the increase in well-being of members of the society. We could perhaps induce people to save more by exposing them to more risk. But that won't necessarily improve their welfare.

Chapter 3

Pinochet and the Chicago Boys privatize Chile's pension system

While a number of industrialized countries have now made moves to privatize their social security systems, Chile was the first country to completely replace a pay-as-you-go public pension program with a privatized mandatory savings scheme. The World Bank's 1994 report on *Averting the Old Age Crisis* draws heavily on the Chilean experience in explaining "how mandatory savings schemes work." Chile's privatized system was the only fully implemented decentralized scheme when the report was being prepared. As the ILO has noted, the Chilean model has now come to represent "the epitome" of privatization schemes. The endorsement of the World Bank seems to have given it added credibility—even among advanced industrialized countries with established public pension plans.

In the United States, where there is now a strong lobby for the privatization of Social Security, the neoliberal Cato Institute appointed José Piñera, whom it describes as "the architect of Chile's successful private pension reforms," as co-chair of its Social Security Privatization project. The Advisory Board for the project includes a number of senior people from investment firms and the insurance industry, and prominent right-wing economists such as Gary Becker and Laurence Kotlikoff. Piñera, who was Minister of Labour and Social Security in the Pinochet regime, has been conducting an active privatization campaign through consultations with governments and others interested in privatization of public pensions, as well as speeches and articles and an Internet site devoted to the project.

In Canada, the Chilean system has also become the favoured option of the right—although, more recently, the Reform/Alliance Party and its supporters seem to prefer the

British system of privatization (the subject of the next chapter). This system allows people to opt out of the state earnings-related public pension program and instead have their contributions directed to a personal pension plan: a defined contribution arrangement roughly equivalent to an RRSP. Presumably, even though the old Reform Party has now transmogrified into the Canadian Alliance, we can expect the party's position on privatization will not change—especially since the Alliance is now led by Stockwell Day who, as Alberta Treasurer, tried in vain to get the other provincial finance ministers to agree to allow opting-out from the CPP.

Proponents of privatization of the CPP have been praising the Chilean model since the early 1990s. For example, the *Globe and Mail* promoted it in a 1994 series of articles by Andrew Coyne—now a columnist for the *National Post*—followed by an editorial endorsement which called for getting rid of the CPP to turn Canada into "a nation of savers." The Reform Party rallied to the cause with a proposal called *Renewing CPP* released in October 1995. The Chilean model has since been endorsed by other neoliberal commentators and research organizations, including the C.D.Howe Institute and the Fraser Institute.

The influence of the Chicago Boys

Chile's privatization of public pensions in 1981 was dreamed up by the notorious Chicago Boys, a group of monetarist economists, followers of right-wing economic guru Milton Friedman, who were to decide not only the future of Chile's social security system, but also the structure of the entire Chilean economy. Just who were these men who wielded such power over Chile's economy and social programs? Following the coup of September 11, 1973, when Augusto Pincohet seized power from President Salvador Allende, several right-wing economists were vaulted into key economic management positions. They quickly became known as the Chicago Boys. Archibald Ritter, who was working in Chile at the Economic Commission for Latin America during the latter period of Allende's Unidad Popular and the first months of the junta, explains that the label referred to the general neo-classical, Friedmanesque, free market orientation of the junta's economic managers. Ritter says the term "came to imply intolerance, neoliberal fanaticism, an inhuman preoccupation with efficiency, and a disregard to equity." The term was also based on the academic linkage between the University of Chicago Economics Department and an inner core of the junta's new economics team.

Under a 1956 agreement signed between the University of Chile and the University of Chicago, the U.S. Agency for International Development funded scholarships for promising Chileans to study economics at Chicago. A number of Chileans earned Chicago economics degrees under the program and in the process, says Ritter, they became imbued with the atmospherics and the theoretical policy orientations of the Chicago school and its major gurus—in particular Milton Friedman and Arnold Harberger, who became "el Padrino" to the Chicago Boys. When they returned to Santiago, some of them converted the economics department at the University of Chile to a bastion of the Chicago school, teaching neo-classical economic theory and promoting a neoliberal approach to economic policy,

According to Ritter, when it seized power the junta initially appeared to be devoid of a clear idea of how to manage the economy. But one of the four men in the junta already had an indirect personal contact with the Chicago Boys, who had been working on an alternative approach to economic management. Their blueprint document was on the desks of the members of the junta the day after the coup. And the authors of the blueprint were soon installed in key economic positions in the government, where they dominated policy-making until the mid-1980s.

Although the Pinochet regime had apparently planned to initiate a reform of the social security system very early after taking power, the social security issue was not dealt with until 1979 when the reappearance of the issue coincided with the consolidation in power of the Chicago Boys. With a stroke of the pen and without any prior announcement or discussion of any kind, the government enacted a decree which radically changed the pension system. New legislation, introduced in 1980, abolished the pay-as-you-go public pension plan, which was based on a collectivist ideology, and replaced it with a system of individual accounts, transforming the social security system into a compulsory private insurance scheme.

According to political scientist Silvia Borzutsky of the University of Pittsburgh, it is clear that the neoliberal economic model and the authoritarian state converged in their need effectively to silence the entire society, and especially those groups—such as organized labour and professional associations of white collar workers and civil servants—perceived as having political power and interfering with the free functioning of the market. At the same time, the regime enacted laws that entirely changed Chile's labour legislation and were a crucial component of the process of depoliticization and fragmentation of society pursued by the regime.

With these laws, Borzutsky says, the regime effectively destroyed the old labour movement, limited the right to strike, and deprived the workers of both political and economic power as well as internationally recognized rights. She says the social security reform was central to this process. Effectively, it transferred power to the new pension funds—the *Adminsitradora de Fondos de Pensiones,* or AFPs, and their new private sector owners, as well as the major banking and publicity concerns involved in the new system. According to Borzutsky, Piñera himself was associated with the Cruzat family economic group, one of the two largest of the new funds. The real measure of the pension industry's political and economic power is its value, says Borzutsky: controlling the private pension funds of five million workers.

It's important to note, as Borzutsky points out, that the Chilean system was developed by an authoritarian regime that had suppressed almost all forms of political expression —although it stressed the principles of individual responsibility—and eliminated the notions of equity and solidarity for all except for the very minimum pensions. In an authoritarian context, the reforms came from the state itself, without the participation of the society.

Limited democratization and the Concertación

The approach to economic management instituted by the Chicago Boys held sway in Chile until March 1990, when Pincohet's military rule ended and a Christian Democrat-led coalition of centre and centre-left parties known as the Concertación took office. But it should be noted that, at the core of the negotiations for the Concertación, after its electoral success in 1989, to take over from the Pinochet dictatorship was the Concertación commitment to maintaining the neoliberal economic model—although they promised to deal with existing social inequities and the legacy of poverty left by the Pinochet regime.

But it would appear that, as far as the public pension system was concerned, the new government in Chile had no plans to reverse the privatization initiatives taken by the Pinochet dictatorship. Observers point out that privatization of social security is now being advocated by national and international experts as a policy that would reduce public spending, increase domestic savings, strengthen labour markets, and provide a more efficient administration, among other changes. The policies appeal to current political élites in Chile because they see it as minimizing the role of government and cutting corporate taxes. In fact, the state continues to play a major role in the system, as we shall see later. But corporate taxes have been reduced and very powerful private financial entities— most of them foreign-owned—are now in control of the pension system.

Chile's mandatory savings scheme

Chile's system of mandatory private savings accounts replaced the public pay-as-you-go pension plan virtually overnight. But it can hardly be called a pension scheme, since there is no pooling of risk, which is the fundamental characteristic of a true pension plan. Workers must contribute 10% of their monthly earnings into an account with a private fund or *Adminsitradora de Fondos de Pensiones* (AFP) to cover old age pensions, and an additional 3% of earnings to cover administrative costs and an insurance premium for disability and survivor pension benefits.

In addition, there is a mandatory health insurance premium of 7% of earnings, which can be paid either to the government health program or into any of the private health programs. In other words, total mandatory contributions to these programs amount to 20% of earnings, and there are no matching employer contributions.

Employers to remit contributions

Employer contributions were deliberately eliminated as part of the privatization. The neoliberal rationale was that this would lower the cost of labour, in turn reducing the high unemployment rates. However, employers are under a legal obligation to collect worker contributions and to deposit them in the AFP chosen by the worker. After deducting commissions, the AFP invests the money on behalf of the worker.

Observers say that lack of adequate payment controls and high inflation—especially in the 1980s—created an incentive for employers to delay the transfer of salary deductions to the AFPs. Workers in the private scheme are supposed to check the regular quarterly report they receive from their AFP to make sure their employers have actually transferred their contributions into the plan. But many don't do this and others can't understand the reports. In fact, according to a 1994 survey conducted by the Association of AFPs,

71% of those surveyed kept the report without reading it and 48% said they did not understand the report.

The AFPs can prosecute delinquent employers, but many fail to do so because they're afraid the employers will encourage their employees to change AFPs. They have also opposed the introduction of a unified fully computerized system, in part because they fear a powerful state agency could use information against the AFPs.

Switching to the new system

Membership of a personal pension plan was compulsory for wage and salary workers who entered the labour force after 1982. But it is optional for self-employed workers. In fact, in 1993, only about 4% of Chile's 1.3 million self-employed workers belonged to the privatized system. Workers who were already insured under the old program had the option of remaining under that system. However, strong incentives were provided to encourage people to switch, including a net salary increase for those workers who chose to move to the new system, ranging from 7.6% for those who belonged to the blue-collar workers fund to 17.1% for bank employees. By the end of 1982, about 70% of all those insured under the old program had transferred to the new scheme.

Experts suggest that four key elements prompted people to abandon the old social security program:

- a very expensive, skillful and well-orchestrated propaganda campaign that emphasized giving the individual "the freedom of choosing and deciding" as well as "personal effort and reward"—in Piñera's words;
- the net increase in income for those who moved to the new system;
- the desperate situation of the pensioners, who no doubt expected to get much better pensions under the new system; and
- the pressure applied by some employers, some of whom reportedly ordered employees to switch.

Recognition bonds

To fund the transition from the public pension plan to the private savings scheme, the government issued "recognition bonds" which were transferred into the new individual accounts of workers and designed to mature at their retirement. Carrying an interest rate of 4% a year, and indexed for inflation, the value of the bond represented the worker's previous contributions to the old system. It was calculated as the capital required to pay a pension equal to 80% of the insured worker's earnings in 1978/79, multiplied by the proportion of the insured's working life spent contributing to the old system.

According to some estimates, recognition bonds represent from one-half to three-quarters of the accumulated capital of those retiring in the next 13 years or so, or an average of nine years of their pension. These amounts will have to be paid by the government in a lump sum instead of being spread throughout the entire retirement period, as payments under the public pension plan would have been. Observers point out that the state's commitment to the pension scheme—including the recognition bonds and other guarantees—has reduced public funds for other programs, such as health care, for the lowest income groups. The deficit from recognition bonds is estimated at 1% of GDP for the next 20 years, reaching a maximum of 1.2% of GDP in the year 2005. These figures are double what was estimated in the mid-1980s.

AFPs - the new pension funds

In the beginning, ownership of the AFPs was tied to the "economic groups" or large conglomerates that resulted from the privatization policies in the early years of the Pinochet regime. Public enterprises were sold off at firesale prices, promoting a concentration of assets in the hands of a small business and financial élite, and in particular in the hands of the small group of financial conglomerates known as *los Groupos*. Some of the groups went bankrupt as a result of the 1982 recession. Their assets were temporarily administered by the state and later some were sold to foreign creditors under the debt-for-equity swap program designed to reduce Chile's external debt.

The four largest AFPs, responsible for administering about 70% of the funds, are now either partially or totally owned by foreign corporations. The two largest are controlled by the U.S. conglomerates Bankers Trust and Aetna. Observers say privatization has produced a huge concentration of power in the hands of the AFPs, whose assets now represent 40% or more of Chile's GDP.

From all accounts, the huge pension funds are also very profitable operations. For example, it has been estimated that in 1995, when individual investors in the AFPs actually lost money, the pension funds themselves made profits of more than 20%. The return on investment of the funds was –4.7%. The negative yield in 1995 was attributed to the lingering effects of the Mexican financial crisis which affected the Chilean stock market. It was the worst yield since the privatized system began in 1981. But, even in the good years, when the funds were earning double-digit rates of return on their investments, fees and commissions charged by the AFPs were so high that returns for individual investors were actually negative for much of that time. Marketing and publicity costs are a large component of the high costs AFPs incur. Such costs, of course, were not incurred under the old public pension plan.

In the grand neoliberal design for pension privatization, the AFPs were supposed to compete for worker's accounts on the basis of their investment returns, commissions and marketing ability, thereby giving potential investors all the benefits of the "efficiency" of free markets. Reality has proved otherwise. Bankruptcies, mergers and foreign takeovers have reduced the number of funds to 16 from a high of 21 in 1993. There is a high degree of concentration.

The three largest funds covered 60% of insured workers in 1981. By 1995, almost 69% of those insured were enrolled in the three largest funds.

And in spite of the vaunted benefits of free markets to consumers, it seems their choice of AFP is not based on yield, nor on the basis of the commissions charged. Instead, aggressive marketing campaigns, which boost costs significantly, have attracted vulnerable subscribers, who may choose their fund because of promotional gifts and cash payments, because of advice they receive from their peer groups, or even just to do their agents a favour.

Workers can freely switch between AFPs at no cost to themselves, and sellers of the plans concentrate on persuading investors to switch from one plan to another. Experts say that the insured—particularly the elderly and women—usually ignore the differences between AFPs in terms of commissions and yields, and so are easy prey for the sellers. It is reported that 50% of all contributors switch AFPs each year. As one observer comments, switching large numbers of workers around between fund management companies with practically identical portfolios is obviously highly inefficient.

Switching plans may do nothing for the insured worker, but, of course, it's always beneficial is for the seller who can earn a commission on the switch and for the fund that gets the business. All this contributes to the very high costs of the individual accounts. Commenting on the system, one critic observes that it has produced cut-throat competition among companies for the individual accounts, and high prices for all workers.

Government involvement still required

While Chile's system has been hailed by the right in Canada and the U.S. as the ultimate in privatization for public pension programs, in fact, the state is still heavily involved in the Chilean scheme. So much so that some purists believe the Chilean model should not even be considered a "privatized" system.

As mentioned earlier, the government is underwriting the recognition bonds that were given to contributors who switched to the new system from the old public pension plan. The bonds are expected to result in an enormous cost to the government, which according to some estimates has already paid out about 200,000 bonds. As well, the government regulates and guarantees the AFPs, which are required to generate monthly returns not lower than the average returns of all the funds in the last 12 months, minus 2% or one-half of this average, whichever is lower. Regulations also cover the investment portfolios of the funds. And the government guarantees the pension accounts in the event of an AFP failure, as well as a fraction of annuity pension benefits in the event of an insurance company failure.

It also provides a minimum pension guarantee for those who lack sufficient funds in their AFP, provided the insured has at least 20 years of contributions. There is also a public assistance minimum pension—lower than the minimum guaranteed under the privatized system. In theory, at least, this minimum pension would be available for those who are not covered by the privatized scheme or who cannot meet the 20-year requirement to qualify for a minimum pension from the scheme. But the number of public assistance pensions the government will pay is limited to 300,000, and there is a long waiting list.

Both the monthly minimum pension under the privatized scheme (worth about US$100) and the public assistance pension (worth about US$36 a month) are not enough to meet even the most basic needs. And about 37% of those affiliated with the AFP system are unable to obtain a pension above the minimum. As a result, it seems clear that a large proportion of Chile's population will face extreme poverty after retirement. Analysts say that women will form a large part of the extreme poor, since they will not even qualify for the minimum pension from the privatized scheme because of the 20-year requirement.

Providing a pension

The contributions to the personal pension scheme and the accumulated returns are tax-free. Workers are not allowed to borrow against the funds, nor can they draw on the fund until they retire. At retirement, the contributor has three options:

- To purchase a life annuity from an insurance company, which receives all the funds from the AFP and guarantees a monthly pension for the insured and any survivors, based on the worker's age, sex and number of beneficiaries. The insurance company charges a fee for establishing the annuity, and once made, the contract cannot be revoked.
- A "programmed" retirement pension paid directly by the AFP out of the worker's accumulated fund and calculated according to a formula established by the state supervisory authority. The amount of the pension is calculated annually and depends on the size and yield of the individual's fund and the number of the insured's beneficiaries.
- To take a programmed pension for a number of years and purchase an annuity at a later date.

At retirement, contributors may also withdraw some of their savings in the form of a lump sum, provided they have contributed for at least 10 years, and provided certain minimum amounts are left in the fund.

The AFP must provide all the necessary information so the worker can make an appropriate choice among the various retirement options. However, according to some reports, 90% of workers do not understand the complexities involved and hire an expert to help them choose. Fees charged for this advice can vary from about 3% to 5% of the total value of the fund. Disability and survivor pensions are paid by insurance companies contracted for that purpose, not by the AFPs.

Concerns about the privatized scheme

Experts who have looked at Chile's mandatory private savings scheme have raised serious concerns about it, including the high cost of the scheme; the low coverage and the large number of vulnerable workers who are excluded; the inadequate benefits provided by the scheme; and the systemic bias against women.

The high cost of privatized savings schemes

All of the evidence indicates that the Chilean personal savings scheme has much higher costs than a pay-as-you-go public plan. According to one estimate, for an average worker, the costs of their personal pension plan plus the costs associated with purchasing an annuity pension on retirement would be well over one-third of their contributions. By way of comparison, the cost of running the CPP (before the recent reforms) is 1.8% of the contribution revenue.

Even the World Bank admits that marketing costs of these privatized schemes are "a particularly sore point." Where investors are relatively uneducated and uninformed about financial matters, the Bank says, they are susceptible to intensive marketing campaigns that increase costs. According to the World Bank's 1994 report on *Averting the Old Age Crisis,* the promotional costs are estimated to account for as much as 30% of the operating costs of the Chilean system. These costs are eventually passed on to consumers in the form of higher fees.

The individual AFPs are free to set the level of commissions for the services they provide. There are fixed commissions for handling the pension accounts, as well as variable commissions imposed as a percentage of the worker's earnings on which pension contributions are paid. Analysts point out that the structure of commissions has a redistributive impact. Fixed commissions, charged for handling the pension accounts, are regressive because they reduce the pension funds of low-paid workers by a larger proportion than for highly-paid workers. In 1987, for instance, it was estimated that fees and commissions represented an 18% reduction in the deposit of an insured in the 10,000 pesos-a-month bracket, but only 0.9% for an insured in the 100,000 pesos-a-month bracket. For the same reason, in 1981-87, the investment yield for the lowest income bracket averaged 7.6%, compared with 11.3% for the 60,000 pesos-a-month bracket.

Then, in addition to the costs associated with the build-up of the pension fund, there are the costs of making pension arrangements at retirement. For example, it has been esti-mated that insurance company deductions from the pension fund when selling an annuity pension are about 25% of the fund. An important factor in the high costs is apparently the fact that all annuities are contracted on an individual basis and group contracts are not allowed. Each pensioner has to negotiate independently with the insurance companies. As well, the annuity factors redistribute generally from short-lived individuals to long-lived individuals: in other words, from men to women and from low-income workers to high-income workers. And, as noted earlier, many workers who don't understand the complexities of the retirement pension options hire advisers to help them make a selection. Of course that involves even more charges.

High commissions and fees make a huge dent in the much-publicized high returns on AFP investments. In fact, according to one estimate, during the first 14 years of opera-tion of the new system, the net investment yield for the pri-vatized pension funds, after deducting the administrative commissions, was lower than the interest paid by bank deposits. Other estimates indicate that, despite double-digit rates of return on the AFPs in the early years, returns for indi-vidual investors were actually negative.

Rates of return on AFP investments in Chile

Years	Real rate of return for funds	Real retun for individual investors
	%	%
1982	28.8	-3.2
1983	21.3	-1.3
1984	3.5	-5.9
1985	13.4	-2.3
1986	12.3	0.3
1987	5.4	0.5
1988	6.4	1.4
1989	6.9	2.1
1990	15.5	4.2
1991	29.7	7.9
1992	3.1	6.9
1993	16.2	8.0
1994	18.4	9.1
1995	-2.5	7.4

Source: Sinha, Tapen (2000)

Tapen Sinha, a professor of risk management in the Department of Actuarial Studies at Instituto Tecnologico Autonomo de Mexico (ITAM), one of Mexico's best business schools in Mexico City, says it's a common misconception that investors in the AFPs have been getting double-digit rates of return for their funds. As the table shows, the cumulative rate of return has actually been negative for the first decade. The difference between what the fund gets and what the account holder gets is accounted for by the management fees.

Low coverage and the exclusion of vulnerable workers

In a country like Chile, where the privatized personal pension system is the only form of pension provision available, coverage of the scheme of paramount importance. Lack of pension coverage will translate directly into poverty in old age for workers currently in the labour force, and will result in higher government pension liabilities because the government will have to pay the guaranteed minimum pensions for those who are not covered. But, even though membership of a personal pension plan is compulsory in Chile, it has been estimated that over a third of the Chilean labour force is not covered by the program. In contrast, it is estimated that the public pension plan at its peak in the early 1970s covered 76% of the labour force.

Married women, who must take time out of the work force for family responsibilities, are left out. So are unpaid family workers and other workers in the informal sector of the economy. Self-employed workers may contribute on a voluntary basis, but only a tiny minority do so. And, of course, workers who are unemployed can't contribute.

Other estimates suggest that in 1988 56% of the labour force was registered and contributing; 24% was registered and not contributing; and close to 20% was not covered. Many of those who did not contribute were temporary workers and unemployed, as well as others who had withdrawn from the labour force. In 1993, it was estimated that about 90% of the labour force was registered in the private system—but only 53% were contributing. These figures exclude contributors in the public system. If they are added in, coverage increased to 60% in 1993; while adding in the armed forces increased coverage to 61%. Official statistics indicate that the percentage of insured workers in the private AFP system who are actually contributing to their funds has been dropping steadily from 74% in 1982 to 56% in 1995.

Lack of pension coverage is higher among both younger and older workers, according to Armanodo Barrientos, an expert on the Chilean pension system and principal lecturer in economics at the University of Hertfordshire Business School in Britain. He says non-coverage of younger groups is explained by the expansion of tertiary education, but also by higher rates of unemployment for these groups. Unemployment is the main factor behind low pension coverage among older workers, Barrientos notes. And, as another observer points out, not only does the privatized system reinforce the economic inequities produced by the labour market, but, given the impact of the commission structure, mentioned earlier, it also exacerbates the socioeconomic differences that already exist in society.

Low-income workers are particularly disadvantaged by mandatory private savings schemes because they cannot afford to contribute the mandatory percentage of their earnings. Barrientos notes that, for a high proportion of low-paid workers in Chile, the combined health insurance and pension contributions at 20% of earnings is too large, encouraging non-compliance. This, he says, applies particularly to married women, who may suffer from work interruptions such that pension contributions do not generate any benefits, and who may rely instead on benefit entitlements of contributing partners.

According to the ILO, the privatized funds catering to lower-paid workers in Chile report that only 45% to 55% of workers are actually making the contributions they are supposed to make. But the small number of funds catering to better-paid workers are recording compliance rates in the region of 80% to 90%.

Inadequate benefits for many workers

As time goes by, the number of pensioners in the Chilean system is rapidly increasing. But most of those in the privatized system have not yet reached the official retirement age. It appears that most of the annuities paid out so far were paid to individuals who had sufficient balances in their accounts to retire early. It must be emphasized, however, that workers now retiring from the privatized system have benefited from the generously calculated recognition bonds that were given to those who switched from the old system to the new. Future retirees will be much more dependent on the performance of the new system for their retirement pensions.

And for many of those who will retire under the privatized system, pension benefits are likely to be inadequate. Low-paid workers or workers with employment and contribution gaps will, under most scenarios, get lower pensions. Job interruptions have strong effects on pension benefit adequacy. And Barrientos notes that continuous employment is untypical for blue-collar workers and women in Chile. Since the level of the pension is dependent on the contributions, it seems likely that a large group of pensioners will be able to receive only the minimum pension, which in practice will mean extreme poverty.

Even where workers are covered, early estimates suggest that the personal pension funds of 45% of women and 34% of men will generate benefits below the minimum pension level. Under the Chilean system, as mentioned earlier, the government would then be required to top up benefits to a basic minimum, equivalent to only 40% of average earnings, and then only for workers who have at least 20 years of contributions.

Systemic bias against women

Chile's privatized system also reinforces the difference between female and male pensions, making female pensions considerably lower because women have lower wages, retire at an earlier age, and live longer than men. According to one analyst, male-female income differentials increase between the labour and the pension market. Women who begin their working life with about 75% of the male salary will receive 50% of a male salary when they retire and only between 35% and 45% of the average male pension after they leave the labour market.

All Latin American countries have large informal sectors and women account for many of those who work in the informal sector of the economy. According to one estimate, the informal sector in Chile represents about 18% of the country's GDP. But Chile's privatized savings scheme only benefits the formal sector. Studies have shown conclusively that, as a result, the Chilean reform of the pension system has increased income inequality among pensioners.

In addition to these disadvantages, there is an additional systemic bias against women. In theory, the Chilean program is designed to give workers a retirement benefit equivalent to about 70% of their average insured wages over the last 10 years before retirement. But this estimate is based on male workers with male life expectancy and male lifetime work patterns. As in many other industrialized countries—including Canada—women in Chile earn less than men do; they retire earlier and live longer. In fact, the official retirement age of 60 for women under the Chilean system is five years earlier than it is for men. And even when women work in the formal sector of the economy, they may take time out of paid employment for family responsibilities.

All of these factors imply that, under a system of individual savings accounts such as Chile has, women would need a bigger fund at retirement than men do, if they are to have adequate pensions throughout their retirement years. In fact, it has been estimated that, to get the same replacement rate as men, women insured under Chile's fully funded individual scheme would have to contribute 15% or 20% of their insured wages, instead of the 10% amount needed by the average male worker to get the same 70% replacement rate. Given their lower earnings, this would almost certainly be impossible.

A Chilean research institution estimates that salary replacement rates under the Chilean system are 80-86% for men, but only 52-57% for women. Given that women's salaries are lower to begin with, a pension that replaces only a little more than half of those earnings is a virtual guarantee of poverty in old age.

Trading political risk for market risk

Advocates of privatization of public pensions often point to the political risks involved in pay-as-you-go public pension plans. For example, it is claimed that many public pension systems are inefficient because they have been captured by certain interest groups—typically public servants and the military—who receive large pensions paid for from the contributions of the mass of workers who receive very little.

According to the World Bank, large earnings-related pay-as-you-go public pension plans are "prone to political pressure from influential groups. These groups want provisions that will benefit them, they want others to finance these benefits, and pay-as-you-go defined benefit schemes make it easy for them to introduce poor design features that accomplish this goal in the early years of the plan." As well, it is feared that it will be difficult to achieve public consensus over the scaling-down of public pension benefits unless substantial numbers of people—particularly higher earners—have been weaned away from reliance on state benefits.

According to some observers, politicians in Latin America have often used social security as a political tool, doling out benefits and administrative jobs to loyal political supporters. In some Latin American countries, social security pension reserves have been used for personal loans to the élites while low-income workers and peasants had little access to these funds. As well, in Latin America, social security benefits were always subject to political risk because governments often failed to index benefits against inflation, or did not pay what they legally owed. And, as the World Bank notes, "most governments change their benefit promises many times over a typical worker's lifetime." The Bank claims that "not one public defined benefit scheme has held to the same benefit formula over lifetimes of a cohort of members." It then uses the "political risk" argument to advocate replacing public defined benefit pension plans with privatized savings schemes in which the amount of the pension benefit is not specified at all.

In the view of the World Bank, privatized savings schemes have advantages over public pension plans by "being transparent to enable workers, citizens, and policymakers to make informed choices, and being insulated from political manipulations that lead to poor economic outcomes." Significantly, perhaps, in spite of the World Bank's praise for the Chilean model, the military dictatorship that imposed the privatized scheme did not require the military to join it. The armed forces did not join the new system—an option not available to any other group in the country.

But the idea that corrupt and inefficient governments provide a rationale for individual accounts is one of the political economy myths tackled by former World Bank senior vice-president and chief economist Joseph Stiglitz in his landmark paper on the mythology that has developed around social security systems. As one American observer puts it, "Although Social Security has also been used by U.S. politicians to score points among voters, it has always paid its benefits on time, is fiscally solvent, and has never been subject to the episodes of fraud and mismanagement that have occurred in South America. Unlike their Latin American counterparts, would-be privatizers in the United States cannot substantiate rhetoric about government inefficiency ruining Social Security."

Canadian advocates of privatization of public pensions have also tried to make the case that government "mismanagement" of the CPP warrants its replacement with individual savings accounts, but they have produced little evidence to support their rhetoric.

On the question of the political risk of public pension plans, two key points need to be made:

- Replacing a public pension plan with a system of individual accounts does not eliminate the need for government involvement. As we have already seen, in privatized systems, governments must still guarantee some kind of basic minimum pension for those who are excluded from the private system or who can't accumulate an adequate pension from their own savings. As well, governments must regulate the operation of the privatized system. In Chile, for example, the government sets the parameters for the operation of the AFPs, establishes the retirement age, and generally oversees the operation of the privatized scheme. And privatized systems of individual accounts are notoriously difficult to regulate, as we shall see in the next chapter dealing with the British approach to privatization. In that country, the "misselling" of personal pensions by insurance companies, to the detriment of individuals who were persuaded to opt out of the public pension plan, created a huge scandal which is still reverberating.

- Even if continued government involvement were not an issue, eliminating public pay-as-you-go pensions in favour of individual savings accounts simply trades the political risk involved in public pay-as-you-go pension plans for the market risk associated with individual investment accounts. Individuals in Chile's privatized system are left to the vagaries of the "free market" and must bear the entire risk of pension provision themselves. In effect, where public pay-as-you-go pension plans are replaced with a privatized system of mandatory individual savings accounts, the huge sums of money invested will require adequate regulation and will therefore be subject to both political and market risk.

The Chilean model in Canada

Clearly, any attempt to introduce a Chilean-type model in Canada as a replacement for the CPP would raise serious concerns, for all the reasons already discussed. Yet Canadian advocates of privatization still seem to look favourably on this type of system. Where there are reservations, they seem to be not about the design of the system itself, but more about differences between the Chilean economy and the Canadian economy which might make implementation of such a system in Canada more difficult.

For example, economist James Pesando, in a paper on privatization written for the C.D.Howe Institute, acknowledges that "several features of the Chilean economy, including a much younger population and a government that has been running large surpluses, have facilitated the transition from a pay-as-you-go pension system to a fully funded private alternative." Nonetheless, he says, "Chile's experience provides a useful benchmark against which policy initiatives in Canada can be evaluated." The fact that the Chilean model might even be considered an appropriate one for privatization of public pensions in Canada is indeed disturbing.

The Reform Party's "Super-RRSP" proposal

In fact, the Reform Party developed quite a detailed proposal for introducing the Chilean model in Canada in its 1995 document *Renewing CPP*, in which it proposed a system of "Super-RRSPs" to replace the CPP. Recently, however, the party seemed to have modified its recommendations on the privatization of public pensions to conform more to the British model, implemented under Margaret Thatcher's regime in the mid-1980s. It seems likely that the Canadian Alliance, which replaced the old Reform Party, will also advocate privatization in the form of allowing individuals to opt out of the CPP—particularly since this was the option favoured by the party's new leader, Stockwell Day, when he was Treasurer of Alberta.

Just the same, it may be instructive to review the Reform Party's original proposal for "Super-RRSPs." Its proposals illustrate clearly the folly of letting right-wing ideology dominate policy proposals to the exclusion of thoughtful analysis and clear thinking. We can be sure that some version of the Super-RRSP proposal and the Chilean model will resurface during ongoing discussions about CPP reform. And, thanks to new legislation, it seems we are doomed to continue picking at the CPP indefinitely. That's because the last round of reforms, implemented in 1998, committed the federal and provincial finance ministers to review the operation of the CPP every three years instead of the previous five-year interval. The next triennial review is scheduled to get under way in 2002.

The Reform Party's 1995 proposal for Super-RRSPs was that, instead of contributing to the CPP, workers would be required to contribute a percentage of their earnings to a privatized system of mandatory individual savings accounts, based on the existing system of RRSPs. Each worker would then have a "Super-RRSP" which would provide him or her with retirement income.

Significantly, the proposal did not suggest a limited number of private pension funds as the Chilean system has. Instead of the 16 or so large funds Chile now has, the Reform Party's proposed privatized system would apparently have been based on Canada's current private retirement savings plans, consisting of thousands of RRSPs. Numerous studies of privatized schemes that use individual accounts indicate that widely decentralized systems—such as Canada's RRSP system—are much more costly and more difficult to regulate than a limited number of centralized funds.

While the Reform Party's 1995 document did not spell out all the details of the privatization proposal, there was enough information in it to raise some interesting questions:

- **Contribution rates would be even higher.** The Reform Party's proposal would have increased contribution rates considerably higher than they were at the time the proposal was made. Of course, this is consistent with the Chilean model where workers are required to contribute 20% of their earnings for social security and health programs. Reform suggested, "The schedule of planned increases to the CPP payroll tax (which at that point was predicted to grow considerably in size between 1996 and 2030) could be maintained or somewhat accelerated, with the excess funds being diverted into contributors' personal Super-RRSP funds." It even suggested that unemployment insurance contributions could be diverted to the Super-RRSP program. (The proposal was made before the name of the program was changed to Employment Insurance). Presumably this meant that the UI program would be abolished, but this was left vague in the proposal.

- **Recognition bonds for the transition.** People aged 40 and over would not have enough time to accumulate enough money in their Super-RRSPs to compensate for the loss of their CPP retirement pensions, Reform said, so they would be given "Recognition Bonds"—another idea borrowed from Chile. These government-issued bonds would guarantee "all previously made contributions to the CPP." How would the government finance these bonds? By privatizing Crown corporations and giving workers shares in the privatized companies. As to what would happen if the shares of the newly privatized companies failed to maintain their value, Reform did not say. In addition, guaranteeing people receive funds equivalent to what they have contributed to the CPP would presumably not involve guaranteeing them the pension they would normally have expected to receive for their years of contributions, but this too was glossed over.

- **Loss of tax revenue.** Contributions to the Super-RRSP would, of course, be tax deductible. The Reform Party proposal made no comment on the huge loss of government tax revenue this would involve. According to a 1994 estimate by the federal government, the existing RRSP and Registered Pension Plan system, with its tax-deductible contributions and tax-deferred compounding of interest, cost approximately $15 billion a year in lost tax revenues. At the time this estimate was published, only about $3.5 billion was recovered by taxing withdrawals from these plans. But Statistics Canada estimated that the total amount contributed to RRSPs in 1994 was less than 17% of the amount Canadians were entitled to contribute. If everyone were forced to contribute, as they would be under the Super-RRSP proposal, the cost to both federal and provincial governments in lost tax revenues would likely be astronomical.

- **Transfers from low-income to high-income.** The proposal would also involve a major transfer from low-income to higher-income taxpayers. Because the entire amount of an RRSP contribution is deductible from income, those with the highest income get the highest benefit, because their marginal tax rates are higher. For instance, a $1,000 RRSP contribution made by someone in a 30% tax bracket results in a tax rebate of $300. A $1,000 contribution made by someone in a 50% tax bracket produces a $500 tax rebate. The cost of these lost tax revenues is borne by all taxpayers, including those with the lowest incomes who pay taxes but may not have enough spare cash to enable them to contribute to an RRSP. Switching to a mandatory Super-RRSP system would therefore involve a significant transfer from lower-income tax-payers to higher-income taxpayers. Contributors to the CPP are entitled to a credit for their contributions rather than a deduction, so taxpayers receive the same tax benefit for the same amount of contribution, regardless of their income level.

- **High costs of proposal.** The CPP has very low administrative costs. The Reform Party claimed its Super-RRSPs would have low administrative costs, too. However, in effect, the administrative cost is transferred to the individual instead of being absorbed by the fund. It may be hidden in the rates of interest paid by financial institutions holding the RRSPs, but it would also be imposed directly through investment management fees and commissions, just as it is in the Chilean system. And, with all the funds channeled through private financial markets, private financial institutions would compete for funds, passing on their marketing costs to individual workers and reducing the rate of return workers could expect to get from their private Super- RRSPs. As we have seen, in the Chilean system, excessively high costs result in a significant reduction in the proportion of a worker's contributions that actually generates a pension for the individual.

- **Rates of return.** And what about the rate of return on these private savings accounts? The Reform Party did not see this as a problem. It claimed the elimination of the existing foreign content rule, which at that time prohibited individuals from holding more than 20% of their RRSPs in foreign investments, would enable people to get a higher rate of return. Of course, there is no evidence this would happen. And the claim ignores the fact that inexperienced investors investing in high-risk foreign markets may put their entire retirement savings fund at risk and end up without any funds to purchase a pension. Since the Super-RRSPs proposal was first put forward, the federal government has eased the restrictions on foreign investments in RRSPs, but the same considerations still apply.

- **Poor investment expertise.** As for people not having enough investment expertise to get a good rate of return on their Super-RRSP investments, Reform agreed that people who currently have RRSPs tend to buy low-risk investments with lower rates of return, but that results from "individual small-scale investors purchasing low-income fixed-return investment vehicles through RRSPs that are registered at the local bank or trust company," it said. As the size of each person's Super-RRSP grows, the Reform Party claimed, "his [sic] risk-aversion will likely decline, as it will become increasingly easy to hedge various investments within the bounds of the RRSP."

  Experience in Chile indicates otherwise, and it would appear that a flourishing market has developed for "investment advisors" who take a percentage of the retirement fund to help inexperienced investors decide what to do with it.

- **Cashing in before retirement.** Perhaps the biggest unanswered question of the Super-RRSP proposal is how the government would prevent people from using up the money in their plans before retirement. In the Chilean system, workers are not allowed to draw on their private retirement funds or borrow against them until they retire. But, under the existing RRSP system in Canada, there is no requirement that RRSP savings be used for retirement. The government itself has encouraged people to use their RRSP savings to buy homes and to pay for higher education, and there is evidence that many people also cash in their savings plans when they fall on hard times, such as during recession or job loss. Unless funds in the proposed Super-RRSPs were locked in until individuals reached retirement age, many Canadians might end up with little or no income in their retirement years, leaving many more people dependent on the basic income-tested seniors' benefit. But the Reform Party proposal did not address this issue.

- **Disadvantages for women.** As with the Chilean system, the proposed Super-RRSP would have serious disadvantages for women. But the Reform Party claimed to have addressed the needs of women by considering their position as surviving spouses. It said the CPP provides an "ungenerous survivor's allowance," even though CPP surviving spouse benefits are equivalent to 60% of the pension received by the deceased spouse, which is also the standard for most private occupational pension plans in Canada. Of course, Reform did not acknowledge that the reason why CPP surviving spouse benefits are so low in dollar terms is because the basic CPP pension is equivalent to only 25% of average contributory earnings of the deceased spouse. And 60% of 25% does not amount to much of a pension.

Reform said the Super-RRSP proposal would solve the problem because all the money in the Super-RRSP would be transferred to the surviving spouse on the death of the contributor. It did not say what would happen if the RRSP funds had already been used up by the time the holder died, or if poor investment decisions had produced a very small fund. Effectively, there is no guarantee that women as surviving spouses will be any better off under a mandatory private savings scheme than they are under the CPP.

Even more astonishing is the failure of the Reform Party's proposal to address the concerns of women as wage-earners and potential contributors to a mandatory private savings scheme. This is a serious omission, given the evidence on how badly women workers are disadvantaged under the Chilean model. In Canada, at last count (1997), 77% of adult women aged 25 to 54 were in the paid work force. The implication that their retirement income needs have been addressed by considering them only as surviving spouses of male contributors displays a depth of ignorance that is truly remarkable.

The bottom line on the Chilean model

Replacing a social insurance program like the CPP with a mandatory private savings scheme would mean the risks of providing for retirement would be borne entirely by the worker. As the ILO points out, the eventual pension the worker expects to receive will be significantly lower if she or he experiences periods of personal misfortune, sickness, disability, or unemployment during working years. The worker also runs the risk of mismanagement or bankruptcy of the pension fund that manages his or her savings. (The Reform Party said government regulation and deposit insurance can address this problem, but it did not calculate what size of a fund would be needed to insure the huge private savings deposits that it claimed would result from the Super-RRSP scheme, nor what it would cost).

Then there would be risks associated with general economic developments—in particular, slower economic growth or periods of low or negative real interest rates associated with rapid inflation. For low-income workers, there would also be the risk that income in retirement might fall below the poverty level. As for the Chilean model, analysts with the Social Security Department at the ILO in Geneva say, "It contains no elements of mutual insurance between members of the workforce; there are no links of solidarity between social groups; there are no inter-generational transfers, explicit or implicit; neither the government nor employers contribute to the individual's retirement account; and yet the scheme deprives all wage and salary earners of the right to determine how to dispose of 10% of their earnings."

It also contravenes international labour standards and conventions on social security. In fact, say these analysts, it is not clear why such a scheme should exist at all. They point out that the Chilean scheme "departs significantly both from the criteria established by ILO international labour standards concerning social security, and also from the structure of social security schemes established by most developed countries over the last several decades." In addition, the scheme contravenes requirements of various ILO Conventions that Chile has ratified.

Chapter 4
Margaret Thatcher brings opting-out to Britain's pension system

Privatization of public pensions in Britain was implemented under the government of Margaret Thatcher in the mid-1980s. However, rather than replacing the public pension program with a mandatory private savings scheme along the lines of the Chilean system, the Thatcher government, with its 1986 *Social Security Act,* decided to allow individuals to opt out of the public earnings-related system, provided they could demonstrate they had an approved personal pension. Personal pensions were individual defined contribution arrangements, sold mainly by insurance companies and very similar to Canada's RRSPs.

This version of privatization of public pensions now seems to be the option favoured as an alternative to the CPP by the former Reform Party and the Alberta government, among others. A version of it also featured in the platform adopted by the Republican Party candidate George W. Bush in his 2000 campaign for the presidency of the United States.

While opting out of the public pension plan in Britain was voluntary, once the "free market" stepped in, many individuals were powerless to resist. And the Thatcher government provided strong incentives to help the process along. Financial institutions persuaded two million people to opt out of the public earnings-related pension plan in favour of individual savings accounts, even though the pensions they will receive at retirement will be less than they would have received under the public pension plan.

The scandal that followed, euphemistically known as "the mis-selling of personal pensions," resulted in insurance companies being fined an estimated £11 billion, and further changes in the pension system, introduced in the Blair government's 1999 *Welfare Reform and Pensions Act*, to be phased in over a period of several years.

According to pensions expert David Blake, the United Kingdom is now one of the few countries in Europe that is not facing a serious pensions crisis. The reasons for this, says Blake, are straightforward. State pensions (both in terms of the replacement ratio and as a proportion of average earnings) are among the lowest in Europe; the UK has a long-standing funded private pension sector; its population is aging less rapidly than elsewhere in Europe; and its governments, since the beginning of the 1980s, have taken measures to prevent a pension crisis developing. These measures have involved making systematic cuts in unfunded state pension provision and increasingly transferring the burden of providing pensions to the funded private sector, principally on a defined contribution basis.

It's interesting, of course, that Blake claims the UK is "not facing a pensions crisis" when what he clearly means is that the government—or British taxpayers—no longer have the major responsibility of providing for future seniors. That has now been shifted to the individuals who will be the seniors of the future. Whether they, as individuals, will face a "pensions crisis" of their own remains to be seen. From all accounts, it looks as if many of them will.

As Blake also points out, in a recent paper reviewing two decades of pension reforms in the UK, the personal pensions that many individuals have chosen in place of the public earnings-related plan are based on uncertain investment returns and are subject to very high set-up and administration charges, often inappropriate sales tactics, and very low paid-up values if contributions into the plans lapse prematurely. What's more, he admits that, although only four years of data are available, the evidence suggests that very few personal pensions scheme members (only around 16%) are likely to maintain their membership of the scheme for long enough to build up an adequate pension.

Other analysts have noted that the low contributions rate for personal pensions is a cause for concern, since these rates are about 1% of average earnings and are unlikely to build up to a fund value which would generate a pension big enough to live on. It is generally agreed that the introduction of personal pensions in the late 1980s has eroded the importance of the state earnings-related pension scheme (SERPS). The number of people contributing to SERPS, which peaked at more than 10 million in 1987, had dropped to about 7.5 million by 1996, representing only 35% of all individuals with some kind of pension coverage other than the basic state pension—similar to Canada's OAS.

Changes introduced by the Blair government's *Welfare Reform and Pensions Act,* which received royal assent in November 1999, will phase out SERPS, beginning in 2002, replacing it with a new State Second Pension (S2P). The legislation also provides for new Stakeholder Pension Schemes (SPSs), to be introduced in October 2001, which are expected to prove more attractive to opted-out individuals, eventually replacing the existing system of personal pensions. Although these changes are an attempt to correct some of the more serious problems with the Thatcher pension reforms, it appears the Blair government is continuing with Mrs. Thatcher's agenda of trying to reduce the cost to the state of public pension provision, and of transferring the burden of provision to the private sector through the introduction of the Stakeholder Pension Schemes.

Pension provision in the United Kingdom

Effectively, the UK currently has a three-pillar retirement income system roughly comparable to that advocated by the World Bank—with the significant difference that the second pillar is a voluntary rather than mandatory system of individual savings accounts, and that a public, earnings-related pay-as-you-go pension plan still plays a limited role in the second pillar.

The first pillar basic state pension

The basic state pension (BSP), which constitutes the first pillar of the UK retirement income system, is a pay-as-you-go plan that pays a flat-rate benefit. Membership of the basic state scheme is compulsory for all employed and self-employed workers with earnings above a small exemption amount, and contributions are collected through the National Insurance system.

Current pensioners in the UK get the largest share of their income from this basic state pension, which has been in place since 1948, although its origins lie in the National Insurance Act of 1908. Everyone gets the same level of pension, subject to having a sufficient contribution record. But, because contributions are related to earnings, higher earners pay more than lower earners. A system of National Insurance credits and home responsibilities protection ensures that most people are covered by the basic state pension, even when they are not in the paid work force or are earning below the National Insurance contribution lower limit. In many respects, the basic pension may be seen as similar to Canada's Old Age Security (OAS) benefit

There is also a means-tested benefit designed to provide a minimum level of income for the poorest seniors and roughly comparable to Canada's Guaranteed Income Supplement (GIS).

The second pillar state earnings-related pension scheme (SERPS)

The state earnings-related pension scheme (SERPS) constitutes the second pillar of the retirement income system. It is a pay-as-you-go plan, with contributions collected form employers and employees through the National Insurance system. Membership in the plan is mandatory for employees—but not those who are self-employed—unless the employee has contracted out into a private pension scheme.

Like the CPP, retirement pensions paid by SERPS are related to earnings that individuals had during their working lives, and there is both a minimum and maximum limit for earnings on which contributions are paid. SERPS was introduced in 1978, and people reaching state pension age—currently 60 for women and 65 for men—in 1998/99 were the first to receive the full rate of SERPS pension.

In fact, as we shall see later, the majority of employees are now opted out of SERPS and have their National Insurance contributions directed to their individual accounts instead. To this extent, then, the second pillar has been largely privatized—but not quite in the way that the World Bank envisaged for this tier of retirement income systems.

The third pillar forms of voluntary private pensions

As in Canada, the third pillar of the British retirement income system consists of private pension arrangements, of which there are two main types: occupational pension plans and personal pension schemes, roughly equivalent to Canada's RRSPs. And, as in Canada, these private arrangements are effectively subsidized by the government since contributions to the plans are made from pre-tax income.

There is a complex array of options available in these third pillar arrangements. Occupational pension plans may be defined benefit or money purchase plans; mixed benefit or hybrid plans; contracted in or contracted out of SERPS. And individuals may top up their plans with additional voluntary contributions.

As an alternative, individuals may choose a personal pension scheme that is independent of the employer's plan. The options here are a group personal pension scheme—equivalent to a group RRSP in Canadian terms and likely organized by a small employer—or a personal pension scheme. Personal pension schemes are in turn divided into two components. The first is an Appropriate Personal Pension (APP) which is contracted out of SERPS and provides "protected rights" benefits that replace SERPS benefits. These plans are also known as minimum contribution or rebate-only schemes, since the only contributions permitted are the combined rebate on National Insurance contributions with the employee's share of the rebate grossed up for the basic tax relief.

The second type of personal pension scheme is an additional scheme, also contracted out, that receives additional contributions up to the Inland Revenue limits. Since APPs were intended only to replace the relatively low SERPS benefits, people with rebate-only APPs will likely also have an ordinary personal pension scheme to which they can make additional contributions.

Coverage of different types of schemes

It's not easy to sort out who is covered by what type of arrangement in the UK retirement income system. However, according to one 1998 estimate, it appears that, out of about 35 million people of working age, 21% were covered only by the basic state pension and not by any second or third pillar arrangements. Another 20% were covered only by SERPS, and a further 30% by occupational pension plans. About 29% were covered by some type of personal pension scheme, of which 16% were covered by APPs and another 13% by other personal pensions.

A slightly different estimate was provided by a government-appointed task force—the Pension Provision Group — that reported in June 1998. It said there were about 32 million people between the age of 20 and state pension age. Of these, about 25 million were in paid work, of whom about three-and-a-quarter million were self-employed. Another two million were looking for paid work—including those not receiving state benefits—and about five million were not currently in the labour market.

As mentioned earlier, nearly everyone of working age is in effect covered for the basic state pension. But only those in paid work can contribute to second pillar pensions. As for the types of second-pillar provision employees and self-employed people were making, the Pension Provision Group said that the largest single group of 10.5 million were employees in occupational pension schemes and about 85% of these were contracted out of SERPS. About one in four employees had a personal pension. This included people who were currently contributing to a personal pension, as well as those who used to contribute but were no longer doing so. It also included a large number who were currently in an occupational scheme.

Looking at employees and self-employed people, the task force concluded that more than a third of people in paid work were making no private provision for retirement. In other words, unless they had previously built up rights to an occupational or personal pension, they were relying on the prospect of receiving only state benefits in retirement. Clearly, future seniors faced much greater income insecurity in the wake of the Thatcher reforms, and income inequality had increased. In a foreword to the report of the Pension Provision Group, the Secretary of State for Social Security, Harriet Harman, said the income gap between the better-off and the poorest was greater than at any point in the last 30 years. Personal pensions had grown as an alternative source of second tier provision, she said, while SERPS was reduced in value. The changes had widened the gaps in provision between those with and without good second-tier provision, she said.

The Thatcher government encourages people to opt of the public pension plan

The state earnings-related pension scheme, or SERPS, came into effect in 1978 and was intended to provide an additional state pension to employees who didn't have an occupational pension plan. It paid a pension based on average earnings during the best 20 years of each person's working life. And any SERPS earned was revalued in line with the growth in average earnings during the person's working life. Once the pension started to be paid, it was indexed in line with the growth in prices.

The scheme was compulsory for all employees earning above a minimum earnings level. However, those who had an occupational pension plan paying an equivalent or better level of pension could contract out and pay a reduced rate of National Insurance contributions. Only defined benefit occupational pension plans were allowed to contract out. And employees who were contracted out in this way were guaranteed they would not have a lower retirement income than if they had remained in SERPS.

Cutbacks in SERPS benefits

But, with the election of the Thatcher government in 1979, everything changed. Consistent with the New Right ideology, the official view now was that state provision should be minimal and that people should make provision for themselves. The new government set about slashing the SERPs program. It linked the growth in benefits to prices rather than wages; it reduced the retirement pension by 20%—from 25% of average contributory earnings to 20%; it abolished the 20-year basis for the calculation of retirement pensions and substituted calculations based on the worker's entire lifetime earnings instead; it cut surviving spouse benefits; and it increased the age of eligibility. It was estimated that the combined effect of these cuts was to reduce the value of SERPS benefits by about two-thirds.

Personal pensions introduced

Then, with the *Social Security Act* of 1986, personal pensions were introduced, to be effective in 1988. Essentially, these were defined contribution arrangements, similar to RRSPs, sold mainly by insurance companies. The government then encouraged people to opt out of SERPS using defined contribution schemes—either those run by employers or the new personal pension plans. Individuals could also opt out of defined benefit occupational plans in favour of a personal pension. The 1988 changes also made occupational pension plans entirely voluntary. Employers were no longer allowed to require membership of a workplace pension plan as a condition of employment. In fact, new employees had to take the active decision of joining their employer's scheme. Fewer than 50% of them did so.

There was no longer any requirement that transferring from an occupational pension plan to a personal pension scheme was in the best interests of the employee—leading directly to the personal pensions mis-selling scandal that erupted in December 1993. Pensions expert David Blake says that as many as 90% of those who transferred had been given inappropriate advice. Miners, teachers, nurses, and police officers were among the main targets of the insurance company sales agents. Blake says that many of these people remained working for the same employer, but they switched from a good occupational pension scheme offering an index-linked pension into a personal pension scheme towards which the employer did not contribute and which took 25% of the transfer value in commissions and administration charges.

Personal pensions, like RRSPs, may also be used to supplement anticipated benefits from SERPS. But, as the Pension Provision Group noted in its 1998 report, "These schemes offer no commitment to a particular level of benefit." According to Will Hutton, economics editor of *The Guardian* newspaper, the government argued that these measures would lower the future claim of pensioners on the state. But, as he put it in his landmark 1995 book *The State We're In*, "The state is doing all it can to wash its hands of responsibility for future generations of old people."

Opting out of SERPS

Hutton says that two million people were persuaded to opt out of SERPS and into private pension schemes—actually individual savings accounts—when their earnings were too low to allow them to achieve a comparable income in retirement for the kind of payments they had already been making to the state scheme.

The Pension Provision Group says that, for many of the two million people who chose an APP instead of remaining in SERPS, "the additional income an APP will provide in comparison with SERPS is likely to be marginal and may be equivalent to having taken no action. Indeed, some will receive less than SERPS would have provided." A significant minority of people may be worse off, says this report, "particularly if they are modestly paid, are already part way through their working lives, and do not invest in equities for most, if not all, of the time up to retirement."

Incentives to opt out

The Thatcher government provided strong incentives for people to opt out of SERPS. Not only did they receive a rebate on their National Insurance contributions, which was contributed directly into their personal pension scheme by the Department of Social Security, but the rebate was structured in such a way that there were very strong incentives for younger people to opt out of SERPS and purchase a personal pension instead. A "special bonus" in the form of an extra 2% National Insurance rebate was provided for all personal pensions schemes contracting out of SERPS between April 1988 and April 1993. As well, an incentive was provided from April 1993 in the form of a 1% age-related National Insurance rebate to members of contracted-out personal pension schemes aged 30 or more to discourage them from re-contracting back into SERPS, which technically they were allowed to do. But, far from saving the government money,

Blake says the National Audit Office estimated that the net cost of the personal pension schemes during the first 10 years was about £10 billion.

"Mis-selling" of personal pensions

Once they were launched in 1988, personal pensions became a highly attractive proposition for the financial services industry. Not only were they tax-favoured like other pensions, but, if they were used to contract out of the public pension system, contributions into the plans were guaranteed because the employees' National Insurance contribution rebate was paid directly into the pension fund by the government. Financial institutions went to town.

In Britain, personal pension plans are sold mainly by insurance companies, whose aggressive marketing persuaded many people to opt out of the public pension plan. At the urging of the insurance companies, many people also opted out of generous defined benefit workplace pension plans and bought personal pensions instead. They were able to do this because, as one of its 1980 reforms, the Thatcher government had removed the right of employers to make it compulsory for employees to join or to stay members of their occupational pension plan.

The result was the huge "mis-selling" scandal referred to earlier. Will Hutton says that the Securities and Investment Board estimated that as many as 450,000 people left occupational pension schemes with guaranteed pensions related to final salary and with contributions from their employers, to buy private pensions "dependent solely upon stock market gyrations and their own contributions."

Some of the best-known names in the insurance world, including Sun Life, Legal & General, Norwich Union and Guardian Life, were involved in the scandal. The authorities undertook a major review, and the regulatory framework governing occupational pension schemes was tightened to reduce the possibility of fraud and/or mismanagement.

Holders of mis-sold personal pensions must be reinstated into their former occupational pension plans or compensated so they are no worse off than they would have been if they had stayed in the pension plan.

As well as compensation to those they misled, the insurance companies have been forced to pay heavy fines for malpractice, poor record-keeping, and bad advice. A report in the *Globe and Mail* in August 1998, for example, said that Sun Life Assurance Co. of Canada's British operation had been fined a record £600,000 (nearly $1.5 million) and was assessed an additional £125,000 for legal fees and other costs associated with the regulators' investigation. (It would appear that Sun Life has also now become involved in Chile's mandatory private savings scheme by purchasing a one-third share in one of the AFPs which aims its investments at high-income workers.)

Impact on women and other low-income workers

About 85% of individuals who belong to occupational pension plans are now opted out of SERPS. Many of those who opted out have no other coverage apart from their APP. According to the Pension Provision Group's report, part-time women employees are the least likely to have a personal pension. The high fixed cost of personal pensions and the lower levels of women's earnings—especially part-time women employees—means that the amounts they are able to contribute cannot support the costs and provide a satisfactory benefit. If earnings are high enough for a SERPS benefit, then continuing SERPS membership is likely to be more cost-effective and less risky. In fact, it would appear that, instead of a broadly based social security plan, SERPS has now become mainly a program for low-income workers. According to one estimate, the majority of those who remain in the public plan earn less than about £10,000 annually.

The Pension Provision Group also said that the other changes to the SERPS program, introduced in the 1980s, would very substantially reduce SERPS entitlements accruing in the future, with the greatest proportionate impact being on the lowest earners and on women. During the 1990s, the implications of the Thatcher reforms became clear. The diminishing value of state pensions in the future would require more effort on the part of individuals to provide for themselves. However, the options for low and moderate earning workers without access to an occupational pension plan, were very limited. For employees, SERPS was to be of lower value relative to average earnings for those who retired in the future. And personal pensions, as they had developed since their introduction in 1988, had turned out to be more suitable for those with larger sums to invest. Those without stable earnings found personal pensions particularly unsuitable for their needs.

Because of their relatively short life to date, personal pensions have not yet become a significant source of income for pensioners. But analysis shows that higher earners are much more likely to have a personal pension plan. Recent government reports have documented rising inequality among pensioners. And it has been suggested that, when personal pensions become a more important component of average pensioner incomes, they are likely to be a further contributor to inequality among pensioners.

The high cost of personal pensions

True to its free market ideology, the Thatcher government placed no restriction on the charges that could be imposed in personal pension schemes, clearly hoping that market forces alone would ensure that personal pension schemes would be competitively provided. The reality is very much otherwise. There is certainly competition. But, as in the Chilean system, it has actually increased the cost to consumers. And high charges have eaten into the proportion of the amounts contributed to the schemes that are available to generate a pension.

Personal pensions have proved extremely costly, both for the government and for individuals who have chosen them as a replacement for membership in the public pension plan or in an occupational scheme. As the Pension Provision Group pointed out, the costs of running personal pensions are significantly higher than those for most occupational pension schemes. Inevitably, administration costs reduce the share of contributions which result in pension rights, the Group says. For example, it noted that—despite its complexity—the cost of administering SERPS, measured by unit of benefit provided, is low in comparison with an equivalent funded scheme, particularly for those with relatively modest benefits who represent a significant proportion of those who remain fully in SERPS.

Taken as a whole, the weekly administration cost of state pensions in 1995/96 to the Department of Social Security was 60p per beneficiary, or 1.1% of total state pension costs. The administrative cost per unit of benefit provided under personal pension schemes was estimated at 22% higher than this.

The cost to individual investors

Pension expert David Blake says that the average personal pension scheme in the UK takes 19% of the fund value in charges, and the worst scheme takes nearly 30%. The charging structures for personal pensions are high, complex, disguised, and front-loaded. On the one hand, says Blake, such charging structures have the effect of confusing the consumer to such an extent that they are unable to assess whether the scheme they are being invited to participate in for a substantial period of time and with a substantial commitment of resources offers value for money. On the other hand, they give little incentive for the provider to offer value for money on a long-term basis.

He points to research that shows providers of personal pension schemes change their charging structures on a regular basis. This makes it very difficult to compare schemes over time, and he raises the question as to whether particular charging structures and changes to them are used to conceal the impact of costs and thereby to confuse the customer even more.

If consumers are going to be able to compare products and make informed choices, it is important that they be fully aware of all the charges they face. But it is frequently the case, says Blake, that some charges are disguised or hidden. A 1998 survey of fund management fees conducted by benefits consulting firm Towers Perrin documents the myriad of ways in which this is done.

Lack of transparency can also lead to incentive problems, Blake says. For instance, brokerage fees are related to turnover, which provides an incentive to churn or trade stocks in the portfolio unnecessarily. This is especially so, Blake notes, if the transactions are executed by an in-house broker and the brokerage fee is hidden from the client.

A 1997 report from the Office of Fair Trading also commented on the high and front-loaded charges associated with personal pensions. In the wake of the mis-selling scandal, the Office initiated a review of the provision of occupational and personal pensions to identify practices that adversely affect the economic interests of consumers. It said charges can "make a large hole" in the returns from investing contributions. These charges reflect the cost of setting up and running a pension plan, and include commission to the salesperson, documentation charges, fund management expenses, administration costs, and profits for the provider.

The report concluded that many personal pension plans are simply poor value. Their benefits are consumed in the high levels of expenses needed to support the marketing effort and the active management of the funds. These expenses are often loaded on the early years of the plan, so that they bear disproportionately on plans where the contributions are discontinued because of changes in personal circumstances. In comparison with most occupational schemes, said the report, the level of employers' contributions may be inadequate or non-existent.

The Consumers' Association says personal pensions are a "rip-off"

In a 1997 report called *A Blueprint for Better Pensions,* the UK Consumers' Association charged that most personal pensions were a "rip-off." The Association estimated that the charges imposed over the life of a personal pension plan reduce the value of a fund by 24%. According to the Association, the effect of the introduction in 1995 of disclosure requirements designed to bring down charges by promoting competition had only been to reduce average charges from 26% to 24%.

Overall costs of privatized individual accounts in the UK

Three economists who looked at the UK system of personal pensions as part of an ongoing World Bank project on individual accounts in the UK say that, on average, between 40% and 45% of the value of individual accounts in the UK is consumed by various fees and costs. In their 1999 report, these authors warned that "the debate in the United States should take careful note of the results from the UK which suggest that a voluntary privately managed approach to individual accounts could prove to be surprisingly costly." The same stricture might apply to Canada, where advocates of privatization now seem to favour the British approach to privatization of public pensions and propose allowing opting-out of the CPP in favour of individual accounts such as RRSPs.

The three economists based their estimates on actual data from financial providers. Their analysis incorporates typical earnings growth over a 40-year career and is based on individual accounts involving contributions of between

US$2,000 and US$4,000 a year. Costs were broken down into three components:

The **"accumulation ratio"** which captures fund management and administrative costs for a worker contributing to a single financial provider throughout his or her career. They found that the amount of money in the account when the worker retires is 25% lower than it would be without these charges. The authors note that expressing fees in terms of annual basis points may be most familiar to investors. But that's not necessarily the most insightful approach because the accumulated effects of charges over many years may not be immediately obvious. They point out that several other analysts have found that an annual management fee of 100 basis points—or one percentage point —can reduce the value of an individual account by slightly more than 20% over a typical working life.

The **"alteration ratio"** which measures the additional costs of failing to contribute consistently to a single financial provider over an entire career. It includes any costs of switching from one financial provider to another or from stopping contributions altogether. Most previous analyses have ignored the costs of transferring funds or stopping contributions, the authors say. They conclude that such costs are significant in the UK. This factor reduced an account's value by 15% over a career, on average.

The **"annuitization ratio"** which reflects the costs of converting an account to a lifetime annuity upon retirement. In the UK, this factor reduces the value of an account by approximately 10%, on average.

Commenting on the mis-selling debacle, the three economists say that the misleading advice given by insurance companies was motivated at least in part by a desire to gain additional customers. But they also say that the pressures induced by strong competition among providers of personal pensions have not resulted in low costs. A number of features of the UK system—including the need to provide advice, as well as complications involving tax compliance checks—make it expensive for providers, say these authors. But the economists emphasize that "a high level of fees and other charges need not imply excess profitability. In the UK case," they say, "we do not believe that it does."

Clearly, however, the high costs of individual accounts must be borne by the individuals holding those accounts. The authors' finding that almost half of an individual account's value could be lost through charges implies that the advocates of opting-out—not to mention financial advisers who might try to persuade clients to opt out of the public pension plan and invest for themselves—may seriously underestimate the amount individuals would need to save under a privatized system to provide themselves with an adequate retirement income.

The high cost estimates of the UK study have come under fire in the U.S., where critics have accused the three economists of focusing only on administrative costs and ignoring the higher rates of return in a privatized system. While higher rates of return are probably the most popular argument in favour of privatizing social security systems, the authors of the UK study say simple comparisons of the rate of return on individual savings accounts with an assumed rate of return on social security contributions ignore the transition costs of continuing to pay for social security benefits already accrued.

In the UK, for example, the net cost of allowing workers to opt out of that system and into individual accounts is estimated to be over US$20 billion. Transition costs would also be an important issue if Canada were to seriously consider an opting-out provision for the CPP, because some way would have to be found to pay for the CPP entitlements accumulated by those who decide to opt out.

However, the three economists note that the cost of a privatized system depends on the structure of individual accounts. For example, some proposals for individual accounts in the U.S. seek to take advantage aggressively of potential economies of scale through centralized provision —by offering individual accounts only through one provider and by limiting investment options. Such a system would be unlikely to appeal to privatizers in Canada, where there is a well-established system of RRSPs already in place. Most analysts agree that a system of individualized accounts, privately managed and highly decentralized, is substantially more expensive. And the authors of the UK study say that "the UK experience debunks the argument that competitive pressures will automatically reduce costs" in a decentralized system.

Other problems with personal pensions

The Pension Provision Group said that the mis-selling of personal pensions had also greatly tarnished these plans and those who provide them, although it also noted that some of the structural weaknesses in personal pension schemes were beginning to be addressed as some providers began to adapt their policies to better meet the needs of policy holders. And the Blair government has recently started phasing in some changes, providing other investment vehicles that are expected to replace the personal pension schemes eventually. But the British experience with using opting-out as a form of privatization of public pensions still presents a cautionary tale for fans of privatization in Canada and elsewhere.

And there are other problems with the British scheme that remain.

Contributions too low to build up a pension

For example, there is no requirement that any particular amount be contributed to the individual account. Although rebates of National Insurance contributions are contributed directly for those who have opted out of SERPS into an APP, the contribution rates for other personal pension schemes are left up to the individual. As with Canada's RRSPs, tax assistance for contributions is only available up to certain limits. The evidence is that, with current contribution rates, the amounts of money going into individual personal pension funds are unlikely to generate sufficient funds to produce a reasonable pension at age 65.

While average contribution rates to occupational pension plans in the UK represent more than 10% of average earnings, contributions to personal pension schemes are between 1% and 5% of average earnings. Over a 40-year career, that's not going to build up a very big fund— especially given the huge amounts that will be creamed off in fees and commissions. In fact, the British Consumers' Association argues that, with current low contribution rates, an individual at retirement will be "shocked" to discover that there are insufficient accumulated funds to generate an income that will maintain the individual's standard of living.

Individuals stop contributing

Another problem with the personal pension schemes is that a large percentage of them are terminated prior to their maturity date. People stop contributing for one reason or another. And when a contributor stops paying into their personal pension, it is converted to paid-up status, which typically has low maturity values because the plan provider continues to extract the same annual charges as with an active plan. This is particularly a problem where there is significant front-end loading of charges, since individuals will lose a substantial amount if their contributions lapse prematurely.

The Office of Fair Trading report said that 16% of personal pensions were terminated within one year, and 28% were terminated within two years. Another report by the Personal Investment Authority (PIA) showed that persistency rates after just four years of membership were between 57% and 68%. In other words, only 57% to 68% of people who started a personal pension scheme were still contributing four years after they began the scheme.

The PIA report said these rates were "disturbing." It said there could be a number of explanations: people might have been mis-sold personal pension schemes that were either unsuitable or too expensive; regular premium policies might be unsuitable for those with irregular earnings or uncertain long-term employment; a change of employment may lead to a member joining an occupational pension plan and abandoning their personal one; adverse general economic conditions could also make it more likely that people will stop contributing.

The Blair government reforms

Tony Blair's New Labour party came to power in 1997 with a radical agenda for reforming the welfare state. But it appears that Frank Field, who was appointed the first Minister of Welfare Reform at the Department of Social Security (DSS), proved to be too radical for the traditional Old Labour wing of the party and was soon replaced. In July 1997, the government announced a Pensions Review, setting out 10 challenges it said must be met if Britain was to succeed in narrowing the gaps in retirement incomes between the richest and poorest pensioners, between women and men, and between full-time and part-time workers. It also committed to produce a Green Paper with recommendations that would aim to meet those challenges and ensure proper regulation of pension investments, striking a balance between public and private funding.

Publication of the report of the Pension Provision Group in June 1998 was followed by the DSS Green Paper in December 1998, setting out detailed proposals for changes to the pension system. The Green Paper proposals then formed the basis for the *Welfare Reform and Pensions Act*, which came into effect in November 1999. According to David Blake, while the Act that was eventually passed did not fully meet the Green Paper's own objectives, it did make some important improvements on the existing system. However, he says it fails three of Frank Field's tests for a good pension system: it is not mandatory, it is not funded, and it remains means-tested.

Key provisions of the new legislation were as follows:

- **Indexing of the basic state pension** (BSP) will remain linked to prices. But in April 1999, a new Minimum Income Guarantee (MIG) was introduced for pensioners. This will be means-tested and indexed to earnings. The government admits it will save substantial sums of money by not linking the BSP to wages. But Blake says that, as a result, the value of this benefit will "fall relentlessly" as a proportion of national average earnings. In effect, he says, the government is abandoning the first pillar of support in old age and obliging everyone to rely on the second and third pillars. The Green Paper talked about building on the BSP, but this implies building on a sinking ship, he says.

- **SERPS is to be abolished and will be replaced by a new State Second Pension** (S2P) from April 2002 that will initially be earnings-related. But, from April 2007, it will become a flat-rate benefit, even though contributions will be related to earnings. This feature will provide a strong incentive for middle- and high-income earners to contract out of the program. The government says the S2P will give employees on low earnings a much better pension than is currently available from SERPS. The new pension will, for the first time, also include certain caregivers and people with a long-term illness or disability whose working lives have been interrupted or shortened.

- **New Stakeholder Pension Schemes** (SPSs) will be introduced in October 2001, principally intended for middle-income earners, with earnings between £9,000 and £18,500, who have no existing private pension provision. People will be able to use an SPS to contract out of the new S2P plan. The new SPSs will be money purchase arrangements with the same maturity conditions as existing personal pension schemes. However, there will be strict limits on the amounts that providers of the schemes may charge, and the funds will also have to meet certain other minimum standards. They will be set up with a trust structure, and will be subject to other regulations.

Stakeholder pensions are intended to be much simpler, transparent products than the existing personal pension schemes, so that less advice and information is needed. It is anticipated that, once these new pensions are introduced, personal pensions will become uncompetitive, so that anyone opening a new pension would choose a stakeholder over a personal pension.

- **Employers will again be able to make membership of an occupational pension plan a condition of employment.** Employees will only be allowed to opt out if they have signed a statement of rights being given up, certified they have adequate alternative provision, and have taken advice that confirms that the alternative is at least a as good as the S2P.

While these reforms are clearly an attempt to correct the worst excesses left from the Thatcher privatization, it is clear—as noted earlier—that, with the introduction of the new Stakeholder Pension Scheme, the Blair government is continuing the emphasis on private pension provision rather than collective responsibility through public pensions. Effectively, second pillar pensions will be largely private individual accounts, with a small minority of people left in the public pension system. Nevertheless, as David Blake points out, the Blair reforms did place much greater emphasis on redistributing resources to poorer members of society than was the case with the Conservatives.

As Social Security Secretary Alistair Darling put it, "In the long-term, we are aiming for a radical re-balancing of state and private provision, to ensure that those who can join secure, funded, non-state pensions do so." In the long term, he said, state spending on pensions will be reduced from 60% to 40% of the total.

The bottom line on opting-out

Allowing individuals to opt out of public pay-as-you-go pension plans raises serious concerns for those worried about the security of incomes of future seniors. There is clear evidence from the British experience that individuals can be persuaded to opt out of a public pension plan—even though they may be much worse off in retirement—through aggressive marketing by financial institutions which stand to gain by selling private pension arrangements, whether they be personal pension plans as in Britain or the Super-RRSPs suggested by the Reform Party when it was promoting the Chilean model for Canada. This possibility should not be taken lightly by those who advocate permitting opting-out of the CPP—especially given the aggressive marketing campaigns conducted by financial institutions during the peak RRSP buying season each year.

Since the personal pension plans in the British system are defined contribution arrangements, they are really no different from the mandatory savings schemes in which Chilean workers are required to participate. No pension is guaranteed; there is no pooling of risks; women and low-income workers are particularly disadvantaged; and the cost of operating such plans is extremely high, thus seriously cutting into the funds that can be accumulated for retirement.

Few of the five million people who took out a personal pension under the British scheme as a result of the reforms introduced in 1988 have so far retired. At this point, therefore, it is not possible to measure the actual impact of this initiative on the financial security of older people in Britain. The recent changes implemented by the Blair government may go some way toward addressing the problems caused by the Thatcher government's privatization, but it is clear that public pensions are destined to play a much reduced role in the UK retirement income system. In fact, the new Stakeholder Pensions to be introduced under the Blair government reforms are specifically designed to encourage middle- and higher-income earners to opt out of the public pension system in favour of private arrangements. Opting out of public pay-as-you-go pension plans may also seriously undermine the viability of the public plan itself. Such plans depend on pooling of risks and pooling of contributions from all workers at all wage levels. But it would appear from the British experience that those most likely to opt out are higher-income workers with secure jobs. Those who are left in the state plan are likely to be those with the lowest earnings and the least job security. The question then arises as to whether contribution revenue will be adequate to pay the promised benefits. Clearly, even in a system of opting-out, transition costs are also likely to be very significant.

Where opting-out is structured in such a way that only the increase in premiums for the public pay-as-you-go plan would be directed to a private savings arrangement—which seems to be what some advocates of privatization in Canada are proposing—similar considerations apply. The financing base of the public pension plan is also undermined.

As well, the more people who opt out of the public pension plan, the more collective responsibility and social solidarity is weakened. It then becomes a simple matter to abandon the public earnings-related plan completely, forcing low-income workers to rely on means-tested benefits from the first tier of the pension system—always assuming they can qualify.

Opting out of the CPP

Advocates of privatization of public pensions in Canada are now suggesting people be allowed to opt out of the CPP and have their mandatory contributions directed to their RRSPs or some other type of personal savings scheme instead. And it would appear that some provinces are now expressing interest in the idea. For example, at the June 1998 meeting of the federal, provincial and territorial finance ministers on CPP reform, Alberta Treasurer Stockwell Day suggested that, "Where possible and appropriate, individuals and employers should be given the flexibility to design equivalent or better benefits." Is it possible or desirable, he asked, "to set up individual accounts for future retirement benefit accruals?" He also suggested the possibility that employers who sponsor registered retirement plans that exceed minimum CPP benefit levels be given some special recognition in the CPP program.

These suggestions, of course, open the door to the possibility of allowing opting-out of the CPP, along the lines of the British system. This was, in fact, the position adopted by the Reform Party in 1998 and presumably now espoused by its successor, the Canadian Alliance. Despite the 1998 changes in the way the Canada Pension Plan is funded, Reform still maintained that the plan is "not a sound pension plan." It proposed that people be allowed to opt out of the CPP and direct their contributions to a private savings account instead. "With little invested and significant contributions required by the CPP," Reform said, "it will be better for many Canadians to switch to their own individual pension plan."

In a booklet called *Can Your Pension Be Saved?* Reform took up a familiar theme. It claimed younger people would get a very poor return on investment if they stay in the CPP. "Think of how much better you could do on your own if you could control your retirement contributions," says the booklet. According to one of its charts, annual contributions of 7% of "pay" over a 40-year period, earning an average annual real rate of return of 4%, would generate a nest egg big enough to provide an annual pension of $16,700 at retirement, compared with a maximum CPP pension— based on contributions of 9.9% of "pay"—of only $8,900 in 1998 dollars.

While the booklet claimed people will have to contribute 9.9% of their earnings to the CPP, in fact employees contribute only half that rate, with a matching employer contribution, on earnings within a band ranging from $3,500 to $37,600 (for 2000), known as "contributory earnings." And of course generating the nest egg predicted by Reform would depend on being able to make the required contributions every year for 40 years; being able to invest them and get a real rate of return of 4% every year for that period of time; and being able to purchase an annuity 40 years from now, when it is assumed the 4% real interest rate will still prevail. Clearly, there is no way any of those conditions could be guaranteed. And no mention was made of the percentage of individual contributions that would be directed to fees and commissions instead of to providing a pension.

"Wouldn't this money provide more security for your retirement in your own fully funded individual pension plan as opposed to the government-run, unreliable CPP?" Reform asked. As we have already seen, the answer to that question is No. An RRSP (or personal defined contribution "pension plan") is not an alternative to the CPP. It cannot provide the kind of security provided by the CPP, nor can it provide additional benefits available through the CPP such as inflation-proof annuities, disability coverage, survivor benefits, and so on.

The Reform Party's individual "pension plan"—which would apparently be a form of RRSP and not a "pension" at all—shifts the entire risk of providing a retirement income onto the individual, with all the disadvantages discussed earlier. As well, with more and more workers in non-standard jobs, such as part-time, temporary and contract work, as well as self-employment, it may be even more difficult to contribute to a personal pension account regularly every year for 40 years to get the kind of pension Reform seemed to suggest would be attainable under its proposal.

One key issue raised by Reform's opting-out proposal is what to do with the CPP benefits already accumulated by those who might choose to opt out. People might be asked to give them up, Reform suggested. Even more important is how to finance the benefits for those who choose to stay in the CPP. On this one, Reform said "Changes to premium levels, benefit levels and/or general tax levels may be necessary to keep it solvent." Several possibilities are suggested: the age of eligibility could be increased; disability coverage could be handled separately, possibly by the provinces; future benefits could be income-tested; people who choose to stay in the plan could be asked to pay more for their benefits. None of these options seems likely to prove politically acceptable.

Meanwhile, Stockwell Day continued to push his privatization ideas at meetings of the federal and provincial finance ministers, but failed to get any of the other ministers to sign on to the project. In his last hurrah as Treasurer of Alberta, he issued a press release after the completion of the first triennial review of the CPP in December 1999, threatening to take Alberta out of the CPP unless the other finance ministers agreed to a series of reforms proposed by Alberta, one of which was to allow some form of opting-out by directing some part of contribution revenues into individual accounts. Now that he is leader of the Alliance, we can be sure his views of privatization of the CPP will receive even greater prominence.

Chapter 5
Does Social Security have a future in the U.S.?

There was a time when no American politician would dare say anything against Social Security, so popular was the program. People like to refer to it as "the third rail of American politics," presumably alluding to the third rail carrying the electricity that makes the trains run. And just as no one wants to touch that electrified rail, American politicians who valued their political lives did not want to touch Social Security. Social Security was appreciated as the most successful anti-poverty program in America, and its clout came from the millions of voters from all walks of life who received cheques every month without fail.

Almost everyone acknowledges that Social Security has been an enormous success in providing the elderly, the disabled, and survivors with a modest basic income. Two-thirds of retirees receive more than half their total income from Social Security. Without this program, the incomes of approximately 16 million people—about half of all retirees—would fall below the official poverty thresholds. As it is, because of Social Security, only 11% of American seniors live in poverty.

The push for privatization

But lately, Social Security has been losing some of its lustre, thanks to a concerted effort by right-wing think tanks such as the Heritage Foundation and the Cato Institute, ably assisted by a compliant media that has swallowed their privatization message hook, line and sinker. Observers believe the relentless campaign has reinforced the conviction in the political centre that Social Security needs a major overhaul rather than minor surgery.

While the push for privatization now seems to be reaching fever pitch, attacks on Social Security are actually nothing new. According to economist James Schultz, a professor of economics at Brandeis University and a specialist in aging policy, opponents of Social Security have been waging a kind of holy war for decades now, designed to "wake up" the American public to the supposed dangers of an aging population. But the war is not so much about unsustainable Social Security and Medicare, says Schultz, or even about budget deficits. It is really about the age-old questions associated with the appropriate distribution of income in the United States: between rich and poor, whites and non-whites, and the strong and the weak.

Schultz argues that Social Security and other pensions should be seen as one of society's ways of dealing with the growing problems individuals have in finding work as they age. But more important, he says, these programs and initiatives should be seen in the context of ever-changing employment needs and the chronic unemployment characterizing market economies. Free market advocates, of course, see things differently. They may accuse seniors of being dependent on state handouts—as the Association of Canadian Pension Management did when it called for Canada's retirement income system to move away from "an emphasis on entitlement and dependence towards greater individual responsibility and self-sufficiency." They may argue that workers should be given a "free choice," as José Piñera, Pincohet's minister of labour and social security, has argued on behalf of the right-wing Cato Institute.

Either way, the objective is the same: to eliminate any kind of collective responsibility and to shift the risk and responsibility of retirement provision onto the individual. Not only does this conform to free market principles, but the pay-off for private financial interests would be enormous. Even a limited form of privatization, such as allowing people to opt out of Social Security—an approach advocated by George W. Bush in his recent campaign for the presidency— would channel huge amounts of mandatory contributions into private financial institutions, where commissions and fees could be charged. And, if the British experience is anything to go by, persuading people to opt into private savings accounts instead of guaranteed Social Security benefits would not be difficult.

Economist Robert Kuttner, writing in the July-August 1998 issue of *The American Prospect*, said that since the mid-1990s the campaign for full or partial privatization has been abetted by a sophisticated media and lobbying drive by bankers and Wall Street investment houses that stand to make fortunes as account managers, and by conservative groups ideologically opposed to social insurance. According to Kuttner, the State Street Bank has spent millions of dollars promoting privatization. The J.M. Kaplan Fund of New York has financed several right-wing groups advocating privatization, Kuttner says, including the National Center for Policy Analysis, the Institute for Research on the Economics of Taxation, "Third Millennium," a letterhead organization posing as a mass-membership group of Generation Xers, and the National Development Council.

The National Center for Policy Analysis has been promoting privatization of Social Security for the past 10 years, while also lobbying for school vouchers, massive tax cuts for the wealthy, privatized prison labour, and paycheck deception legislation, as well as funding bills opposing patients' rights.

Neoliberal think tanks and right-wing commentators are prominent advocates of the privatization of Social Security. Leading the charge is the Washington-based Cato Institute, whose project on Social Security Privatization is co-chaired by José Piñera, architect of Chile's forced privatization under the Pinochet dictatorship, along with William Shipman, principal of the Boston money management firm State Street Global Advisors. As noted earlier, the Advisory Board for the project includes a number of senior people from investment firms and the insurance industry, as well as prominent right-wing economists. Observers believe that 25% of the funding for Cato's privatization project comes from Wall Street firms, with banks and other major corporations also contributing. And, according to the *Washington Post*, the Investment Company Institute, the lobbying arm of the mutual fund industry, has made revising Social Security a top legislative priority.

The compliant media

There seems no doubt that the media are getting the privatization message across very effectively. Observers have documented considerable media bias in reporting the issue of Social Security privatization, with both print and electronic media reporting only one side of the story. Pro-privatization pundits are interviewed without any presentation of contrary views. And major network anchors fail to challenge misinformation from neoliberal think tanks.

Diana Zuckerman, director of the Social Security Project of the National Association of Commissions for Women, describes one incident where Daniel J. Mitchell, author of a 1998 Heritage Foundation report that falsely claimed Social Security had a US$20 trillion shortfall, repeated the claim on *Good Morning America*. The ABC reporter interrupted him, not to correct him, but to indirectly support his views by pointing out that 84% of participants in a survey on ABC's web-site favoured some sort of privatization. Anchors on CNN's *Your Money*, basing their comments on information from one of the neoliberal think tanks, claimed "Social Security starts having cash-flow problems just 14 years from now," says Zuckerman. In fact, actuaries at Social Security had estimated that at the end of 2015, or 17 years after that broadcast, Social Security would have assets of almost US$2 trillion.

Robert Kuttner tells of a spread in the *Washington Post* that featured Daniel Patrick Moynihan, a supporter of partial privatization, juxtaposed against the American Enterprise Institute's Carolyn Weaver, also a supporter of partial privatization. And FAIR—a New York-based media monitoring organization devoted to Fairness & Accuracy in Reporting—reviewed more than a year's worth of transcripts from the three major networks' nightly newscasts and found a "remarkable unity of views" on Social Security, with the possibility that the system is **not** going broke never being entertained.

According to FAIR, ABC's John Cochran touted the privatization of public pension plans in Chile and Britain. *NBC Nightly News* cited Third Millennium's famous 1994 poll that found that "more young adults believe UFOs exist than believe Social Security will exist by the time they retire" —even though the poll was done by Frank Luntz, who was censured by the American Association for Public Opinion Research for his failure to disclose his techniques in his Contract With America polling for the Republican Party.

Again, there are striking parallels with Canada where, during recent discussions of CPP reform, the media generally accepted without question the view that the CPP is broke, and where the business press regularly comments favourably on privatization proposals without exposing any problems or disadvantages, and without presenting any views in opposition.

How Social Security works

Essentially, U.S. Social Security, like the Canada Pension Plan, is a pay-as-you-go social insurance program, funded mainly by a payroll tax. A small amount of additional revenue is raised by taxing the Social Security benefits of high-income beneficiaries.

American workers contribute 7.65% of their gross wages up to a limit (for the year 2000) of US$76,200, with 6.2% going for Social Security benefits and 1.45% for Medicare. Contributions are referred to as "Social Security taxes" and are matched by an employer contribution of the same amount. For those who earn more than US$76,200, the employer continues to withhold the Medicare portion of the

Social Security tax, or 1.45%, on the rest of their earnings. Self-employed people must pay 15.3% of their taxable income for Social Security and Medicare, up to the same limit of US$76,200 (at 2000 rates). However, there are special deductions that can be used to offset part of the self-employed person's tax rate. The maximum contributory earnings limit changes automatically each year, based on the increase in the average wage for all workers. Contributory earnings under the CPP are adjusted in a similar way.

Medicare benefits provided under the U.S. program help with hospital bills and provide limited coverage of skilled nursing facility stays, hospice care, and other medical services at age 65, or younger if the contributor becomes disabled. The rest of the program is comparable to the CPP and includes retirement pensions; disability coverage; benefits for spouses and children (including dependent adults who have been disabled since childhood) of eligible retired and disabled workers; and benefits for surviving spouses and dependent children of a deceased contributor.

There is no other program equivalent to Canada's OAS. However, a minimum benefit is guaranteed. It is worth noting that U.S. workers pay a combined employer/employee contribution for Social Security of 12.4% of earnings, up to a maximum earnings level equivalent to about C$113,000 (at exchange rates prevailing in the fall of 2000). There is no exemption for the first few thousand dollars of earnings as there is in Canada, where workers do not have to pay contributions on the Year's Basic Exemption (YBE) now frozen at $3,500.

In Canada, payroll taxes to fund public pensions are much lower than they are in the United States. And during the 1997-98 round of CPP reforms, federal and provincial finance ministers decided the combined employer/employee contribution would have to be kept below 10% of contributory earnings, as higher contribution rates would be politically unacceptable. The business community had expressed its strong opposition to CPP combined contribution rates going any higher than 10%, claiming higher payroll taxes would kill jobs and make business uncompetitive.

While it might be argued that Canadians also have access to the OAS—as well as the GIS and Spouse's Allowance—which are funded from general tax revenues, it is significant that, for their CPP benefits, Canadian workers contribute only on earnings up to a maximum (in 2000) of $37,600—less than one-third of the contributory earnings limit for U.S. Social Security. In fact, the earnings base on which CPP contributions are collected represents about 67% of total wage earnings, while the earnings base from which U.S. Social Security taxes are collected covers approximately 86% of total wage earnings.

Partial funding

Legislation enacted in 1977 moved Social Security from pay-as-you-go financing to "partial reserve financing," with the potential accumulation of significant reserves. But poor economic performance prevented these reserves from accumulating. However, Congress made a number of changes to Social Security in 1983, in effect moving to a system of partial funding. It raised Social Security taxes and announced that the age of eligibility for full retirement benefits would be increased gradually from 65 to 67. Together with strong economic performance, these changes resulted in the steady growth of reserves, so that Social Security is now no longer strictly a pay-as-you-go plan.

Congress also stipulated that the reserves accumulating in the trust funds could not be invested in private stocks and bonds, in part because the trust fund managers might have to sell at a loss and such sales could depress values of assets also held in private portfolios. A more important consideration, however, was the fear that political pressures might lead the trust fund managers to interfere with private business decisions. For the same reasons, Federal Reserve chairman Alan Greenspan has also publicly expressed his opposition to investment of the trust funds in the stock market.

Canadian policy-makers, it appears, have no such qualms. The CPP fund, now accumulating as a result of the recent sharp increase in contribution rates, is being invested in equities by the CPP Investment Board. With $2.4 billion in assets under management, the Board's 2000 annual report, released in June 2000, announced it had earned a 40.1% rate of return on its investments in its first full year of operations as a result of investing solely in equities. However, the Board president cautioned that such a spectacular return could not be expected again because the Board intended to broaden its asset allocation base, thus decreasing the volatility of its investment portfolio.

The trust funds

Social Security and Medicare taxes are divided among several trust funds, which are governed by a Board of Trustees required by law to report annually to Congress on the financial condition of the funds and on estimated future operations. If income of a trust fund is not enough to pay the benefits and administrative costs, the fund's assets serve as a temporary contingency reserve to cover the shortfall temporarily. And if there are recurring shortfalls, the availability of trust fund assets allows time for the enactment and implementation of legislation to restore financial stability to the program.

There are two Social Security trust funds:

2. The federal Old Age and Survivors Insurance (OASI) trust fund is used to pay for retirement and survivors benefits.

3. The federal Disability Insurance (DI) trust fund is used to pay benefits to people with disabilities and their families.

These two funds are described together as OASDI. There are also two Medicare trust funds:

4. The federal Hospital Insurance (HI) trust fund is used to pay for the services covered under the hospital insurance (Part A) provisions of Medicare: that is, in-patient hospital and related care.

5. The federal Supplementary Medical Insurance (SMI) trust fund is used to pay for services covered under the medical insurance (Part B) provisions of Medicare: physician and out-patient services.

The 7.65% Social Security tax deduction is allocated as follows: 5.35% to the OASI trust fund; 0.85% to the DI trust fund; and 1.45% to the HI trust fund. Social Security taxes are not used to finance the SMI trust fund. Most SMI revenues come from the general fund of the Treasury. The remainder comes from premiums paid by enrollees.

Any Social Security reserves not needed for the payment of benefits or operational expenses—which are consistently less than 1% of revenues—are invested only in U.S. government securities and earn the prevailing rate of interest. These are normally special obligations issued specifically for the trust funds. The amount of interest earned is substantial. For example, in 1998 the Social Security trust funds earned US$49.3 billion in interest, representing an effective annual interest rate of 9%.

The Social Security Administration points out that there is a persistent—but false—rumour that trust fund money has been used for purposes other than Social Security payments or operational expenses. It suggests confusion arises because of the trust fund investment procedures. The trust funds are financial accounts in the U.S. Treasury. The only purposes for which these trust funds can be used are to pay benefits and program administrative costs. Money invested in government bonds by Social Security is used for various government purposes. But, as with any other bonds it issues, the government must pay interest to the Social Security trust funds, and it must redeem the bonds—or pay back the borrowed money—when they mature or when they are needed to pay benefits.

Benefit levels

Social Security replaces about 40% of the average worker's pre-retirement earnings. In comparison, CPP retirement benefits are intended to replace 25% of earnings up to the average wage. But a full OAS benefit is equivalent to about 14% of the average wage. So, for those entitled to a full OAS benefit, CPP and OAS combined are equivalent to about 39% of the average wage—about the same as U.S. Social Security.

However, Social Security pays a minimum fixed benefit to everyone, no matter how little they've paid into the system. In effect, then, benefits replace a much higher percentage of the pre-retirement income of low earners than of high earners. According to one estimate for 1997, replacement rates ranged from 80% for low-wage earners to 25% for high-wage earners.

Benefits are indexed to the Consumer Price Index and adjusted annually to account for inflation. Reduced benefits are payable starting at age 62, but up to now the standard retirement age at which individuals can receive a full retirement benefit has been 65. For people born in 1938 or later, the full retirement age is scheduled to rise gradually to reach 67 in 2022—although reduced benefits will still be available at age 62.

Is Social Security broke?

The idea that Social Security is broke—or will be bankrupt any day now—has become so much a part of the conventional wisdom that almost no one even questions it.

So effective has the right-wing message been that economist James Schultz says apocalyptic predictions about Social Security now represent the accepted opinion of the bulk of the American population. There are clear parallels with the attack on the CPP in Canada and with the widespread—but erroneous—belief that the CPP is broke.

The reality, as it turns out, is that the Social Security Trust Fund is in surplus and is expected to remain that way for at least the next 35 years or so, by which time the baby boom generation will have retired. The surplus, which currently stands at about $124 billion, has been accumulating since 1983, when the payroll tax was increased. And it will help finance the baby boomers' retirement, which is why the program will not have any trouble meeting its obligations when the boomers are retiring.

The trustees of the Social Security system estimate that it will not be until some time after 2015 that the program will take in less in taxes (or Social Security contributions) than it pays out in benefits. And even then it will have more than $1 trillion in the Social Security trust fund left from previous years. In fact, assets in the trust funds are expected to continue growing over the next 25 years, to reach US$6.05 trillion in nominal dollars by the end of 2024. Assets in the funds will then start declining as they are used to supplement Social Security tax revenues to pay the benefits. In their 2000 annual report, the trustees projected that the trust funds would be adequately financed until 2037, which is three years longer than they had projected in their 1999 report. The improvement was attributed to the better-than-expected performance of the U.S. economy.

By 2037, when it is expected that the trust fund will be exhausted, revenue from Social Security taxes will no longer be enough to pay all the benefits that are anticipated. But even then, the trustees expect there will be Social Security payroll taxes to pay 72% of the planned benefits on a pay-as-you-go basis.

Economists Dean Baker and Mark Weisbrot, in their book *Social Security: The Phony Crisis*, observe that the system's revenues may have to be increased at some point in order to maintain its commitments, but they don't expect this to place an undue burden on the post-2034 labour force. Even if payroll taxes were to be increased to cover the shortfall, these economists say, the added cost would barely dent the average real wage in 2034, which will be over 30% higher than it is today. At the moment, however, payroll tax rates for the programs are not scheduled to change.

Conservative projections for the Social Security Fund

While Social Security is likely to be in good shape for at least the next 30 years or so, analysts suggest the projections leading to this conclusion are based on very conservative assumptions. In other words, the prognosis for America's public pension program may be even better than anticipated. Actuaries for the fund are projecting an economic growth rate over the next 75 years of 1.4% a year, which is less than half the average of the past 75 years, and below the average of the 1930s. Their long-term population growth rate projection is about half of what the Census Bureau is projecting. And not only is the growth of the working-age population projected to slow to a crawl, but the share of that population at work (the employment/population ratio) is also projected to decline—a violation of all historical precedent.

However, in their 2000 report, the trustees were somewhat more optimistic. They based their new projections on an assessment that some of the recent favourable economic performance, with low unemployment and faster-than-expected growth in both GDP and employment, will carry through into the early years of their 75-year projection period. Compared with their 1999 report, they said, the 2000 report generally reflects assumptions of lower unemployment rates, higher productivity gains, faster labour force growth, and a higher ratio of wages to total compensation throughout the first 10 years of the projection period. In combination, the trustees said, these changes produce higher levels of employment, productivity, real wages, and real GDP throughout the balance of the 75-year projection period. In fact, the trustees said "the strong economy of the past four years has weakened the argument that Social Security must be radically changed because it is absolutely unaffordable."

Possible options to bolster Social Security

As in other countries with pay-as-you-go public pension programs and aging populations, proposals have been made to bring the U.S. Social Security system into long-term, balance: that is, over the 75-year period generally used by the trustees of the Social Security funds for long-range planning purposes. Some—but not all—of these proposals involve partial or full privatization.

The 1994-96 Advisory Council on Social Security proposals

In 1994, for example, President Clinton appointed a bipartisan 13-member Advisory Council on Social Security, chaired by Edward M. Gramlich, to develop proposals to deal with the long-term viability of the program.

The Advisory Council reported in 1997 and a plurality of six members recommended incremental changes similar to those made in the past, that would reduce, but not eliminate, the projected deficit, which at that time was expected to be slightly more than 2% of projected payroll tax revenues. These reforms included:

- increasing the working period over which a retiree's benefits are computed from 35 years to 38 years;
- changing the way in which Social Security benefits are taxed, so that any benefits a retiree received beyond what he or she contributed to the system, as a worker would be taxed as ordinary income; currently, only beneficiaries with incomes above certain

annual thresholds owe taxes on their benefits, and just a portion of those benefits is subject to tax;

- extending Social Security coverage and participation to 3.7 million state and local government employees who are currently excluded from the program; this would bring more revenues into the system.

- accelerating the scheduled increase in the retirement age so that it becomes 67 by 2011; the retirement age would be indexed to longevity thereafter; this would reduce how much the system pays out and improve the long-term financial picture for Social Security; it is estimated that this change would eliminate about 22% of the projected funding gap;

- adjusting the Consumer Price Index (CPI); the calculation of the CPI is currently the subject of considerable controversy in the U.S., with some people claiming it overstates inflation; because the CPI is the basis of indexing for Social Security benefits, the claim is that overstatement of the index has unnecessarily increased costs.

It was estimated that these incremental changes would eliminate more than 70% of the projected long-term shortfall in Social Security funding. Other options proposed to eliminate the rest of the shortfall include investing the trust funds in the stock market and means-testing Social Security benefits. The Advisory Council agreed that means-testing should not be implemented.

The Robert M. Ball plan

Former Commissioner of the Social Security Administration Robert M. Ball put forward a plan in 1998 to restore long-run financial balance to Social Security by increasing payroll taxes, making modest cuts to benefits, and investing part of the trust fund reserves in equities. It was estimated that investing up to 40% of the reserves in equities by 2015 would close roughly half of the projected long-term deficit. The proposal would also allow workers to invest up to an additional 2% of their pay in voluntary supplementary retirement accounts administered through Social Security. This would supplement but not replace Social Security contributions and benefits.

Essentially, the Ball plan is similar to the one proposed by the six-member group of the 1994-96 Advisory Council on Social Security. But critics say it would probably not permanently solve the Social Security fiscal imbalance because it proposed only modest changes.

Maintain structure plan

Richard Leone and Greg Anrig Jr. of The Century Foundation, in their 1999 book on *Social Security Reform*, say that, while Social Security is important and successful, "even its most ardent supporters acknowledge that the program has shortcomings." Social Security' structure reflects the economic, social and demographic conditions of mid-20th century America, not the circumstances of a nation entering the 21st century, these authors say. However, they argue that Social Security should be modernized and strengthened, not privatized.

Among the changes that could strengthen and modernize the program, they say, the most important are:

- to modify benefits provided to spouses in recognition of the increased labour force participation of women;
- to improve the adequacy of benefits for older survivors;
- to make annual cost-of-living adjustments more accurate;
- to increase the age of initial eligibility for retirement benefits, in recognition of the improved health and longevity of the elderly; and

- to speed the accumulation of financial reserves and diversify the assets in which Social Security reserves are invested.

The distinctive characteristic of this plan, its authors say, would be the creation of a new Social Security Reserve Board (SSRB), modelled on the Federal Reserve Board, that would manage the operations of the Social Security system and would be removed from the budget presentations of the executive and legislative branches. The SSRB would be charged with achieving, over the course of several decades, reserve balances similar in magnitude to those that would be required of private pension funds under the Employee Retirement Income Security Act (ERISA). The trust fund investments would be diversified among government bonds and private stocks and bonds. But the proposal envisages benefit cuts—actually larger cuts than under the Ball plan— that would be "designed to reflect changes that have occurred in the labour force and in life expectancy since the program was enacted."

Proposals to introduce individual accounts

A number of other proposals have been put forward which would introduce private individual savings accounts into the system—in most cases, allowing individuals to divert part of their Social Security taxes to their individual accounts.

The Moynihan-Kerrey Plan

Democratic Senator Daniel Patrick Moynihan's proposal represents a limited form of privatization through individual accounts. Along with Democratic Senator Robert Kerrey, he introduced legislation in 1998 to implement his proposal.

Workers would be authorized to set up voluntary individual retirement savings accounts. Over a five-year period, Social Security payroll taxes would be reduced by two percentage points from a combined employer/employee rate of 12.4% to 10.4%. Workers would then be permitted to spend or save the one percentage point cut in their portion of the payroll tax. They could save it, either in voluntary personal accounts modelled on the Thrift Savings Plan and administered by a new government board, or in special Individual Retirement Accounts managed by a financial institution of their choosing. If an employee established a personal account, the worker's employer would have to match the worker's contribution. Withdrawal of account balances at retirement would be unrestricted.

After 2024, the Moynihan-Kerrey plan would have Social Security payroll taxes start increasing again to keep contribution revenues in line with benefit payments. But critics say that reducing average payroll taxes over the next 75 years would mean significant cuts in Social Security benefits. The plan would erode benefits steeply, and in ways that could hurt vulnerable groups the most.

In addition, the proposal fails the acid test of supporters of public pensions, articulated clearly by Richard Leone and Greg Anrig Jr.: that Social Security's long-term financing problem should not be aggravated by diverting the program's revenues to private accounts, and benefits should not be reduced to make room for private accounts; any such accounts should be supplementary to Social Security, treated entirely as add-ons.

The Breaux-Gregg (21st Century Retirement) Plan

This plan, proposed in 1998 by Democratic Senator John Breaux, Republican Senator Judd Gregg, and others would divert two percentage points of the current Social Security payroll tax to individual accounts modelled on the Thrift Savings Plan and cut Social Security benefits an average of 25% to 30%. Cuts of this size would be necessary both to close the current projected long-term deficit and to free up two percentage points of the payroll tax for individual savings accounts.

The Feldstein-Samwick plan for 2% accounts

Harvard economist Martin Feldstein, a leading proponent of privatization of Social Security and chief economist in the Reagan administration, together with economist Andrew Samwick, proposed a plan in 1998 whereby each worker would deposit 2% of his or her earnings, up to the maximum subject to the payroll tax, into a personal retirement account. Workers would receive an income tax credit to offset the cost of these deposits. For low-income workers with little or no tax liability, the tax credit would be refundable.

When workers reached retirement age and began to draw pensions from their personal retirement accounts, their Social Security benefits would be reduced by US$3 for every US$4 withdrawn. Overall, it is estimated retirees would receive about 60% of their benefits from Social Security and 40% from their personal accounts. Higher earners would depend more on their personal accounts, and some would receive nothing from Social Security. The reductions in Social Security benefits would eventually be sufficient to close the projected long-term Social Security deficit.

But, in a critique of the proposal, Brookings Institution economists Henry J. Aaron and Robert D. Reischauer charged that the Feldstein-Samwick plan would raise, not lower, the baby boomers' pensions, which they regard as imprudent. More generous benefits would be possible under the plan, say these economists, because it uses the budget surpluses projected for the next two decades to support deposits into individual accounts. But when these surpluses begin to shrink, taxes dedicated to retirement pensions will have to be raised, other spending cut, or deficits incurred for several decades.

And another critique of the Feldstein-Samwick proposal from the Congressional Budget Office said the proposed tax credits would cost the government about US$800 billion over the next 10 years. Rather than raise taxes or reduce government spending over that period, Feldstein and Samwick believe that anticipated federal budget surpluses could be allocated to pay for the tax credit. Then, whenever federal budget surpluses become insufficient, Congress could determine how to raise the money. But, as Richard Leone and Greg Anrig Jr. point out, because federal budget surpluses reduce the federal debt, creating a new tax credit and diverting the surpluses to private accounts would increase the government's long-term obligations and interest costs. As the Congressional Budget Office report said, "The policy would implicitly increase the tax burden on future workers if no further adjustment were made in the spending side of the budget."

The privatization option proposed by the 1994-96 Advisory Council on Social Security

Five members of the Advisory Council on Social Security, in their 1997 report, put forward a plan that would effectively have meant a partial privatization of Social Security. They proposed replacing part of Social Security with government-mandated but privately-managed Personal Security Accounts (PSAs) that individual workers would invest in a range of financial instruments. In effect, Social Security would gradually be replaced with two other benefits: a guaranteed minimum benefit and an additional amount that reflected the returns individuals earned on their PSAs. Both components would be financed by the payroll tax. But, because the guaranteed part of the benefit would be based only on a portion of the payroll tax, it would be significantly lower than the benefit that low-income retirees now receive. Each individual's additional benefits would depend on the performance of his or her PSA, which the worker would control.

Essentially, it appears the plan would have met the framework of the World Bank's ideal retirement income system, with a first pillar consisting of a minimal basic flat rate benefit intended to reduce poverty, and a mandatory private savings arrangement in the second pillar replacing the public earnings-related public plan. The suggestion was that the new system would be phased in over a long period of time so that no retiree would receive benefits entirely under the new system for about 40 years.

The five-member group also proposed that payroll taxes be increased by 1.52 percentage points for about the next 70 years to fund the transition. The added tax would be needed because continued Social Security benefits for current retirees and older workers, the new flat pension, and deposits into personal accounts would cost more than the current 12.4% payroll tax would generate. But, even with the tax increase, it was estimated that the new system would run a deficit for the first few decades, forcing the government to borrow approximately US$2 trillion (in 1998 dollars). Eventually, as Social Security was phased out, revenues would exceed costs and the debt would be paid off. When all the initial borrowing had been repaid—around the year 2070— it was suggested the supplemental payroll tax could be repealed.

The Advisory Council's proposals have all the disadvantages of other privatization proposals discussed in earlier chapters of this book. Whether or not workers accumulated sufficient income for retirement would depend on their investment skills; workers who failed to provide adequately for themselves would be dependent on a much smaller minimum income guarantee or on the support of their families; fees and commissions charged by financial institutions to manage the individual accounts would seriously reduce the portion of workers' contributions that could generate an income at retirement; and there would be huge transition costs. Cynics said the big advantage would be that privatization of Social Security in this way would relieve the government of the obligation to raise taxes to provide the promised benefits.

Whether or not future retirees would have enough to live on seems to have been beside the point. And all indications are that this kind of privatization would significantly reduce benefits. Robert Eisner, professor emeritus of economics at Northwestern University and a prolific author on economic issues, says that, if five percentage points of the 12.4% Social Security payroll tax were diverted to private investment, as advocated in the PSA proposal put forward by the five-member group, it would come to an average US$100. "Imagine brokers or mutual funds handling monthly investments in amounts that would be this small (and for many of the 150 million covered workers much less still) and then making monthly payments to as many as 50 million retirees," says Eisner. For those that would be willing to handle such small accounts, service charges would have to be large, he points out.

Clinton's 1999 Social Security "fix"

In his 1998 State of the Union address, President Bill Clinton had pledged to use the budget surplus to help reform Social Security. But the White House did not bring forward any kind of detailed plan for Social Security, nor did it endorse any of the different proposals that had been put on the table by both Democrats and Republicans. Democrats generally had been opposed to privatization. They had argued that introducing private savings accounts and giving individuals full responsibility for their investment choices would place too many Americans at serious financial risk. Others also said that the investment risks associated with individual accounts would undermine the fundamental goal of the Social Security program, which is to guarantee a retirement income for retirees.

Progressive commentators say that the fear of raising taxes —even by a small amount—currently pervades the political debate in Washington. This leaves the most common-sense solution to the Social Security problem—increasing the Social Security tax—with little support in Congress or the White House. Instead, they say, President Clinton proposed a "second-best" plan for Social Security. In his 1999

State of the Union address, the President set out a proposal to transfer about US$2.8 trillion of the projected US$4 trillion government budget surpluses over 15 years to the Social Security retirement income fund. Transfers would be made from the U.S. Treasury to the Social Security trust fund each year for 15 years, and the amount transferred each year would be specified in law, so that by 2015 about US$2.8 trillion would have been transferred.

The President also proposed that about US$600 billion of the new money paid into the trust fund would be invested in the stock market to earn a higher return. Each year from 2000 through to 2014, a portion of the funds would be transferred to the market until such time as 14.6% of the trust funds were in private investments. Funds would be invested in broad market indexes by private managers, not by the government. On average, trust funds invested in the market would represent no more than 4% of the stock market. It was suggested that these two initiatives would place the Social Security system in balance until 2055. And the President called for a bipartisan effort to take further action to extend that solvency at least until 2075.

As well, Clinton proposed a new initiative that would divert around 12% of the surplus, or an average of about US$36 billion a year, to establish universal savings accounts—or USAs. These accounts would be separate from Social Security and not a substitute for the guaranteed benefit. In making the announcement, the President said, "With these new accounts Americans can invest as they choose and receive funds to match a portion of their savings, with extra help for those least able to save. USA accounts," he said, "will help all Americans to share in our nation's wealth and to enjoy a more secure retirement." The proposal was that workers would receive a tax credit to contribute to their own saving accounts, and an additional credit to match a portion of their savings—with their own choice about how to invest the funds and additional help for lower-income workers who might have a harder time saving.

Testifying before the House Ways and Means Committee, Kenneth Apfel, the Social Security Commissioner, said no resources for these accounts would be drained from the Social Security system. And he claimed that "USA accounts, separate from Social Security, will mean hundreds of dollars in targeted tax cuts for working Americans who choose to save more for retirement, with more help for lower-income workers."

Reaction to the proposal from Republicans was predictable. They were opposed to the investment of Social Security trust funds in the stock market because of the risk of political interference in the marketplace. As the Cato Institute put it, "Allowing the government to invest the trust fund in private capital markets would amount to the socialization of a large portion of the U.S. economy. The federal government would become the nation's largest shareholder, with a controlling interest in nearly every major American company." Right-wing critics also said that the surplus should be returned to taxpayers, who could then invest their money as they chose in private savings accounts, without the potential for corruption.

But even progressive economists have expressed opposition to investing trust funds in the market. For example, Dean Baker of The Century Foundation lists several "thorny issues" raised by Clinton's proposal, including:

- the expected rate of return on stock holdings, which he suggests may be overly optimistic;
- the potential loss to Social Security reserves from bear markets;
- the questions of corporate governance when the government holds stock; and
- the political effect of the government having a major stake in private corporations.

These concerns, of course, are also significant for Canada, which has already started investing part of the CPP fund in the market and which has yet to have any public discussion of the "thorny issues" Baker raises.

The Clinton plan has also been criticized because it would devote a large part of the federal budget surplus over the next 15 years to Social Security and debt reduction, raising the possibility that other pressing public needs will continue to be ignored and that discretionary domestic spending will be insufficient to provide an adequate level of services. Ultimately, as Edith Rasell and Jeff Faux point out in a *Briefing Paper* for the Economic Policy Institute, the essential problem facing Social Security is less dire or complicated than it may seem from the hyperbole produced by the current debate. The fact that people will live longer than their parents is cause for celebration, these authors say, and the obvious implication— that they will spend more time in retirement receiving Social Security and therefore have to pay a little more in taxes to support the program—should not be unbearable for most voters to accept. Unfortunately, they say, "neither the White House nor congressional leaders seem willing to make this simple, honest case to the people."

George W. Bush and the Republicans propose opting-out

In the meantime, advocates for privatization continue their campaign, with George W. Bush adopting a version of opting out of Social Security as part of his platform during the 2000 presidential race. No doubt based on the views of his campaign adviser Martin Feldstein (whose 2% privatization plan was described earlier in this chapter), Bush proposed allowing workers to divert part of their Social Security payroll tax— possibly two percentage points—into their own individual savings accounts. At the same time, he said benefits for current retirees and those nearing retirement would be maintained, as would benefits for disabled workers and survivors. Bush also said he would not raise payroll taxes, nor would he invest Social Security trust funds in the stock market.

It would appear that Bush's plan—like all similar privatization proposals—was based on the assumption that returns in the stock market will be the same as they have been in the recent past. Overly optimistic assumptions about stock market returns were apparently not matched by any assumptions at all on what percentage of contributions to individual accounts would be consumed by fees and commissions. Nor did the plan take into account transition costs involved in moving to the new system. According to the Washington-based Center on Budget and Policy Priorities, Bush's privatization plan would cost something like US$900 billion over the first ten years. Transition costs this high would result because the Social Security system would have to simultaneously pay out current benefits, while privatization drained over 16% of the money coming into the system—assuming that two percentage points of the current 12.4% contribution rate would be diverted to the individual accounts.

Economists who analyzed his plan pointed out that Bush's proposed tax cuts—also part of his platform—would consume virtually the entire projected non-Social Security surplus, leaving no room for transfers to Social Security without causing a non-Social Security deficit. In other words, the only way the Bush plan could be implemented would be to cut Social Security benefits. Four economists looked at how large those cuts would have to be and whether the proceeds of investments in individual accounts could compensate for them.

The economists concluded that, if Social Security benefits were cut equally for all workers aged 55 or younger in 2002, benefits would have to be cut by 41% to maintain solvency of the system over the next 75 years. But they pointed out that this approach would weigh most heavily on workers in their early 50s, who would have little time to build up individual accounts before retirement. Alternatively, benefit cuts could be phased in so that total benefits—that is, Social Security benefits plus assumed average individual accounts—would be reduced equally for workers of all ages. Using this method would require reductions in Social Security benefits of only 29% for people aged 50 or older in 2002, but benefits for those aged 30 or younger would have to be cut by 54%.

Not only would average benefits be cut relative to current law, but workers would have to shoulder substantially increased risk under individual accounts—a typical outcome when public pension programs are replaced with individual savings accounts, even when such privatization consists of the kind of limited opting-out that the Bush proposal envisages. The four economists concluded that the Bush proposal could cut Social Security benefits by more than 50% for young workers, and that the proceeds from the individual accounts would, on average, make up only a portion of that cut while exposing individuals to significant risk. In fact, they said, "the implied reductions for future retirees are so substantial that they raise questions about the viability of protecting benefits for current retirees, older workers, disabled workers, and survivors while diverting payroll taxes to individual accounts."

Two of the four economists later noted that Feldstein had disputed their conclusions. But they also said that "the assumptions he makes are so unrealistic that he unwittingly confirms our original contention: The Bush plan would cripple Social Security, expose workers to increased risk, and reduce their pension income." Feldstein's arithmetic, they said, requires that the Social Security trust fund go into the red and stay there for about 20 years, which is contrary to current law and to a previously inviolable 65-year-old pledge. During that time, it would have to borrow about US$2 trillion from the Treasury in order to meet Social Security pension obligations, while diverting revenues into private accounts. "Is this scenario politically credible?" they ask. "More important, is it good public policy?"

Coalitions fight back

With Bush now in the White House, the pressure for privatization of Social Security is likely to continue. The financial industry stands to make billions of dollars if even a small part of Social Security contributions can be channelled through individual savings accounts. And the industry has the clout and the resources to make its voice heard in the corridors of power—not just in the United States, but in Canada too. As many commentators have pointed out, privatization of Social Security has more to do with ideological preferences and economic interests than with the solvency of Social Security. And, as we have also seen, privatization has nothing to do with ensuring an adequate income for future seniors, either.

The extensive resources available to the privatization advocates have allowed them to capture the agenda. And a dutiful media seems to have been able to convince people that radical changes are needed in Social Security. High stock market returns, combined with a massive amount of misinformation in the media, have softened up Americans for some form of privatization—at the very least, perhaps, a partial privatization though opting out into individual accounts. For all the reasons discussed earlier, such a move would seriously undermine the financial security of future seniors. Even more important, however, is that it is unnecessary.

For example, economist Dean Baker set out a detailed blueprint for "Saving Social Security in Three Steps," in a 1998 *Briefing Paper* for the Economic Policy Institute. He advocated a program that would:

- commit a portion of the federal government's projected budget surpluses to the trust fund, or, alternatively, index the payroll tax to increases in life expectancy;
- fully incorporate the impact of recent changes to the consumer price index into the projections for the trust fund; and
- raise the cap on wages that are subject to the payroll tax so that it keeps in step with the upward distribution of income.

Other thoughtful analysts have demonstrated that radical surgery is not required. But the advocates of privatization still seem to have the upper hand. Writing just over two years ago, in the summer of 1998, Robert Kuttner described the apparent disarray in which the usual defenders of Social Security found themselves. While individual groups such as the Twentieth Century Fund (now known as The Century Foundation) and the Campaign for America's Future are doing heroic work, he said, "there is simply no liberal counterpart to the right's multi-pronged campaign."

At that time, it seemed, the most logical defenders were "otherwise engaged." Liberal economists and policy analysts, Kuttner said, had played a mainly defensive game, supporting a series of policy adjustments that many commentators derided as "nip and tuck." The problem, as Kuttner saw it, was that the debate is "numbingly technical" and "the liberal side lacks the drama and excitement of what appears to be a big new idea consonant with the pro-market sentiment of the age."

More recently, however, a number of organizations have been fighting to raise public awareness of the attack on Social Security and to mobilize people against the privatizers' plans. For example, the AFL-CIO put stopping Social Security privatization at the top if its legislative agenda for the year 2000, and, with its affiliate unions, is engaged in extensive education activities throughout the country. It has also endorsed a coalition of various progressive organizations, called The New Century Alliance, which is dedicated to seeing that Social Security reforms benefit working people.

Progressive think tanks, such as the Center on Budget and Policy Priorities, The Century Foundation, and The Economic Policy Institute, regularly publish papers on Social Security privatization, most of which are available on the Internet at their various web-sites. And a Social Security Information Page at http://userdata.acd.net/demarco.chris/sspriv.htm collects information on Social Security privatization, providing links to various web-sites containing the facts about privatization:

facts that the major media tend to ignore in their analyses. The individuals operating this particular site hope to get out information to as many people as possible so they can "build a grass-roots movement against bankrupting Social Security to improve the bottom line of Wall Street firms."

Chapter 6
Replacing the Canada Pension Plan with individual accounts

Should we get rid of the Canada Pension Plan and force Canadians to save for their own retirement? Should we at least let people opt out of the CPP if they want to, and have their contributions directed to their private savings accounts instead? Advocates of privatization say it's time to make these kinds of radical changes in the CPP. It's the only way to deal with our aging population, they say. Public pension plans—and especially pay-as-you-go plans like the CPP—will be unsustainable in the face of the "demographic time bomb." We can't afford to maintain entitlements to seniors—and anyway, they've become much too dependent on the state. It's time for seniors to become more self-reliant.

These arguments are all too familiar. And, like many ideas put forward by the right in Canada, they are more than a little reminiscent of the position of Republicans in the United States. In Canada we hear the same references to "greedy geezers" and "Ponzi schemes" that have become part of the rhetoric used by neoliberal opponents of U.S. Social Security. We've seen how Canadian advocates of privatization, like their American counterparts, have used apocalyptic demography to construct a "demographic time bomb" and claim that public pensions are no longer affordable; to fan the flames of inter-generational conflict and promote a "war between generations" over pensions; and to give their arguments the veneer of economic respectability by claiming that replacing our public pension plan with a system of individual accounts will increase national savings and bring all sorts of other economic benefits—none of which can be demonstrated with any confidence.

The tactics of the privatizers in Canada are also strikingly similar to the kind of strategies being used by advocates of privatization south of the border. The key to getting radical changes adopted, of course, is creating a crisis mentality. If people can be convinced our public pension program is in crisis, they will be much more amenable to making major changes.

In Chapter 1, we looked at the blueprint for guerilla warfare against U.S. Social Security and those who support it. The libertarian Washington-based Cato Institute was promoting it as long ago as 1983. The first step for those who want to see radical changes in the public pension system — according to this approach—is to calm existing beneficiaries and older workers by assuring them that proposals to respond to the "crisis"—such as privatizing or means-testing—will not affect them. Opponents of public pensions must then take every opportunity to demonstrate weaknesses in the current program, while developing a fully privatized alternative.

Next, they must work to sell this privatized alternative to the young, the majority of whom question the future of social security. And finally, it's necessary to activate powerful private interests, including the banks, insurance companies, and other institutions that will gain from privatization.

What's wrong with the CPP?

It's remarkable how closely Canadian advocates of privatization have been following this blueprint. They've been using inter-generational equity as a cornerstone of their argument. They claim that the CPP is unfair to young people because they will be asked to pay more than their parents did, and they will have to pay more than their benefits are worth. They've also claimed that the rate of return on the CPP is so low that it is not a good deal for young people; they would have a much better return on their investment if their contributions were directed towards private savings arrangements.

As well, the privatization advocates argue that the high payroll taxes that would be required to sustain the CPP as the population ages would be politically unacceptable and detrimental to employment, too. And they suggest that savings and investment would be greatly improved if the CPP were replaced with a privatized savings scheme. We looked at many of these arguments in detail in the first two chapters of this book. In this chapter, we'll bring them all together and see why we should resist the attack on our public pensions.

"Young people will pay more than their parents did"

It's worth noting that all of the CPP actuarial reports, including those before its inception, projected increasing contribution rates in the future because of the maturing of the plan and the changing of Canadian demographics causing the population to age. Because the CPP is essentially a pay-as-you-go plan, contribution rates have to increase as the population ages, so that enough money is coming in to pay all the benefits. But this is nothing new. It was anticipated in the way contribution rates were set so far in advance. In fact, before the recent CPP reforms, contribution rates were set by federal and provincial finance ministers on a 25-year schedule and adjusted at each five-year review, as required by legislation.

"Young people will pay more than their benefits are worth"

Claims that young people will pay "more than their benefits are worth" or that they will pay more into the plan than they will ever receive in benefits are simply not true. Experts expect that all future generations will receive in current dollar benefits over five times what they and their employer contributed, contrary to the belief that they will receive less in benefits than the amount contributed.

"The CPP is not a good investment for young people"

As we saw earlier, the implicit rate of return on a mature pay-as-you-go pension plan will be equal to the rate of growth in the earnings base on which contributions are assessed. Current estimates for the CPP indicate that this is about 1.5% a year, after allowing for inflation. This kind of return is obviously puny compared with the spectacular returns stock market investors have been achieving recently, and advocates of privatization have seized on this as "evidence" that the CPP is a bad bargain for Canadians.

They have also claimed that today's young people will get so little out of the CPP in relation to what they've put into the plan that they'd be better off putting their money into an RRSP or some kind of mandatory savings arrangement. But, as we saw earlier, the comparison is not appropriate for a number of reasons. It's like comparing apples and oranges.

"High payroll taxes make the CPP unsustainable"

It was inevitable that, as Canada's population was aging, contribution rates needed to fund the CPP would have to increase. Critics of the plan claimed they would have to go to such high levels that people would be unwilling to pay the cost. High payroll taxes, they said, would make the CPP unsustainable. They also said payroll taxes were killers of jobs.

In 1995, as the federal and provincial finance ministers began their regular five-year review of the CPP rate schedule, as required by legislation, they had in front of them projections prepared by the Chief Actuary, which he was required to provide as the basis for their discussions. The ministers were also required by law to set contribution rates at a level where sufficient funds would be generated to pay the benefits and maintain a reserve equivalent to two years' worth of benefits.

The Chief Actuary's report said that, to meet the requirements of that law, contribution rates would have to be increased at a faster rate than he had projected in his previous report. He determined that, if finance ministers decided to increase contribution rates right away, instead of waiting until the year 2015 when they were scheduled to go up again, combined employer/employee rates might reach 13.91% of contributory earnings in 2030, rising to 14.07% in 2050 and reaching a peak of 14.44% in 2100.

The finance ministers decided that combined contribution rates close to 14% in 35 years' time would be unacceptable. They used these rate projections to justify a change in the funding of the CPP so that the combined contribution rate could be kept below 10% of contributory earnings. The ministers claimed this could be done by switching to partial funding of the CPP. Ironically, to generate surplus funds for investment, it was necessary to increase CPP contribution rates much more sharply over the next few years than they would have been under the old rate schedule designed for what was essentially a pay-as-you-go plan.

As for the impact of payroll taxes on jobs, it is perhaps interesting that they seem to have had little negative impact in the U.S., where Social Security taxes are 12.4% of contributory earnings, compared with what was a combined rate of 5.6% in Canada when the 1996 round of CPP reforms began. In actual fact, although advocates of privatization argue that high payroll taxes are "killers of jobs," there is very little evidence to support that view. Although there is still not much research on the relationship between payroll taxes and employment, what evidence there is indicates that payroll taxes are almost entirely passed on to employees in the form of lower wages. The 1994 OECD Jobs Study, for example, concluded: "It is all but impossible to find a simple relationship between taxes on labour and employment." And it said that reducing payroll taxes and shifting to some other form of tax would have only "a limited effect on employment."

In a mandatory privatized pension system, employees and employers would still be required to contribute to the program—although, in the Chilean system, there is no matching employer contribution to the scheme. In fact, the ILO argues that payroll taxes would be just as large in a privatized system as they are under pay-as-you-go social insurance programs.

If mandatory contributions do indeed have an impact on job creation and employment, it is difficult to see how that impact would be lessened if the contributions were directed to a private savings scheme rather than a public social insurance program such as the CPP. However, privatization advocates in Canada have argued that mandatory contributions to a privatized savings scheme "would be seen as the purchase price of a pension benefit, not simply as an increase in the payroll tax," and for this reason, "the long-run disincentive effects of required contributions to mandatory RRSPs would be small or non-existent, unlike similar contributions to a reformed CPP." The credibility of that conclusion is certainly suspect.

Advantages claimed for individual accounts

We all know Canada's population is aging. Within the next 30 or 40 years, about one-quarter of our population will be 65 or older. If we are concerned about making sure these future seniors have adequate incomes in retirement, we have to ask ourselves: just how would it help to replace the CPP with a system of individual savings accounts, or to allow some people to opt out of the public plan and replace it voluntarily with their own private savings accounts?

For the advocates of privatization, switching to individual accounts—whether on a mandatory or voluntary basis—would have important benefits. As they see it, individual accounts would:

- **Reduce or eliminate the cost of public pensions.**
  Pay-as-you-go pension plans like the CPP use contributions from those in the current work force to pay the pensions of those who are retired. Aging populations require increasing contributions from those of

working age, since there are more pension claimants in relation to contributors. Replacing the public plan with individual accounts is seen as a way of avoiding continuous contribution increases from the population of working age.

- **Eliminate intergenerational transfers.** Replacing a contributory public pension plan with a system of mandatory individual savings accounts still requires mandatory contributions, but they are directed to the individual's own account, instead of towards paying for the pensions of others. Inter-generational transfers are thus avoided: another objective of advocates of privatization. Allowing opting-out of the public plan would reduce but not eliminate inter-generational transfers within the plan.

- **Eliminate collective responsibility and shift risk to individuals.** Public pay-as-you-go pension plans pool the risks of providing for retirement and protect those who are most vulnerable. Private individual savings accounts shift the risk to individuals who must then fend for themselves. Advocates of privatization characterize this as putting pension provision under individual control. They also see it as reducing the role of the state, which is an ideological objective.

- **Direct pension contributions to the "free market."** A system of mandatory individual savings accounts or voluntary opting-out would direct mandatory contributions collected from individuals and their employers into the financial markets where financial institutions, brokers, advisers, and others can earn commissions and fees on the funds.

- **Other economic reasons.** Advocates of privatization through individual accounts also claim such systems increase national savings and promote economic growth.

A number of different schemes have been proposed to privatize of the CPP by converting it to a system of mandatory individual savings accounts, or by allowing people to opt out of the plan and have their mandatory contributions directed to their individual savings accounts. While initially most proposals seemed to favour the Chilean model, in recent years the British system of opting-out seems to be the preferred option.

The neo-liberal think tanks and commentators

Privatization of the CPP has long been a favourite hobbyhorse of the neoliberal think tanks in Canada, along with their friends in the media and assorted right-wing pundits. A recent salvo from the Fraser Institute, for example, was its release in June 2000 of a survey of investment managers, reporting on their response to the 2000 federal budget and related issues, including the CPP. A spokesperson for the Institute said: "There is little agreement regarding the exact nature of reform for the CPP other than complete unanimity on the unsustainability of the status quo. It is quite clear everyone surveyed favours some type of privatization." That was hardly surprising, given that investment managers would benefit handsomely if the CPP were converted to a system of individual savings accounts—particularly if such private accounts were mandatory.

The corporate-funded C.D.Howe Institute has published numerous studies and commentaries advocating privatization of the CPP—many of them written by economist William Robson, a senior policy analyst at the Institute. Robson is in demand as a speaker and media commentator who will support the widely-held view that the CPP is beyond repair—a myth that advocates of privatization like to promote. He called for its abolition as long ago as January 1996, when he wrote, in a Commentary for the C.D.Howe Institute, that Canadians should contemplate winding up the

CPP in favour of an expanded private pension system, which would include mandatory RRSP contributions.

Reflecting the classic neoliberal stance on privatization of public pensions, Robson claimed privatization through individual accounts would mean a "switch from the current state-run system, which sets important political risks against the economic advantages of more complete funding, to a more secure system based on individual responsibility and control." It was not made explicit, of course that the "political risk" of having a public pension system, established by the demographic will of Canadians, would be traded for the market risk of individual savings accounts, putting individual Canadians at risk of ending up with insufficient income in retirement.

Robson proposed that CPP contribution rates should be raised to a "sustainable level." At that time, he was proposing a combined rate of 7.5%, starting in 1997 and continuing indefinitely. Benefit growth should be reined in, he said, by raising the eligibility age for normal retirement pensions to 70 over a 20-year period; future benefit accruals should be scaled back to 60% of projected levels; and the disability portions of the CPP should be hived off into a separate program.

But even those changes would still not make the CPP attractive to younger Canadians, Robson alleged. The most complete answer to those remaining problems, he claimed, would be to phase out the CPP in favour of a universal private system founded on individual money purchase retirement accounts for all those not covered by occupational defined benefit pension plans. His prescription strongly favoured the Chilean model.

As to how to get from here to there, Robson suggested no further accrual of CPP benefits after a given date, but with full payment of all then-existing entitlements as they come due. "While it may appear abrupt to some and insufficiently vigorous to others," Robson said, "it represents one route by which the CPP could be wound down without dramatically altering already accrued benefits, yet without requiring exorbitant taxes for those who will never become entitled to benefits." He suggests CPP benefits might cease to accrue 10 years after implementing the first round of reforms—that is, increasing contribution rates, cutting benefits, and raising the age of eligibility.

Suppose, for the sake of illustration, said Robson, the door is shut on further benefit accruals after 2008. At that point, he claimed, much of the plan's current structure, including the existing base on which contributions are levied, could be radically modified. The cost of benefits not covered by the CPP account could be paid out of the federal budget—perhaps through selected taxes on retirement income or deficit financing. According to his calculations, the cost of winding down the plan during the first three decades after 2008 could be covered by an additional flat personal income tax levied at a rate around 2.5%. Alternatively, some deficit financing from the federal budget—to the tune of 1.5% of GDP—could be undertaken.

Robson manages to gloss over the inevitably huge transition costs that would be involved if the CPP were to be abandoned. And, while acknowledging that the CPP contributed to an increase in the incomes of older Canadians during the 1970s and 1980s "that is one of the major achievements of modern social policy," he fails to mention what would happen to the incomes of future seniors if the CPP were now to be abandoned. True to his philosophical roots, however, he asserts the virtue of "requiring each generation to save for its own golden years."

Stockwell Day and the Alberta government

In federal-provincial negotiations during the 1996/97 round of CPP reforms, the Alberta government, led by its then Treasurer Stockwell Day, had tried unsuccessfully to convince the other finance ministers that some form of privatization of the CPP should be introduced. Changes to the

CPP require the consent of two-thirds of the provinces having two-thirds of the population, so Alberta would have had to convince at least five other provinces, including Ontario, to have any hope of its proposals being adopted. Then, following the introduction of the federal government's Bill C-2, tabled on September 25, 1997, which implemented the reforms agreed to by federal, provincial and territorial governments, Alberta struck its own committee in December 1997 to look at CPP reform.

Based on the committee's deliberations, the Alberta government on June 15, 1998 released a discussion paper called *Next Steps to CPP Reform*. According to Day, who issued a press release accompanying the paper, "Bill C-2 related to Canada Pension Plan reform was a step in the right direction, not a panacea. It doesn't solve the funding shortfall and inter-generational inequities that are eating away the confidence our youth have in the CPP. We can't ignore it—it's our responsibility to correct those problems."

The provincial agenda for the first triennial review

At the same time, in mid-1998, as federal and provincial governments were going into the first triennial review under the new legislation, Day put forward seven principles from *Next Steps to CPP Reform* for the finance ministers to consider as a starting point. They were:

- The plan's universality and full portability should be preserved;
- The funding basis must be credible and reliable, and must minimize the inter-generational transfer of debt;
- There must be a readily discernible relationship between what people pay and what they get. Contributors should be demonstrably better off by being members of the plan, as a retirement and general insurance scheme;
- Contribution rates must leave room for individual/private initiatives for retirement savings;

- Where possible and appropriate, individuals and employers should be given the flexibility to design equivalent or better benefits;
- All generations should in some way share in the cost of dealing with the CPP's problems; and
- Plan governance must be cohesive and accountable.

One of the key items Alberta wanted the finance ministers to consider during this review was an assessment of "the merits of turning the retirement component of the CPP into mandatory, individual RRSP-style accounts." Alberta's *Next Steps to CPP Reform* had urged consideration of whether responsibility for managing the disability component of the CPP could be delegated to the provinces. And its final point had said that "perhaps it is time to re-examine ways to provide greater flexibility to employees and employers in the provision of retirement and related benefits mandated under the CPP."

For example, the document asked, "Is it possible or desirable to set up individual accounts for future retirement benefit accruals? Should employers who sponsor registered retirement plans that exceed minimum CPP benefit levels be given some special recognition in the CPP program? Can we give this sort of flexibility to individuals and employers and still maintain the positive features of universality and full portability?"

The "Alberta solution" for the CPP

Day failed again in his efforts to get the other finance ministers fired up about his privatization proposals during the 1998/99 triennial review. But it seemed that, instead of arguing for the replacement of the CPP with mandatory individual savings accounts, as it did in *Next Steps to CPP Reform*, Alberta was now advocating a form of limited opting-out. At the end of the first triennial review of the CPP, in December 1999, Day issued a press release which claimed that, while progress had been made on CPP reform, "an Alberta solution is still possible." It listed several points for further study, including a new governance structure; elimination of the foreign content limit; removing disability coverage from the CPP; more detailed reporting to CPP contributors and more detail in the CPP actuarial reports; and "whether cost savings from improved governance, increasing investment returns, and better administration could be directed towards individual retirement accounts."

Limited opting-out would seriously undermine the CPP

Clearly, the kind of limited opting-out that Alberta proposes would seriously undermine the financial base of the CPP. In some ways, what the province appears to be suggesting might be compared with the treatment of surplus under a fully-funded registered pension plan. Most jurisdictions impose strict limits on the withdrawal of surplus from an ongoing plan. Where such plans have an actuarial surplus, the plan sponsor may take a contribution holiday; in rare cases, plan members may be given a contribution holiday; or the surplus might be used to improve benefits, consistent with the maximum benefits allowed by the Canada Customs and Revenue Agency (formerly Revenue Canada).

However, the CPP is not a funded pension plan. It remains essentially a pay-as-you-go plan, in spite of the move to partial funding with the new Investment Fund. If the CPP is able to generate cost savings from improved governance, increasing investment returns, or better administration, it is difficult to see why such a "surplus" should be paid out to individuals to invest in their individual retirement accounts, as Alberta seems to be suggesting. In fact, a strong case could be made for retaining any such funds within the CPP, where they would contribute to maintaining the stability of contribution rates and to funding the promised future benefits. Such unexpected "windfalls" might also be used to improve benefits: for example, by expanding the various dropout provisions, or making other improvements that would help ensure adequate pensions for future seniors— especially those with low earnings.

Privatization and opting-out would introduce inequalities

To withdraw "surplus" funds from the plan and allow individuals to invest them privately for their own benefit would also contravene the principle of pooling risks through social insurance. And it would create inequities between individuals, for all the reasons outlined earlier in relation to defined contribution savings plans. It should be emphasized that individuals who wish to save on their own for retirement already have access to generous tax assistance for RRSPs, much of which is not being fully used.

Alberta threatens to withdraw from the CPP

At the conclusion of the federal-provincial talks in December 1999, federal Finance Minister Paul Martin said Alberta's proposals would be studied, but no commitment was made to take action—at least, not publicly. Day also said that Alberta had been looking at the possibility of setting up its own pension plan if the reforms it had proposed for the CPP were not achieved. He noted, however, that, "if the economic benefits that could be achieved with an Alberta-only plan could also be implemented across the entire plan, Alberta would not need to opt out, and all Canadians would benefit." In other words, opting out through individual accounts could benefit all Canadians—if only the other finance ministers would go along with the idea.

While Alberta's stance on the CPP has been characterized by some observers as simply posturing and not to be taken seriously, it must be noted that it has been hailed by the business press as both innovative and potentially damaging to the CPP. For example, in the *Globe and Mail* on Jan. 27, under the headline "Foolish to ignore Alberta call to fix CPP," columnist John Ibbitson praised Day for his ideas, including those that would "increase individual control" by "creating individual accounts that citizens could contribute to, tailoring the plan to their own needs." A report in the *Financial Post* of December 1, 1999 was also sympathetic and said "Alberta's withdrawal from the CPP would be a critical blow to the national plan."

Could Alberta set up its own plan?

Whether or not Alberta could actually withdraw from the CPP and set up its own plan, perhaps based on individual accounts, is another question. For one thing, it would appear that the other provinces would have to agree to let Alberta go. And the amending formula for the CPP is even more restrictive than the constitutional amending formula. To repeat, two-thirds of the provinces—including Quebec—with two-thirds of the population would have to approve.

But even if that hurdle could be overcome, there would be the question of what portion of CPP costs would Alberta have to assume to ensure the payment of accumulated benefits promised to CPP participants. In other words, who would pay the CPP benefits of retired Albertans? And what about the CPP benefit entitlements earned prior to Alberta's withdrawal by Albertans who are still working?

According to some estimates, the province would have to assume an approximately $50 billion share of the CPP's accrued liabilities if the province decided to withdraw from the plan. This estimate emerged from a conference on *A Separate Pension Plan for Alberta?* organized by the Institute for Public Economics and held at the University of Alberta in Edmonton, in January 1999.

Economist William Robson, from the C.D.Howe Institute, was a featured speaker at the conference, where he repeated his now familiar criticisms of the CPP and said that the latest round of reforms had not gone far enough. According to Robson, "It makes sense to examine further reforms that combine a move toward pre-funded individually controlled retirement accounts with a shift to some other tax base to finance current obligations." Significantly, Robson claimed that "individual provinces can play a role in this process out of proportion to their voting weight in the CPP's amending formula by examining separate pension plans that could enhance their citizens' confidence in receiving the promised benefits, and that could be implemented if other provinces and the federal government do not run the exiting plan responsibly." And, in a closing comment that seemed to come very close to recommending a form of blackmail, Robson said that, for reasons to do with demographics, economics and political culture, "Alberta seems uniquely well placed to play such a role."

Another paper presented at the conference suggested that a separate pension plan for Alberta might be more costly than for the province to remain within the CPP. That's because of the many uncertainties, which include the cost of administering and setting up an infrastructure to administer a separate Alberta Pension Plan; the added cost of pooling risk over a smaller population; uncertainty regarding Alberta's share of the existing CPP fund; and the impact of the volatility of Alberta's economy on the level of contribution rates. In fact, the authors of this paper called it "Checking Out of the Hotel California" after the old Eagles song that says, "You can check in any time you want, but you can never really leave."

While Alberta has not yet made public what kind of pension plan it might set up if it decided to withdraw from the CPP, actuary Robert Brown, director of the Institute of Insurance and Pension Research at the University of Waterloo, who also presented a paper at the conference, assumes that the province does not intend to opt out of the CPP and establish a highly similar plan in parallel. The only logical model Alberta could have in mind, Brown said, would be replacing the present defined-benefit CPP model with a defined contribution system of mandatory retirement savings plans—with all the disadvantages such a system entails. And, as we have already seen, while the Chilean plan was forced on that country's population by a military dictatorship, it seems highly questionable that a free and democratic government could force citizens to channel their mandatory contributions to individual accounts run by private financial institutions, when there is—as Brown pointed out—no element of income redistribution or general welfare purpose.

The Reform Party/Canadian Alliance proposals

Before it transformed itself into the Canadian Alliance, the Reform Party issued two policy booklets on privatization of public pensions. The first, in 1995, proposed the abolition of the CPP and its replacement with a mandatory system of "Super-RRSPs" modelled on the Chilean system. More recently, the Reform Party apparently changed its position. Perhaps feeling that Canadians were not yet ready to abandon the CPP completely, Reform began to recommend voluntary opting-out instead. Its new stance was outlined in the party's 1998 booklet called *Can Your Pension Be Saved? Should you have the choice to take control of your own retirement?* The latest iteration proposed a system that would allow people to opt out of the CPP and appeared to be modelled on the British system introduced in the 1980s when Margaret Thatcher was in power.

The Canadian Alliance policy platform, adopted at its founding convention in January 2000, when it replaced the Reform Party, contained no specific reference to the CPP. However, its policy declaration did make a commitment to "honour obligations under current state-run programs to retired Canadians and those close to retirement," and to "maintain support for low-income seniors." It's interesting how closely this statement reflects the first step of the blueprint for getting rid of public pensions, outlined earlier.

The Alliance went on to say: "We will provide future retirees with a greater choice between a government mandated pension plan and mandatory personal plans." As well, the party said it would "allow individuals greater opportunity to save for their own retirement, giving Canadians greater control over their own affairs."

It's not difficult to decipher the code words. "Providing future retirees with greater choice" can only mean allowing opting-out along the lines of the British scheme. And the reference to a choice between "a government mandated pension plan" and "mandatory personal plans" is clearly a reference to the British model, which permits individuals to opt out of the public earnings-related plan as long as they can demonstrate they have an appropriate personal pension. The Alliance reference to "giving Canadians greater control over their own affairs" is classic neoliberal doublespeak for letting future seniors fend for themselves, with no collective responsibility for ensuring any particular pension at retirement— except for the very lowest-income people.

Alliance leader Stockwell Day's threat to take Alberta out of the CPP unless the other ministers agreed to Alberta's reform proposals would appear to reflect his strong personal commitment to privatization of the CPP by introducing opting-out in favour of individual savings accounts. We can expect the issue to figure prominently in the policy platform of the party in the new federal Parliament.

We looked at the Reform Party's opting-out proposal in Chapter 4 and we saw how misleading calculations and misinformation about public pensions were used to try to persuade people that privatization would offer them a more secure retirement income. It should be clear by now that individual accounts offer no security and no guarantees at all. Not only that, but introducing a system of opting-out of the CPP would undermine the stability of the public program, weakening it for those who must count on it for a significant part of their retirement income.

In its 1998 booklet, Reform claimed that privatization based on individual accounts was working successfully in other countries, including Chile, the UK, and Australia. We've already seen how far from the truth that statement is. Reform also said its plan would give workers the "choice" to establish their own private alternative to the "government-run CPP." But "choice" can only be a free and equitable one if people have full information on which to base their decisions. Surveys show Canadians know very little about public pensions and the advantages they offer. That seems hardly surprising, given the amount of misinformation about the programs that is constantly repeated in the media and elsewhere. Combine that lack of information with misleading calculations from Reform/Alliance and its sympathizers, along with high-pressure sales tactics from those who stand to gain from privatization through the introduction of individual accounts, and there may be serious cause for alarm.

The reality of privatization through individual accounts

In reality, privatization of public pensions by the introduction of individual accounts would raise very serious concerns, as we have seen in earlier chapters of this book. While the advocates of privatization like to present individual accounts, personal pensions or RRSPs as superior to the CPP, it is never made explicit that these "private" arrangements are not comparable to the CPP at all. Private arrangements such as RRSPs were designed to help individuals supplement what they will receive through the public programs— not to replace those programs.

It's worth briefly reviewing again the issues that would be raised by the introduction of individual savings accounts as a replacement for some or all of the CPP.

Converting from defined benefit to money purchase

Effectively, the CPP is a defined benefit pension plan where the retirement pension is defined and guaranteed in relation to earnings and length of service. A savings scheme based on individual accounts is a defined contribution plan, where only the contribution is defined and no benefit is guaranteed. Introducing individual savings accounts as a replacement for the CPP—whether on a mandatory basis or through opting-out—would therefore mean replacing a defined benefit pension with a defined contribution or money purchase plan, with all the disadvantages that entails:

- **No pension guaranteed.** An RRSP or personal savings scheme is not a pension. Some critics have attempted to demonstrate that investing in an RRSP offers a "better rate of return" to young people than investing in the CPP. They have tried to do this is by calculating the dollar value of the benefits a typical CPP contributor might get: a retirement pension, a period on disability benefits, a benefit for the surviving spouse, and so on. They have then related that to the amount paid in contributions and claimed that investing the same dollar amount in an RRSP would generate a larger lump sum than the assumed value of the benefits the person might receive from the CPP.

However, such calculations overlook a number of important differences between the CPP and an RRSP. In a sense, it's like comparing apples with oranges. Unlike the CPP—which provides a defined benefit pension—an RRSP cannot guarantee any particular amount at retirement. As with any money purchase pension plan, an RRSP is simply a way of saving money, with tax assistance from the government. Whatever amount is accumulated in the RRSP fund may eventually be used to purchase a pension, by converting the RRSP to a Registered Retirement Income Fund (RRIF) and withdrawing amounts over a period of time, or by using the accumulated lump sum to purchase an annuity—assuming, of course, that the investor has not cashed in the RRSP and used the funds for something else prior to reaching retirement age.

- **No element of social insurance.** An individual account cannot provide the kind of security provided by the CPP; it is just a fund of money. The CPP is a social insurance program, not simply a retirement plan. Disability benefits, survivor benefits, benefits for dependent children, child-rearing drop-out provisions, general drop-outs protecting workers who are temporarily unable to contribute because of illness, unemployment, enrolment in training and education, or other reasons—all of which are available in the CPP—are not provided for in an RRSP. Some countries with privatized systems also require individuals to purchase life and disability insurance separately. For example, the Chilean system requires workers to contribute an additional 3% of earnings to cover administrative costs, disability and survivor benefits, on top of the 10% contribution they are required to make to the private pension savings scheme. Canadian advocates of privatization through individual accounts generally manage to avoid discussing what would happen to individuals who could not afford to purchase individual disability coverage, or who might not qualify for such coverage because of age, illness or for other reasons.

- **No pooling of risk and no collective responsibility.** The argument that contributing to an RRSP or an individual savings account would be a "better investment" for young people than contributing to the CPP ignores the fact that the CPP is not a personal investment plan; it is a social insurance program through which Canadians agree to accept collective responsibility for and to future seniors.

The CPP pools the risk of providing for retirement among all those who contribute so that all can be guaranteed at least a basic earnings-related pension at retirement (or on disability). With RRSPs—as with the kind of mandatory savings scheme advocated by the World Bank—there is no pooling of risk. In fact, the entire risk of providing a pension is shifted to the individual. As a result, some individuals may end up with an adequate retirement income, but others may end up with inadequate incomes in retirement, and some may end up with no retirement income at all. Replacing a social insurance pay-as-you-go public pension with a personal savings scheme eliminates the collective responsibility and social solidarity that has been the foundation of Canada's public earnings-related pension system for the past 30 years or more.

- **Personal circumstances determine the pension.** The amount of any pension generated under a mandatory savings scheme will depend on a variety of personal circumstances. People would end up with lower pensions if they had periods out of the workforce because they were ill or unemployed; if they had extended periods of further education and training; or if they took time out of the paid workforce to raise children. And, if an individual were downsized or laid off at the age of 50, they might end up with no pension at all because they would have had to use up their retirement savings long before they got to retirement age. Most of these situations are accommodated in the CPP without penalizing the individual.
- **Financial markets and individual investment expertise also determine the pension.** Lower pensions would also result for individuals who made poor investment decisions; if the stock market dropped so that the rate of return on their investments was much lower than they had anticipated; or if interest rates were low when they retired and used their funds to buy an annuity. In reality, there is no private sector equivalent to the CPP, because of the security it provides.

Issues of special concern to women

Privatization of pensions through individual accounts would raise special concerns for women. Evidence from countries such as Chile and Britain, which have replaced their public pension programs with private savings arrangements, shows clearly that women are disadvantaged by such schemes.

- **Lower earnings** make it difficult for women to contribute. This phenomenon is already evident in Canada in the lower participation of women in RRSPs.
- **Employment in the informal sector** also means that women are often excluded from mandatory privatized schemes. Whether they work part-time or full-time, and whether they are employees or self-employed, women workers are included in the CPP as long as they earn more than the Year's Basic Exemption, currently $3,500.
- **Intermittent workforce attachment** means that women frequently cannot contribute to a private savings plan. The CPP retirement pension is based on average earnings over a work life from age 18 to age 65. But all workers are allowed to exclude up to 15% of that period to account for years when they may have been unemployed, sick, or engaged in higher education. In addition, a parent may also exclude years when she or he had a child under age seven. This provision is particularly helpful for women, who must take time out of the paid work force to bear and raise children. In a private savings scheme, of course, years when a person had no earnings would also be years when they were not contributing to their personal savings plan. The result would be a much lower fund from which to purchase a pension at retirement.
- **Greater likelihood of non-standard work.** More and more workers are now employed in non-standard jobs, including part-time jobs, temporary or part-year work, contract work, self-employment, and multiple part-time jobs. In 1994, for example, 40% of women's jobs and 27% of men's jobs were non-standard jobs, compared with 35% and 22% respectively in 1989. Much of this employment offers low wages

and little job security, making it very difficult for women to save.

- **Different retirement age.** Women tend to retire earlier than men, generally for family reasons. Under a private savings scheme, the earlier the person retires the less opportunity they have to build up retirement savings. The CPP permits early retirement at age 60 with an actuarially reduced benefit.
- **Greater life expectancy.** Women live longer than men do, so they would need to build up larger lump sums in a private savings account to provide themselves with pensions that would last for the rest of their lives. With lower earnings and the other considerations outlined above, the possibility of being able to do this is remote, to say the least. This problem does not arise with the CPP.

Turning the contributions into a pension

If people were required to direct their CPP contributions to a private savings arrangement instead of a public social insurance plan—or even if they were permitted to do so on an optional basis—they would have to be responsible for turning the fund into a form of pension once they reached retirement age by purchasing annuities or registered retirement income funds (RRIFs) on the private market.

In the Chilean system, for instance, decisions that have to be made at retirement present serious problems. According to some experts, at least 90% of pensioners-to-be do not know enough about the scheme and are thus not able to judge the different alternatives for themselves. Many individuals therefore use the services of an "independent expert," who provides advice, recommends the choice of an insurance company, and negotiates on their behalf. Apart from the additional cost this involves, there is obvious potential for abuse here and the recent British experience with mis-selling of personal pensions does not inspire confidence.

- **Negative redistribution in annuity purchase.** There may be hidden redistribution from the poor to the better-off when it comes to purchasing annuities with funds accumulated through a privatized savings scheme because higher-income earners live longer. While it is claimed that participants in a defined contribution savings scheme can all expect to earn much the same rate of return by participating in the plan, poor people, who have relatively short life expectancies, will earn a lower return than the wealthy unless some adjustment is made when they purchase annuities.
- **Preventing early withdrawals.** Current RRSP rules permit investors to withdraw funds at any time for any purpose, subject only to the requirement that amounts withdrawn be included in income on which income tax is paid. The federal government encourages RRSP holders to use their funds for other purposes, such as buying a home or paying for post-secondary education. Replacing the CPP with mandatory RRSPs, or allowing people to direct their CPP contributions to RRSPs instead, would then raise the possibility that the private savings funds might be used up well before the holder reached retirement age.

    There is considerable evidence that people have tapped into their RRSPs before retirement age—especially when they have lost their jobs. Cutbacks in employment insurance have been so severe that is now estimated that less than a third of Canadians who are unemployed can qualify for EI benefits. This makes it even more likely that those with private savings plans will want the right to tap into those plans in financial emergencies.
- **Locking in would be required.** If the CPP were replaced with a mandatory savings scheme, funds in individual accounts presumably would have to be

"locked in" to prevent individuals from cashing in their savings prior to retirement, potentially increasing claims on the OAS and GIS. Currently, funds transferred from registered pension plans must be placed in a locked-in account and used to provide lifetime benefits. But funds in regular RRSPs are not locked in.

- **Pressure to unlock funds.** Under the existing system, locked-in vehicles include Locked-In Retirement Accounts (LIRAs), Life Income Funds (LIFs) and Locked-in Retirement Income Funds (LRIFs). Pension regulators are under increasing pressure from those who feel they should be able to control their own funds to unlock funds in these locked-in accounts. In early 2000, for example, Ontario introduced legislation to permit this, within limits, under circumstances of financial hardship or shortened life expectancy. Unlocking undermines financial security in retirement, since it allows individuals to use funds set aside for retirement for other purposes.

Continuing need for a minimum guarantee

Where a system of mandatory individual savings accounts replaces a pay-as-you-go public program such as the CPP, basic first-tier programs such as the OAS and GIS are still required to prevent poverty. Those who favour privatization, including the World Bank, believe this first tier should be kept as small as possible and focus only on the very poor. But amounts paid out under this tier would depend on the effectiveness of the second-tier private savings arrangements in providing retirement income. To the extent that such arrangements are not successful, claims on the basic guarantee, or first tier, will increase. Governments would then be faced with the option of expanding the basic guarantee, or accepting much higher rates of poverty among seniors in the future.

Poverty rates among seniors in Canada have improved significantly over the past two decades—thanks mainly to the maturing of the CPP—although almost half of all elderly women on their own still have incomes below Statistics Canada's low-income cut-offs. Privatization could well result in increasing rates of poverty among the elderly in the future, if people are not able to make adequate provision for their senior years through their own individual investments. However, advocates of privatization seem to have foreseen this possibility, too. They now claim that measures of low income such as Statistics Canada's low-income cut-offs do not accurately reflect the financial situation of seniors and others with low incomes. In other words, redefining poverty with more restrictive measures would supposedly solve this problem.

Continuing need for government regulation

Implementing a system of individual accounts does not eliminate the need for government regulation. Just as RRSPs are regulated in terms of permitted investments, foreign content, contribution limits, and so on, individual accounts would also have to be subject to regulation—especially if they were to be the main vehicle through which individuals were expected to provide for their retirement.

The experience of other countries where public pension programs have been privatized indicates strict government regulation is required. For example, the personal pension scheme in Chile has required a great deal of government intervention. It has relied on tax and other incentives, the active supervision and steering and the constant fine-tuning provided by the government.

In advocating mandatory private savings schemes, the World Bank report lists a number of areas where government regulation is still necessary, including ensuring the solvency of funds and the integrity of managers; keeping investment risk within reasonable bounds; regulating the amount that funds may invest in overseas assets; possibly regulating fees and commission; keeping a lid on operating costs; regulating annuities; monitoring compliance by investment companies; and guaranteeing pensions and pension returns.

Advocates of privatization who hope to eliminate the need for government regulation by replacing public pension programs with private savings plans will clearly be disappointed. Ironically, the "private" savings arrangements, such as RRSPs, favoured by those who advocate privatization of the CPP are anything but "private." They rely very heavily on tax subsidies to make them attractive.

High costs

Even the advocates of privatization admit there are high costs involved in private savings schemes. One 1997 paper on privatization from the C.D. Howe Institute, for example, concedes that administrative costs of the Chilean system to date are "relatively large." Fees and commissions paid to financial institutions eat up huge amounts of potential retirement income in countries with privatized mandatory savings schemes. Neoliberal corporate-funded research institutes cannot therefore be considered completely disinterested participants in the debate when they advocate the mandatory allocation of billions of dollars of workers' savings through the private sector.

In Chile, it is estimated that more than one-third of amounts contributed to the privatized AFPs goes in commissions and fees; in the Netherlands, which also has a partially privatized system, administrative costs for individual pensions are estimated to be 24% of contributions; in Britain, administrative costs of personal pensions are estimated to be 22% higher than the costs of running the state earnings-related pension plan. In contrast, the cost of running the CPP is 1.3% of contribution revenue.

Lost tax revenues are another concern that is almost always overlooked by the advocates of privatization. It should also be emphasized that proposals to replace public pensions with individual accounts seem to assume that people contributing to those accounts would receive a tax break for their contributions, just as we now subsidize RRSP contributions. These tax subsidies, of course, are also a public cost, but advocates of privatization generally don't like to admit that.

Transition costs

It is generally agreed that countries that already have pay-as-you-go public pension programs in place would face high transition costs if they decided to move to a private savings scheme instead. Some way must be found to pay for the benefits promised to people who have contributed to the public pension plan in the expectation of receiving pensions (and other benefits) at retirement. The generation of workers caught in the transition may have to go on contributing to the public plan to pay the promised benefits to retirees, while at the same time allocating contributions to their own private savings plan.

The Reform Party suggested that the government could issue "recognition bonds" financed through the privatization of Crown corporations. It appears these were to be shares in privatized corporations, which individuals would then be able to sell to provide themselves with funds for retirement and to make up for pension benefits they might have expected to receive from the CPP. Alternatively, Reform said, CPP contribution rates could be jacked up even higher and the excess diverted to the privatized system.

Suggestions from other advocates of privatization include proposals that, during the transition period, the payout of previously accrued retirement benefits would be financed either through a payroll tax (as at present) or through general tax revenues. In either case, this suggestion implies, the government would need to increase borrowing temporarily while it pays the bulk of previously accrued benefits.

A privatized scheme would boost savings and investment. Advocates of privatization continue to argue that replacing a pay-as-you-go social insurance pension program with a mandatory private savings scheme will increase savings and investment, even though there is no hard evidence to support this claim. It would appear that they are willing to make the leap of faith in the interests of bolstering their argument for the abandonment of public pension plans.

For example, the Canadian Institute of Actuaries Task Force on the future of the CPP, which did not support privatization, nevertheless argued in favour of a form of partial funding of the CPP on the grounds that, among other things, it would "increase domestic savings and make use of resulting economic benefits." The Task Force apparently assumed that generating a large CPP investment fund—in effect, what federal and provincial finance ministers decided to do in the 1997/98 round of CPP reforms—would increase savings because it would build up CPP assets. However, it produced no evidence of the impact on the savings of individuals who would be required to pay higher CPP contributions to generate the fund. Nor was there any discussion of how the overall savings of Canadians might be affected if the CPP were partially funded.

Similar arguments have been made by advocates of privatization writing for the C.D. Howe Institute. For example, James Pesando, professor of economics at the University of Toronto, suggests that privatization could be accomplished by directing the proposed increase in CPP contributions to individual RRSPs, while retaining existing CPP contributions to finance disability, death and survivor's benefits as well as paying for the benefits already promised—which he refers to as servicing the "unfunded liability." As to the impact on savings and investment, Pesando says, "An increase in CPP contribution rates with an unchanged (or reduced) level of CPP retirement benefits, should increase personal savings."

His paper includes a separate discussion of how CPP contribution rates might affect personal savings, which presents contradictory evidence of the impact of pay-as-you-go public pension plans on savings. He quotes economist Martin Feldstein, a leading advocate of privatization of U.S. Social Security, who believes that "the existence of a pay-as-you-go public pension plan will depress personal savings and thus reduce the stock of domestic capital." But he also notes that other studies have found that, "under a pay-as-you-go public pension plan, households may reduce their consumption and increase their savings (and ultimately their bequests) to offset the higher "tax burden" their children face."

Despite these contradictory viewpoints, Pesando apparently felt justified in deciding that, "on balance, it seems appropriate to conclude that an increase in CPP contribution rates [directed to RRSPs, as he is advocating] will yield an increase in personal savings and in the domestic capital stock." And he states categorically that, "under a fully-funded or privatized CPP, higher contribution rates would lead to an increase in personal savings. This savings increase, in turn, would lead to a higher level of real investment and ultimately to a higher level of output, which is the primary source of the efficiency gains to be derived from full funding."

As Henry Aaron observed, in a 1982 paper for the Brookings Institution, "a person determined to find a respected theoretical argument to support a preconception can find one, and [that] a person without preconceptions will find a bewildering diversity of answers in economic theory about whether social security is more likely to raise or lower consumption or labour supply."

In fact, channeling mandatory contributions through private savings arrangements may even decrease savings— especially if the private savings arrangements receive tax subsidies, according to economist Larry Willmore of the United Nations Department of Economic and Social Affairs. In a 1998 paper on *Social Security and the Provision of Retirement Income,* Willmore points out that savings grow faster within a tax shelter than outside it, so a person can save less in a tax-sheltered private savings arrangement and still attain his or her savings target. As well, he notes, for national savings to increase, someone's consumption must fall. The government can finance its pensions with taxes, thus causing the general public to reduce consumption. But governments can achieve the same result with tighter fiscal policy or conventional public pension reform, with no need to privatize social security. In any case, Willmore points out, "the desire to increase national savings is a poor reason to privatize social security."

In a paper in defence of pay-as-you-go funding for social security, Canadian actuary Robert Brown notes there is an abundant literature on the impact of pre-funding of social security on gross national savings, "but no clear conclusion." In a brief review of the relevant literature, Brown notes that the gross national savings rate in Chile in 1980, when the pay-as-you-go public pension program was in place, was 21%. But he says Chile's gross national savings rate dipped substantially during the 1980s, after the public pension program was replaced with a mandatory private savings scheme. By 1991, Brown says, that country's gross national savings rate stood at 18.8%.

Concerns about allowing individuals to opt out of the CPP

Much of the discussion about privatization of public pensions in Canada has focused on replacing the CPP with a system of mandatory private savings accounts along the lines of the Chilean model. In recent years, however, advocates of privatization seem to be promoting a system of allowing people to opt out of the CPP if they can demonstrate they have an appropriate personal savings arrangement—a proposal modelled on the British system. This is the option apparently favoured by the Canadian Alliance and by the Alberta government, among others.

While opting-out may seem at first glance to be less of a threat to the CPP than complete abolition of the plan, it would actually raise serious concerns about the continued viability of the plan. And virtually all the concerns discussed so far in this book in relation to privatization of public pensions through individual savings accounts apply equally to voluntary opting-out arrangements as to mandatory savings accounts that might replace the public plan.

- **Opting out could seriously undermine the viability of the public plan itself.** Public pay-as-you-go pension plans depend on the pooling of risks and pooling of contributions from all workers at all wage levels. Based on the British experience, those most likely to opt out are higher-income workers with secure jobs. Those who are left in the public plan are likely to be those with the lowest earnings and the least job security. The question must then be raised as to whether contribution revenue will be adequate to pay the promised benefits if contributions from higher-income workers are diverted to the private individual savings accounts of these workers.

- **Increased costs for the public plan if opting-out is allowed.** Questions also arise about how to finance the benefits for those who chose to stay in the CPP if opting- out were allowed. For instance, the Reform Party said that "Changes to premium levels, benefit levels, and/or general tax levels may be necessary to keep it solvent." Several possibilities were suggested in the party's 1998 booklet: the age of eligibility could be increased; disability coverage could be handled separately, possibly by the provinces; future benefits could be income-tested; people who chose to stay in the plan could be asked to pay more for their benefits. All these options would penalize those who opted to remain in the plan, making it likely that lower-income earners might be forced out of the public plan against their will and against their best interests.

- **Limited opting out would also seriously undermine the CPP,** since it would raise the same concerns as an unlimited opting-out provision. But Alberta's proposal that administrative cost savings realized by implementing improved governance and other measures be paid out to individuals to invest in their own private accounts raises even more serious problems. Effectively, it would result in hiving off funds that could have been retained within the CPP, where they would contribute to maintaining the stability of contribution rates and to funding the promised future benefits.

- **Privatization through individual accounts or opting-out would introduce inequalities.** Alberta's proposal to withdraw "surplus" funds from the plan and allow individuals to invest them privately for their own benefit would also contravene the principle of pooling risks through social insurance.

- **It would weaken public policy levers.** Recent Canadian studies indicate the important contribution made by the public pension programs—and particularly the CPP—to reducing poverty and inequality among seniors. Allowing opting-out would reduce the effectiveness of this policy lever. A reduction in the state's involvement in social security by returning social programs to a social assistance function for those most in need, while encouraging marketplace solutions for income security and maintenance, would likely lead to an increase in rates of poverty and income inequality among future generations of Canadian seniors.

- **It would weaken support for the public pension plan.** The more people who opt out of the public pension plan, the more collective responsibility and social solidarity would be weakened. It might then become a simple matter to abandon the public earnings-related plan completely, forcing low-income workers to rely on means-tested benefits from the first tier of the pension system—always assuming they can qualify.

Chapter 7
The bottom line on privatization of public pensions in Canada

So far, policy-makers in Canada have rejected calls to abolish the CPP and replace it with a mandatory system of individual savings accounts. According to the federal government, the 1996 public consultations on reform of the CPP revealed that "most Canadians believe in the CPP and want it preserved." The government said that strong support came from organizations and individuals who said the plan is "an important and key pillar of the retirement income system because it provides full coverage, portable benefits, inflation protection, low administration costs, and a major source of income to seniors."

Polling conducted in December 1996 for the federal Finance Department had also shown there was still strong support for the CPP among Canadians. The poll found "a massive majority of Canadians which wants the CPP to continue," and that "this desire cuts across all age groups and all income levels."

According to the government's report on the consultations, a key theme that emerged was "a strong desire to see the CPP remain a public pension plan rather than privatized." However, there was a vocal minority involved in the public consultations, led by two of three participating taxpayer associations, which argued in favour of privatization. They criticized the pay-as-you-go approach and the proposed significant increases in contribution rates. And they suggested the CPP be replaced with a mandatory, defined-contribution, fully-funded, privately- managed plan.

The third group expressed concern about the impact of the CPP on younger generations and suggested that the government offer people under 30 a chance to opt out. But the government reported that most participants wanted the public system preserved, fearing that its many benefits would be lost if the plan were privatized.

Investing the CPP fund in the market

While federal and provincial ministers ultimately rejected the idea of introducing individual accounts as either a mandatory or voluntary replacement for the CPP, they did opt for a form of privatization by deciding to establish a fund, managed by private financial institutions, that would be invested in the stock market. This should allow the government to avoid significant contribution rate increases over the next 30 years—at least, in theory.

According to sociologists John Myles and Paul Pierson, the choice to increase funding to finance the current program came to the top of the agenda when the nationalist and left-leaning Parti Quebecois made clear Quebec would not support reform proposals that involved significant benefit cuts. Together with the two provinces ruled by social democratic governments—British Columbia and Saskatchewan—Quebec had the potential to block any reform initiative under the legislation creating the plan.

Under considerable pressure from the business community, the finance ministers decided that combined employer/employee contribution rates could not be allowed to exceed 10% of covered earnings. With that as a starting point, they decided on a sharp increase in contribution rates over a six-year period to reach a combined employer/employee rate of 9.9% of covered earnings by 2003. According to the ministers, this level, known as the "steady-state rate," should be enough to sustain the CPP indefinitely so that no further rate increases will be required. At the same time, they implemented measures to slow the growth in costs by tightening up the administration of benefits—particularly of disability benefits—and by changing the way some benefits are calculated.

The new higher contribution rate will generate more than enough revenue to pay current benefits. The objective in moving to a higher rate so quickly was to use surplus contribution revenue to build up an investment fund equivalent to about five years' worth of benefits. Prior to this, as mentioned earlier, legislation required the finance ministers to set contribution rates at a level that would generate sufficient revenue to pay current benefits and maintain a contingency reserve equivalent to two years' worth of benefits. This contingency reserve was invested in 20-year non-marketable securities of provincial governments at the federal government's cost of funds—somewhat lower than provinces would pay on their own market borrowing. But —contrary to widespread popular misconception—not at "bargain basement" rates.

Building up a larger fund and earning a higher rate of return through investment in the market is intended to help pay for the rapidly growing costs that will occur once baby boomers start to retire, around 2010. Earnings on the fund will be used to supplement contribution revenue, so that contribution rates will not have to be increased to the levels originally suggested by the Chief Actuary's Fifteenth Actuarial Report, released just prior to the 1996 consultations. The adoption of this form of privatization was presented as a way of strengthening the publicly-managed plan so it will continue as a social insurance arrangement for the foreseeable future.

As well, it is clearly intended to improve public confidence in the stability of the plan—in effect, resisting the pressure for more radical measures such as replacing the CPP with mandatory individual savings accounts. To the extent that it achieves this goal, the establishment of the investment fund seems to have received fairly wide support.

The mandate of the CPP Investment Board

An arm's-length Investment Board has been appointed to manage the invested assets. The members of the Board are all from the financial community and were proposed by a special nominating committee, the members of which were themselves nominated by federal and provincial governments. There are no labour representatives on the Investment Board and no board members nominated to represent the interests of the plan beneficiaries, as there might be on the board of trustees of a private registered pension plan.

As part of the package of CPP reforms, implemented at the beginning of 1998, the federal government had abolished the CPP Advisory Board: a body of outside individuals, including labour representatives, appointed to advise the government on policy and program design issues relating to the CPP. It was implied that the Advisory Board would no longer be needed, now that an Investment Board was to be appointed. However, the mandate of the Investment Board is simply to invest the CPP funds and not to advise on program policy or other matters relating to the CPP. With the abolition of the Advisory Board, there is no longer any external input on CPP program policy.

In fact, according to the Investment Board president, the Board is actually more like an investment management company than a full-service plan sponsor. And he says one of the Board's biggest challenges will be "getting Canadians to understand that we operate independently of the Canada Pension Plan, …even though our ultimate goal is to increase the value of assets available to the Plan to pay future pensions."

Managing the investments of the fund

As a transitional measure, once the investment fund was established, provinces were given the option of rolling over existing CPP borrowings at maturity for another 20-year term. For the first three years, provinces also have access to the 50% of new CPP funds that the Board chooses to invest in bonds. After this three-year period, to ensure the fund's investment in provincial securities is consistent with market practice, new CPP funds invested in provincial securities will be limited to the proportion of provincial bonds held by pension funds in general.

As a result of these transitional arrangements, the share of CPP assets managed by the Board at first was quite small. In determining its initial asset mix, the Board took into consideration the amounts that were already invested in government bonds and, as a result, 100% of new investments were allocated to equities. The policy resulted in a huge return of 40.1% for the first year of the fund's operation—clearly achieved at some risk. And, in releasing the Board's first annual report in June 2000, the president cautioned that, as the fund broadened its asset allocation base, the volatility of the portfolio would decline, "as will the likelihood of achieving such outstanding annual results again."

At least for the first three years, the Board was required to adopt a passive investment program, which replicated various domestic and foreign stock market indices. Active investment will likely be permitted when the finance ministers complete their next review of the CPP, now required every three years instead of the previous five-year interval. It is expected that the next triennial review will be completed by the end of 2003.

The fund is expected to grow steadily over the coming years, from about $3 billion at the beginning of 2000 to more than $100 billion within 10 years, making it the biggest pension fund in the Canadian marketplace. The Board president says that managing these assets "will inevitably involve exploring a full arsenal of investment strategies,... passive and active investing in public equity and debt securities, merchant banking, private equity and debt, infrastructure projects, venture capital opportunities, real estate investments, and derivative contracts."

However, the size of the fund and a shift to a more active investment approach is bound to raise issues such as the potential impact of such a large fund on the market; the exercise of proxy voting rights by the fund managers; and the limitation on foreign investments, which are currently restricted to 30% of the book value of assets as of 2001. It remains to be seen how these questions will be addressed. There is no indication that the fund will adopt any ethical investment criteria. In fact, given the composition of the Board, it seems highly unlikely that it will show any interest in this issue.

In comments on the role of pension funds in the Canadian economy, the CPP Investment Board president observed that many of these funds are becoming increasingly active as shareholders. Most large pension funds, he said—including public sector funds—take a keen interest in the governance practices of directors and the commitment of management to enhancing shareholder value. For our part, he said, "in exercising our voting rights,… we will act sensibly, responsibly, and with a long-term view."

He also noted that, as leading owners of corporate Canada, pension funds are growing in influence. Just how the CPP Investment Board will exercise that influence could become a matter of some concern, especially since there appear to be no guidelines, and no representation from labour or plan beneficiaries—nor, indeed, any external input—to help develop them. "For public companies," the Board president said, "the good news in this development is that it inextricably aligns the retirement income of Canadians with the financial well-being of the private sector." The better Canadian firms perform financially over the long term, he said, the better off Canadians will be in their retirement years.

But introducing this element of market risk into Canada's public pension system may have its downside, too. For instance, if the returns on the fund fail to live up to expectations, pressure may escalate to raise contribution rates again. Alternatively—and perhaps a more likely scenario—there may be renewed calls for abolition of the CPP entirely, and its replacement with a system of mandatory individual savings accounts.

It is also important to note that, even when the new investment fund is fully up and running, the CPP will still be essentially a pay-as-you-go plan. At the end of 1997, for example, the plan's assets of $36 billion represented about 8% of liabilities. Under the new funding formula, assets will eventually reach 20% of liabilities.

The CPP Investment Fund as a privatization compromise?

The creation of a CPP investment fund was essentially a compromise on privatization. While it did not go as far as the neoliberal advocates of privatization through individual accounts would have liked, it will, in fact, channel a significant portion of the CPP contribution revenue through the private market. When it is finally up and running, the CPP fund could be more than three times bigger than the Ontario Teachers' Pension Fund—now, at $40 billion in assets, the biggest trusteed pension fund in Canada. As the *Globe and Mail* noted in a story which ran in its *Report on Business* after the changes were announced in February 1997, "Bay Street is in line for a big financial windfall under the federal government's plan to shore up the Canada Pension Plan reserve fund by investing it more aggressively in stocks."

The same newspaper later reported that Toronto-Dominion Bank and Barclays Global Investors Canada Ltd. have "won the coveted roles of investing the Canada Pension Plan's multi-billion-dollar portfolio." Commenting on the fact that —at least initially—the fund would be an index fund that will match the Toronto Stock Exchange 300 index and the Morgan Stanley Capital International Index, the writer said that, "While this mandate is a high-profile win for TD Bank and Barclays, running a passive portfolio is not nearly as lucrative as actively picking stocks. Industry experts say fees are likely less than five basis points of the assets under management. [A basis point is 1/100th of a percentage point]. In contrast, active fund managers may charge 100 basis points to run a pension portfolio." But fees are clearly about to increase, because the Board will now be moving to an active investment policy. Fees paid to the private investment managers, of course, reduce the amount of CPP revenues that generate pensions for Canadians in the same way that fees and commissions on individual savings accounts do.

Problems with partial funding

Partial funding of the CPP was agreed to by federal and provincial finance ministers on the assumption that this would allow CPP contributions to be maintained at a combined rate of below 10% indefinitely. Many progressive commentators questioned this assumption. They pointed out that, while the government has said the two objectives of the new CPP financing are 1) to maintain a stable contribution rate (the 9.9% "steady state" combined employer/employee rate), and 2) to maintain a stable fund-to-expenditure ratio; it is impossible to do both.

Bob Baldwin of the Canadian Labour Congress pointed out that, in defined contribution pension plans and RRSPs, the short-term instability of investment returns translates directly and immediately into changes in the level of benefits provided to retirees. Indeed, the uncertainty of investment returns, he said, "is one of the many factors that make it impossible for these plans to make a reasonably certain promise of the benefit that will be provided to retirees."

If the key objective of partial funding for the CPP is to keep the combined contribution rate steady at 9.9% indefinitely, then the size of the investment fund will inevitably vary from time to time, because rates of return will fluctuate. Therefore, there will inevitably be periods when the size of the fund is declining. (In other words, the fund would be actually contributing to a saving decline during those periods.) This also raises the possibility that such periods, when the rate of return on the fund may be below expectations, may lead to pressure to increase contribution rates again, or even to cut benefits further.

Advocates for full privatization by way of individual accounts kept up the pressure, even as the Investment Fund was being put in place. The C.D. Howe Institute, for instance, published a study in early 1999 that claimed the 9.9% "steady state" contribution rate would not be enough to sustain the plan indefinitely. If that turns out to be the case, they said, "an increasing number of Canadians will surely feel that the CPP is still too unsustainable to rely on."

Alternatives to privatization

But, even if it were the case that the 9.9% "steady state" contribution rate could not be maintained indefinitely, other options could be pursued. Some of them were raised during the CPP reform discussions before the finance ministers decided on a move to partial funding. For example, British Columbia had suggested expanding the base on which CPP contributions are applied by raising the ceiling on contributory earnings, currently set at roughly the level of the average wage. As we saw earlier, contributions for U.S. Social Security—currently at a combined rate of 12.4% of contributory earnings—are applied to earnings up to the equivalent of C$113,000, or about three times the average Canadian wage.

As well, in the U.S. system there is no basic exemption from contributions for the first few thousand dollars of earnings. Abolition of the Year's Basic Exemption (YBE) in the CPP—now frozen at $3,500—had also been proposed during the 1996 CPP reform discussions. While this would have represented a significant increase in contributions for lower-income earners, it had been suggested they might be compensated with an enhanced tax credit. In fact, the government itself proposed this option in its February 1996 discussion paper, which formed the basis for the public consultations, saying it would "improve employer compliance and would decrease the contribution rate."

There are certainly many ways to moderate the increasing inter-generational transfers involved in pay-as-you-go pension plans where there is an aging population. For example, Myles and Pierson, in their paper on *The Comparative Political Economy of Pension Reform*, note that, unlike programs financed from general revenues, transfers financed exclusively from payroll taxes impose all of the cost of an aging society on wage income. Since covered earnings are often limited to the bottom half or two-thirds of the earnings distribution, rising pension costs fall disproportionately on lower—and especially younger—wage-earners, they noted.

While all the consumption of the inactive population must ultimately come from wealth created by the working age population, these authors point out, financing population aging primarily through payroll taxes places most of the burden on wage income. But they also suggest that, where pension systems result in a large volume of interpersonal transfers (horizontal or vertical) among beneficiaries, the division between "earned" and "unearned" benefits is being made more transparent, so that financial responsibility for redistributive transfers can be shifted from payroll taxes to general revenues. Pension systems are essentially a code of laws stipulating who may make claims on the state and under what conditions, these authors note. They emphasize that reneging on past contracts by unilaterally reducing benefits creates a profound problem of legitimacy for governments.

In fact, there is absolutely no reason why countries with aging populations and pay-as-you-go public pension plans must abandon those plans and replace them with private individual savings accounts. Canada's choice—at least for the moment—has been to move to a system of partial funding for the CPP, where investment earnings will be used to supplement contribution revenue, while retaining the essential character of the CPP as a social insurance program. Other countries have also chosen approaches that will retain their public pension programs in the face of population aging.

A different approach in the Netherlands

The Netherlands, for example, has capped social security taxes and will make up any funding shortfall in its public pension program through a special fund financed by an allocation from general tax revenues—in other words, funded partly by seniors themselves through their taxes. According to Maarten Camps of the Netherlands Ministry of Finance, there is broad consensus in the Netherlands in support of the public pension, and recognition that switching to an individualized system of retirement savings would involve high transaction costs and "people would lose money." People who are concerned about the possibility of future benefit reductions from the public pension system have been accumulating private retirement savings through the "third pillar" of the retirement income system to supplement what they will receive from their occupational pensions. But Camps says there has not really been any public discussion of the possibility of allowing opting-out of the public pension system or replacing it with a system of mandatory private savings accounts.

The Dutch pension system has been widely praised by commentators, who argue that it has been a significant success in accommodating various social and economic interests in the context of outstanding economic growth. As one observer has pointed out, "The economic virtues of social solidarity are significant and deeply implicated with national politics" in the Netherlands. Analysts describe the Dutch pension system as falling under the schematic model of "citizenship," in which old age public pension systems were designed for universal coverage and the entitlement to a retirement income according to citizenship (or legal residence) and prior earnings."

Public pensions play a key role in the Dutch retirement income system, combining with workplace pensions to provide retirees with a pension of 70% of final earnings (before taxes) after a 40-year career. All income earners under 65, whether self-employed or employees, are required to contribute to the Netherlands public pension plan—known as the AOW (Algemeine Ouderdoms Wet or General Old Age Act)—and there is no matching employer contribution. Contributions are levied as a percentage of income in the two bottom tax brackets of the income tax system. No contributions are required on the first roughly 8,000 guilders of income, and (as in Canada) this basic amount of income is also exempt from income tax.

Employers collect AOW contributions from the employee's salary and remit them to the tax authorities; self-employed people pay their contributions directly. But everyone is entitled to benefits at age 65, whether they have contributed to the scheme or not, and whether or not they are retired at that point. And the AOW benefit is taxable.

Contribution rates are currently running at 17.9% of covered earnings. As part of a restructuring of funding arrangements for the public pension program, the Dutch government has capped contribution rates at 18.25%. In addition, the government has moved to strengthen the pay-as-you-go public system by setting up a separate fund in 1997 with an initial contribution from general tax revenues of NLG 750 million (equivalent to about $526 million at current exchange rates). A booming economy and higher-than-expected tax revenues enabled a further contribution of NLG 1.5 billion to the fund in 1998.

For the next 20 years, the government is required by law to contribute a minimum of NLG 250 million each year to the fund. The money will remain within the government sector and, in return, the government will pay interest to the fund, thus increasing available capital. At this point, there is no intention of investing the fund in the market, although the possibility has not been ruled out, once government finances reach a surplus position in about four years' time.

Legislation does not allow the government to withdraw amounts from the AOW Savings Fund until 2020, when the baby boom generation will be retiring. At that point, amounts accumulated in the fund can be used as needed to supplement contribution revenue to pay for public pensions. Until then, any shortfall in public pension contribution revenue will be made up from the government's general tax revenues—even if that means increasing taxes. Since pensioners themselves pay taxes, this approach effectively will require seniors to contribute to the cost of their own pensions.

Virtually all Dutch workers have an occupational pension plan through their work, and there is heavy emphasis on this second pillar of the retirement income system, although current seniors still get almost half their income from the public pension system. Unlike Canada's extensive system of RRSPs, individual retirement savings play a much more limited role in the Netherlands. Workers are covered through a sectoral system of industry-wide occupational pension plans, negotiated through collective bargaining between employer organizations and trade unions. And, while occupational pension plans are not mandatory, regulations allow the government to compel all firms in the sector or branch of industry to participate in the sectoral pension plan if a sufficiently representative group of employers' organizations and trade unions request it.

Occupational pensions are designed to build onto the state pension, and the AOW benefits an employee will receive are taken into account in structuring the occupational pension so that the person's total retirement income will reach the target replacement rate. Of course, there are exceptions. Some workplace pension plans provide pensions based on career average earnings, for instance. As well, workers without continuous work force attachment, two-earner families, and single individuals generally don't manage to reach the 70% goal.

While the Netherlands pension system is obviously far removed form the kind of retirement income system in place in Canada, there are lessons to be learned from the way the problem of adapting a pay-as-you-go public pension plan to accommodate an aging population has been dealt with. For example, the allocation of funds from general tax revenues to establish an investment fund that will supplement future contribution revenues is a way of tapping into revenues from future seniors to fund their own pensions

Of incidental interest, too, is the fact that contribution rates to the public pension plan will be capped at 18.25%, while finance ministers in Canada felt compelled to keep CPP contribution rates below 10%. But it is important to note that the replacement rate for public pensions in Canada is relatively low, compared with the Netherlands and with many other European countries. For a worker whose final salary is about US$20,000, the Netherlands public pension replaces about 66% of final salary. At the same income level, Canada's public pension system—including the CPP and the OAS—replaces roughly 34%.

Pressure for privatization continues

There is no doubt, however, that, even with the creation of the CPP Investment Fund which will channel a significant portion of contribution revenue through private financial institutions, pressure for privatization through individual accounts will continue. Neoliberal commentators and think tanks, the Alliance Party, the Province of Alberta, and the business press will continue to push for this, whether it takes the form of replacing the CPP with a system of mandatory private savings accounts, or simply allowing individuals to opt out of the CPP and have their contributions directed to their own personal savings accounts instead.

Some observers suggest that private sector business opinion has been led by the financial sector and has swung in the direction of supporting full funding—whether partial funding of the CPP or a mandatory privatized system—on the condition that private investment managers get to manage (and earn fees and commissions on) public funds. The operation of this approach is evident each year during the RRSP sales season, when financial planners and others sell RRSPs by telling people the CPP will not be there for their retirement. This strategy of deliberately undermining the CPP in this way prepares the ground for privatization.

But partial funding of the CPP clearly does not meet the neoliberal ideological objectives of eliminating citizenship entitlements, reducing the role of the state, and shifting the risk and responsibility for retirement provision away from the collectivity and on to the individual. The rationale for their approach was clearly articulated by the ACPM in its 2000 report on *A Retirement Income Strategy for Canada*, when it said: "We believe that Canadians, if they understood the financial implications 20-30 years hence of today's rules, would prefer the path of self-reliance to financing their retirements over the path of entitlement and state dependence which is the orientation of much of today's retirement income system."

High stock market returns undoubtedly have proved attractive, especially to younger people, who are now particularly susceptible to the argument of the privatization advocates that young people would be "better off" investing for retirement on their own rather than contributing to the CPP. Recent surveys indicate that many Canadians—and particularly younger people—know little about the public pension program and the kind of benefits it provides. Associated with this lack of knowledge is the finding that confidence in the stability of the CPP to be there for individuals' retirement is also very low. Individuals aged 25 to 34 are the most likely age group to believe they will not receive anything from public pensions. In the circumstances, there is fertile ground for anyone trying to make a case for individual accounts and private investment as a replacement for collective responsibility and social insurance.

Notably lacking in the debate so far is any public discussion of the high cost of individual accounts, especially in a decentralized system such as Canada now has, and the very high transition costs of moving from a pay-as-you-go plan to individual savings arrangements—even when those take the form of opting-out from the earnings-related pay-as-you-go plan.

The consequences of privatization through individual accounts

Whether privatization took the route of abandoning the CPP and replacing it with a mandatory savings scheme along the lines of the Chilean model; whether it took the form of allowing people to opt out of the CPP and have their contributions directed to their RRSPs instead; or whether it took the form of allowing only the additional CPP contributions to be directed to RRSPs; the immediate question that must be asked is "What is to be gained from privatizing Canada's public pension system?"

Canada's retirement income system has a mix of public and private arrangements that is generally acknowledged to be a reasonable balance between collective and individual responsibility for retirement provision. As well as first pillar government programs which provide a basic income guarantee to seniors, it includes a relatively modest second tier consisting of the public earnings-related Canada/Quebec Pension Plan. There is an extensive system of private savings arrangements in the third tier, which receive considerable tax subsidies.

Canada's public pensions have reduced poverty and inequality.

According to sociologist John Myles, Canada's old age security system has made a big difference in the financial situation of seniors in this country, and at a cost well below what most other OECD countries spend on public pensions. In a study of the maturation of this country's retirement income system, he found low-income rates among Canadian seniors, measured by the usual "relative" international standard—persons with adjusted incomes of less than 50% of the median—are now among the lowest in the OECD.

According to this measure, Myles says low-income rates among Canadian seniors had fallen to about 5% in 1994, compared with a U.S. rate in excess of 20%. And, among the population aged 70 and over, Canada's low-income rate was below that of Sweden, which he says is "the usual winner in the international league tables on poverty reduction." In the mid-1970s, Myles notes, low-income rates among Canadian seniors were still well above those of their American peers. And the first truly comparative studies of low-income rates among seniors for the early 1980s placed Canada at the lower end of the international league tables.

Commenting on the changes, Myles says this "enviable position" has been achieved despite the fact that public spending on income security for seniors in Canada is modest by international standards and is expected to peak at levels well below those anticipated by other Western nations in the next century. For instance, the OECD projects that Canadian spending on public pensions will rise to 9.1% of Gross Domestic Product in 2040 from 5.2% in 1995. In contrast, average expenditures on public pensions in the continental European countries were 10% of GDP in 1995 and projected to rise to 16% in 2040.

Describing it as "a remarkable turnaround from a few decades ago," Myles says these developments have been driven by "what is arguably the main change in Canada's retirement income system over the period"—the maturation of the public pension system and the continued development of private plans. Not only did these earnings-related programs—both public and private pensions—produce a substantial increase in average real incomes, he says, but also a substantial reduction in income inequality among the elderly, due mainly to benefits from the Canada and Quebec Pension Plans.

Income gains among lower-income seniors have been "substantial," he says. And, unlike the United States, where declining poverty rates among seniors have taken place against a background of rising inequality, Myles says, rising incomes among the elderly in Canada were dominated by rising CPP/QPP benefits, and that reduced income inequality. However, he also notes that the CPP/QPP was "rushed" to maturity by legislation that provided full benefits after only 10 years of contributions. The full impact of expanded coverage and rising benefits from employer plans and personal retirement accounts, he says, will take longer to appear.

Despite the improvements, Myles says it would be "extremely difficult" to make a case for the claim, heard in some quarters, that Canadian seniors have now become "too rich." While average incomes among Canadian seniors have risen substantially since the early 1980s, virtually all of the gains have taken place at the lower end of the income distribution scale, he notes. Dividing the elderly population into five income groups or quintiles, Myles points out that there was very little increase in the proportion of seniors in the top two quintiles. Just 14% of seniors were in the top income quintile in 1995, compared with about 13% in 1980.

However, compared with the population as a whole, there has been a significant shift out of the lower-income groups. In 1980, for example, almost 40% of all elderly persons were in the bottom quintile—twice the rate of the population as a whole. By 1995, just over 17% of the elderly were in the bottom quintile, compared with 20% of the entire population.

Privatization is not concerned with incomes of future seniors.

Significantly, none of the advocates of privatization claims that it would ensure adequate incomes for the seniors of the future. In fact, even the World Bank admits that "mandatory savings schemes can still leave considerable old age poverty." Pensions generated from such schemes may fall below subsistence levels because of inflation or unexpectedly low returns. And low-income workers may never accumulate enough in their pension accounts to support themselves in old age, the Bank admits.

The focus of privatization is not, in fact, on the income of future seniors, but on "economic efficiency," "inter-generational equity," and "investment activity." In effect, privatization through individual savings accounts would eliminate—or severely reduce—the claims of future seniors to a public earnings-related public pension, and make them dependent on their own individual initiative and investment expertise to provide themselves with an income in retirement. While some individuals might fare well under such a system, many more would not—especially those with lower earnings and those without a long-term record of full-time paid work.

No redistribution in privatized schemes

Advocates of individual accounts have tried to coat their views with a veneer of economic respectability, but empirical studies suggest that choice of a pension regime in itself has little impact on savings, investment or growth. However, it can change markedly the distribution of income and wealth. By moving from defined benefit to defined contribution, reformers hope to reduce the amount of redistribution that occurs within pension systems. Pension reform for this reason is more a political than an economic issue.

The progressive nature of Canada's public pension programs increases the relative income share and the average

income of the poorest seniors. Recent studies have demonstrated that Canada has a more equal distribution of income
in old age compared with countries with similar old-age welfare systems, such as the United States. Privatization of public pensions will jeopardize the ability of the state to reshape
income inequalities in later life. Reducing the state's involvement in social security by returning social programs to a
social assistance function for those most in need, while
encouraging marketplace solutions for income security and
maintenance, would likely lead to an increase in rates of
poverty and income inequality among future generations of
Canadian seniors.

Resisting the pressure for individual accounts

While some critics believe the move to partial funding is
a first step along the road to complete privatization, there are
signs that the federal Finance Department would not favour
a system of individual savings accounts as a replacement for
the CPP. In a Working Paper published in June 1997, Steven
James, of the Department's Economic Studies and Policy
Analysis Division, concluded that "a well-managed public
CPP can effectively deal with all the concerns of those
favouring privatization, thereby maintaining the many benefits of a public program. In addition, it is argued that privatization does not deal with the key problem presently beset-
ting the CPP: the liabilities resulting from past promises that
must be funded publicly regardless." While the Working
Paper was issued with a disclaimer stating that it does not
reflect the views of the Department of Finance, it may almost
certainly be taken an indication of current thinking in
Ottawa—at least, around the time that the latest CPP reforms
were put in place.

Arguments in favour of a public CPP, said James, generally rest on its unique ability to provide social insurance and
thereby overcome market failures, its low administration
costs, its comprehensiveness and its portability. His paper

makes a number of key points, most of which have already been dealt with in this book. Several are worth repeating here:

- Privatization does not solve the problem of how to pay for CPP benefits already promised to Canadians who have been contributing to the CPP. The government cannot simply walk away from this, James says. The benefits have to be paid for by someone.

- The CPP insures against the risk that people will live long enough to exhaust their savings. Markets cannot efficiently provide these types of insurance through personal savings vehicles. James also points out that the failure of private markets to provide efficient longevity insurance is not mentioned by C.D. Howe economist William Robson in his proposal for replacing the CPP with individual savings accounts. And it is discussed only in passing in the main body of the World Bank report.

- Private systems are subject to significantly higher administrative costs than public systems. Higher administrative costs imply wasted resources and reduced social welfare.

- A fiscally strapped government might make access to other programs conditional on first using the funds in a retirement account.

- Extensive private options already exist in Canada, including significant scope for the tax-sheltering of retirement savings.

- The problem of political risks must be taken seriously. They can be overcome by putting in place institutions and rules of governance to ensure efficient management of the CPP. This applies particularly to the investment of CPP funds and the need to avoid using the CPP as a cheap way to finance expenditures. James also points out that political risks would remain even under full privatization. For example, there could be calls for earlier access to the funds in individual accounts for other purposes such as education and house purchase, significantly outweighed by the potential costs. As we saw earlier, Ontario has already given in to such pressures by allowing access to locked-in retirement accounts in circumstances of "financial hardship."

- On balance, the evidence suggests that the potential gains from privatization are significantly outweighed by the potential costs. Any flaws in the CPP can and should be addressed within the framework of a continued public system.

Rethinking public pension reform initiatives

There are also signs that some of those who previously favoured privatization through individual savings accounts may now be having second thoughts. For example, Peter Heller, of the Fiscal Affairs Department of the International Monetary Fund, published a paper under the title *Rethinking Public Pension Reform Initiatives* in April 1998, in which he argued that there are significant risks, limitations and complications associated with reliance upon mandatory defined contribution, fully-funded schemes as the dominant public pension pillar. This is particularly the case for schemes that rely on the private sector for the collection, management and investment of contributions, as well as the payment of pensions.

Heller makes three principal arguments:

- The purported advantages of defined contribution schemes can be attained only at the expense of higher underlying risks to the incomes of future pensioners. Policies to limit such risks may result in the government being re-injected into the financing of social insurance, thus raising questions as to the relative merits of defined contribution over defined benefit schemes or the desirability of private sector solutions.

- Since defined contribution schemes by themselves do not redistribute income intragenerationally, or provide safety nets, income security measures need to be developed to complement a defined contribution scheme. These must be financed and managed by government. Authorities should ask whether it is more efficient and cost-effective to build such redistributional/safety net elements directly into the social insurance system, rather than make them a separate pillar. At a minimum, the cost of such elements must be factored into any overall assessment of the relative merits of defined contribution and defined benefit schemes.
- If these mandatory social insurance schemes are pursued within the private sector, both the management of fiscal policy and the assessment of the economic impact of fiscal instruments are likely to prove more difficult.

In sum, says Heller, the force of these arguments suggests that a defined contribution, full-funded pillar, while potentially playing a legitimate role in a multi-pillar system for the accumulation of pension savings, should not be the dominant mandatory pillar of the provision of pension incomes. "The principal source of old-age support," he says, "should arise from a well-formulated, public defined-benefit pillar, with a significant amount of pre-funding."

Resisting the attack on public pensions

Those who want to replace the CPP with a system of individual savings accounts—whether that takes the form of mandatory private savings plans or simply allowing people to opt out of the CPP if they wish to—are clearly following their own political and ideological agenda. Their warlike imagery of demographic time bombs and inter-generational warfare would make a fascinating study in itself. But it's clear that, by presenting the situation in terms of crisis and conflict, radical solutions may be more likely to find public acceptance.

We should recognize these threats for what they are. They represent an attempt to justify reducing the role of government and eliminating collective responsibility for our aging population under the guise of preventing inter-generational conflict. Many of those who advocate privatization through individual accounts have a thinly-disguised self-interest in the outcome of this debate. They would like to see the mandatory contributions of workers and their employers directed to private financial markets where fees, commissions and other charges can be levied on them—reducing the portion of workers' contributions that can be used to generate a pension.

Canada has already taken action to address the concerns raised by a pay-as-you-go pension plan in the face of population aging. A wide range of further acceptable options is available to policy-makers, if necessary, without resorting to privatization and individual accounts. Canada's retirement income system already has a reasonable balance of public and private arrangements, and it has done a good job of reducing poverty and inequality among seniors. If we are really concerned about protecting the financial security of future seniors and ensuring them an adequate income in retirement, we must resist the attack on public pensions. Our retirement income system is worth fighting for.

Notes to Chapter 1

Page 5   "low-spending Australia, Myles says." [Myles, John and Paul Pierson: 1999]

Page 5   "those countries averaged 9.2% of GDP" [World Bank: 1994]

Page 6   "social and economic ideals are at stake" [Schultz, James H.: 1999]

Page 7   "namely, the growth of the economy" [Baker, Dean and Mark Weisbrot: 1999]

Page 9   "from 4:1 to 2:1 over the next 30 years" [Association of Canadian Pension Management: 2000]

Page 9   "old age dependency ratio for Canada of 0.19" [Desjardins, Bernard: 1993]

Page 10   "not likely to be exaggerating Canada's favourable position" [Wolfson, Michael and Brian Murphy: 1997]

Page 10   "old age dependency ratio would increase from 0.22 in 1991 to 0.57 in 2041" [Denton, Frank T., Christine H.Feaver and Byron G. Spencer: 1998]

Page 11   "so her daughter can work outside the home is considered a dependent" [Gee, Ellen: 1998]

Page 12   "translate into an increased burden on future working age generations." [Wolfson, Michael and Brian Murphy: 1997]

Page 13   "it is projected to have dropped to 0.38" [Wolfson, Michael and Brian Murphy : 1997]

Page 15   "what we have already experienced when the baby boom generation were children" [Denton, Frank T., Christine H.Feaver and Byron G. Spencer: 1998]

Page 15   "will not be any more costly than what Canada has already had to deal with [Gee, Ellen: 1998]

Page 15   "are not available for other uses, such as private investment, collective investment consumption by either government or workers" [International Social Security Association: 1998]

Page 16   "residual role of providing a safety net, he says" [Mullan, Phil: 2000]

Page 17   " Leone points out" [Leone, Richard C.: 1999]

Page 18   "per capita income (inflation adjusted) that – at about US$35,659 - is almost three times as large" [Schultz, James H.: 1999]

Page 19   "working at the department of Health and Welfare" [Messinger, Hans and Brian J.Powell: 1987]

Page 22   "when they were children, after allowing for inflation" Projections prepared for the author by Informetrica.

Page 23   "Study Warns of Age War Over Pensions" *National Post*, January 26, 2000.

Page 23   "may never recoup their contributions" [World Bank: 1994]

Page 24   "With support from Medicare's private competitors" [Baker, Dean and Mark Weisbrot: 1999]

Page 24   "save it up and give it to their children"
           [Hamilton, Malcolm: 1999]

Page 24   "Where is the fairness in this?" [Association of
           Canadian Pension Management: 2000]

Page 25   "taken from Statistics Canada's income data
           for 1997" [Statistics Canada: 1999a and 1999b]

Page 27   "social exchange that occurs between genera-
           tions occurs along non-monetary lines" [Gee,
           Ellen: 1998]

Page 27   "the title *Averting the Old Age Crisis*" [World
           Bank: 1994]

Page 28   "growth-inhibiting problems associated with a
           dominant public pillar" [World Bank: 1994]

Page 28   "face imminent problems with their old age
           systems" [World Bank: 1994]

Page 29   "problems of elderly welfare at a global level
           from a neoliberal perspective" [Lloyd-
           Sherlock, Peter and Paul Johnson, Editors:
           1996]

Page 29   "to construct a crisis out of change" [Johnson,
           Paul: 1996]

Page 29   "an exercise in positive economic analysis"
           [Johnson, Paul: 1996]

Page 30   "typified by the International Labour Office"
           The International Labour Office, based in
           Geneva, is a United Nations agency, estab-
           lished in 1919, with a special interest in the
           protection of workers. Among its activities is
           the development of standards and formal con-
           ventions on social security for member states.

Page 30   "financed by the state alone and generally
           available, though often means tested" [Lloyd-
           Sherlock, Peter: 1996]

Page 30   "neoliberal organizations such as the World
           Bank" [Lloyd-Sherlock, Peter: 1996]

Page 31   "the epitome of the 'private' approach as
           opposed to 'public' systems" [Gillion, Colin
           and Alejandro Bonilla: 1992]

Page 31   "political vulnerability of public pensions"
           [Baldwin, Bob: 1998]

Page 32   "cuts across all age groups and all income
           levels" [Government of Canada: 1996b]

Page 33   "the Canada Pension Plan should be aban-
           doned" [Government of Canada: 1996a]

Page 34   " changes are required to the public pension
           system to ensure it is affordable" [Government
           of Canada: 1994]

Page 34   "reducing the scope of the public sector in all
           areas of the economy" [Lloyd-Sherlock, Peter:
           1996]

Notes to Chapter 2

Page 36   "simply the price we have to pay for a longer
           life" [Johnson, Paul: 1996]

Page 37   "should not fare very differently in the face of
           demographic change" [Barr, Nicholas: 1987]

Page 37   "a number of key features of the World Bank's
           argument" [Lloyd-Sherlock Peter: 1996]

Page 38   " Canada's public pensions are fully indexed
           for inflation" [MacDonald, J. Bruce: 1995]

Page 39   "from China to Costa Rica, from Sierra Leone to Sweden" [Orszag, Peter R. and Joseph E, Stiglitz: 1999]

Page 42   "much like an extension of the informal system" [World Bank: 1994]

Page 42   "passing the hidden costs on to others in their own or future generations" [World Bank: 1994]

Page 42   "a more positive effect on national saving, labor productivity, and growth, according to the Bank's analysis" [World Bank: 1994]

Page 44   "the whole economy goes down the tubes" [Baker, Dean and Mark Weisbrot: 1999]

Page 44   "A 1995 report from the Canadian Institute of Actuaries (CIA), called *Trouble Tomorrows*" [*Canadian* Institute of Actuaries: 1995]

Page 44   "In its 2000 budget" [Government of Canada: 2000a]

Page 45   "The median growth projection for this period was 2.5% a year" [KPMG: 1999]

Page 45   "is projected to fall rather than rise over the 40-year period from 1991 to 2031" [Denton, Frank T. and Spencer, Byron G.: 1999]

Page 46   "views supporting privatization by way of individual accounts were featured prominently" National Symposium in Aging, held at Westin Harbour Castle Hotel, Toronto. May 1 and 2, 2000.

Page 46   "the orientation of much of today's retirement income system" [Association of Canadian Pension Management: 2000]

Page 46   "has made a significant contribution to reducing poverty and inequality among seniors" [Myles, John: 2000]

Page 47   "lessening the risk faced by any single individual" [Government of Canada: 1979]

Page 48   "should not result in a reduction of the claims of younger Canadians" [Baldwin, Bob: 1997]

Page 48   "60% of new retirees claim their CPP retirement pension prior to age 65" [Government of Canada: 2000b]

Page 51   "start preparing for a future without the CPP [Robson, William B.P.: 1996b]

Page 51   "collapsing underneath the hapless Generation X or perhaps their progeny [Baker, Dean and Mark Weisbrot: 1999]

Page 52   "first popularized by U.S. economist Lawrence Kotlikoff of Boston University in the early 1990s" [Kotlikoff, Lawrence J.: 1993]

Page 52   "100% of their incomes will be eaten up by taxes" [Baker, Dean and Mark Weisbrot: 1999]

Page 53   "And it is being used to justify cuts in government transfer programs" [Gee, Ellen: 1998]

Page 53   "an additional 11.6 percentage points to less than 40%" [Baker, Dean and Mark Weisbrot: 1999]

Page 53   "these private transfers have been unrecognized by the media and by policy makers" [Gee, Ellen: 1998]

Page 54   "reform of public pension programs was "the most obvious example."" [Statistics Canada: 1998]

Page 54   "The primary goal of the tax/transfer system," he said, "is not to ensure intergenerational equity." [Murphy, Brian: 1998]

Page 54   "framing the issue of the sustainability of government tax/transfer arrangements, including public pensions, in terms of generational equity may be seriously misleading" [Wolfson, M.C., Rowe, G., Lin, X., and Gribble, S.F.: 1998]

Page 55   "the legacy of productive capacity which this generation of Canadians will leave to the future" [Osberg, Lars: 1998]

Page 57   "intergenerational transfers within the CPP will have been virtually eliminated by that time" [Baldwin, Bob: 1997]

Page 57   "contrary to the belief that they will receive less in benefits than the amount contributed" [MacDonald, J. Bruce: 1995]

Page 57   " the present value of the streams of contributions that a person makes over their lifetime, related to the benefits they might be expected to receive" [Baldwin, Bob: 1997]

Page 57   "an expected real rate of return of 2.73% on his contributions to Social Security, compared with 1.37% for someone born in 1943" [Baker, Dean and Mark Weisbrot: 1999]

Page 58   "the average real rate of return for those born in 1988 and reaching age 65 in 2053 will be 1.6%, and 1.5% for those who turn 65 in 2073" [MacDonald, J. Bruce: 1995]

Page 58   "equal to the sum of the rate of growth in the
            labour force and the rate of growth in produc-
            tivity" [Samuelson, Paul: 1958]

Page 58   "the rate of growth in the earnings base on
            which CPP contributions are assessed"
            [Baldwin, Bob: 1997]

Page 58   "estimated long-term growth in real earnings
            at 1.5% a year" [Office of the Superintendent
            of Financial Institutions: 1998]

Page 58   "only at the expense of reduced consumption
            and returns for intervening generations"
            [Orszag, Peter R. and Joseph E, Stiglitz: 1999]

Page 59   "reflecting a very limited historical perspec-
            tive on what constitutes reasonable rates of
            return" [Baldwin, Bob: 1997]

Page 60   "Although they were strong in the 1990 to
            1995 period and they have been quite irregu-
            lar from decade to decade" [Canadian
            Institute of Actuaries: 1996]

Page 60   "are significantly higher than those for most
            occupational pension schemes" [Government
            of the United Kingdom: 1998]

Page 61   "could consume about 20% of the value of the
            account accumulated over a 40-year work
            career" [Orszag, Peter R. and Joseph E,
            Stiglitz: 1999]

Page 61   "Final benefits at retirement are 15% to 20%
            lower than they would have been in the
            absence of the fees" [Sinha, Tapen: 2000]

Page 61	"the costs associated with purchasing an annuity pension on retirement would be well over one third of their contributions" [Barrientos, Armando: 1996]
Page 62	"between 40% and 45% of the value of individual accounts in the U.K. is consumed by various fees and costs" [Murthi, Mamta, Orszag, J. Michael, and Orszag, Peter: 1999]
Page 63	"people who choose to stay in the plan could be asked to pay more for their benefits" [Reform Party: 1998]
Page 63	"1994 report on *Averting the Old Age Crisis*" [World Bank: 1994]
Page 64	"arguments most frequently used to promote individual retirement accounts, say these authors, are often not substantiated in either theory or practice" [Orszag, Peter R. and Joseph E, Stiglitz: 1999]

Notes to Chapter 3

Page 70	"getting rid of the CPP to turn Canada into "a nation of savers" [Coyne, Andrew: 1994]
Page 70	"a proposal called *Renewing CPP* released in October 1995" [Reform Party: 1995]
Page 70	"research organizations including the C.D.Howe Institute" [Robson, William B.P.: 1996b]
Page 70	"but also the structure of the entire Chilean economy" [Borzutsky, Silvia: 1998]
Page 71	"an inner core of the junta's new economics team" [Ritter, Archibald R.M.: 1992]

Page 73   "are now in control of the pension system" [Borzutsky, Silvia: 1998]

Page 74   "total mandatory contributions to these programs amount to 20% of earnings and there are no matching employer contributions" [Barrientos, Armando: 1996]

Page 74   "in turn reducing the high unemployment rates" [Borzutsky, Silvia: 1998]

Page 75   "they fear a powerful state agency could use information against the AFPs" [Mesa-Lago, Carmelo and Alberto Arenas de Mesa: 1998]

Page 75   "only about 4% of Chile's 1.3 million self-employed workers (in 1993) belong to the privatized system" [Mesa-Lago, Carmelo and Alberto Arenas de Mesa: 1998]

Page 75   "from 7.6% for those who belonged to the blue-collar workers fund to 17.1% for bank employees" [Borzutsky, Silvia: 1998]

Page 75   "By the end of 1982, about 70% of all those insured under the old program had transferred to the new scheme" [Mesa-Lago, Carmelo and Alberto Arenas de Mesa: 1998]

Page 75   "four key elements prompted people to abandon the old social security program" [Borzutsky, Silvia: 1998]

Page 76   "the proportion of the insured's working life spent contributing to the old system" [Gillion, Colin and Alejandro Bonilla: 1992]

Page 76   "These figures are double what was estimated in the mid-1980s"[Mesa-Lago, Carmelo and Alberto Arenas de Mesa: 1998]

Page 77	"The two largest are controlled by the U.S. conglomerates Bankers Trust and Aetna" [Borzutsky, Silvia: 1998]
Page 77	"The return on investment of the funds was –4.7%" [Mesa-Lago, Carmelo and Alberto Arenas de Mesa: 1998]
Page 78	"almost 69% of those insured were enrolled in the three largest funds" [Mesa-Lago, Carmelo and Alberto Arenas de Mesa: 1998]
Page 78	"or even just to do their agents a favour"[Queisser, Monika: 1999]
Page 78	"it has produced cut-throat competition among companies for the individual accounts and high prices for all workers" [Queisser, Monika: 1999]
Page 79	"as well as a fraction of annuity pension benefits in the event of an insurance company failure" [Barrientos, Armando: 1996]
Page 79	"the number of public assistance pensions the government will pay is limited to 300,000 and there is a long waiting list" [Mesa-Lago, Carmelo and Alberto Arenas de Mesa: 1998]
Page 80	"they will not even qualify for the minimum pension from the privatized scheme, because of the 20-year requirement" [Borzutsky, Silvia: 1998]
Page 80	"At retirement, the contributor has three options"[Mesa-Lago, Carmelo and Alberto Arenas de Mesa: 1998]

Page 81   "Fees charged for this advice can vary from
               about 3% to 5% of the total value of the fund"
               [Mesa-Lago, Carmelo and Alberto Arenas de
               Mesa: 1998]

Page 81   "the costs of their personal pension plan plus
               the costs associated with purchasing an annu-
               ity pension on retirement would be well over
               one third of their contributions" [Barrientos,
               Armando: 1996]

Page 81   "Even the World Bank admits that marketing
               costs of these privatized schemes are a partic-
               ularly sore point." [World Bank: 1994]

Page 82 "   the investment yield for the lowest income
               bracket averaged 7.6%, compared with 11.3%
               for the 60,000 pesos bracket"[Mesa-Lago,
               Carmelo and Alberto Arenas de Mesa: 1998]

Page 82   "in other words from men to women and from
               low-income workers to high-income work-
               ers"[Barrientos, Armando: 1996]

Page 82   "lower than the interest paid by bank
               deposits" [Mesa-Lago, Carmelo and Alberto
               Arenas de Mesa: 1998]

Page 83   "it's a common misconception that investors
               in the AFPs have been getting double digit
               rates of return for their funds" [Sinha, Tapen:
               2000]

Page 84   "over a third of the Chilean labour force is not
               covered by the program" [Barrientos,
               Armando: 1996]

Page 84   "Other estimates suggest that in 1988" [Mesa-
               Lago, Carmelo and Alberto Arenas de Mesa:
               1998]

Page 84   "the percentage of insured workers in the private AFP system who are contributing to their funds has been dropping steadily from 74% in 1982 to 56% in 1995" [Mesa-Lago, Carmelo and Alberto Arenas de Mesa: 1998]

Page 85   "it also exacerbate the socioeconomic differences that already exist in society" [Borzutsky, Silvia: 1998]

Page 85   "the small number of funds catering to better-paid workers are recording compliance rates in the region of 80% to 90%" [Gillion, Colin and Alejandro Bonilla: 1992]

Page 85   "It appears that most of the annuities paid out so far were paid to individuals who had sufficient balances in their accounts to retire early" [Queisser, Monika : 1999]

Page 86   "workers now retiring from the privatized system have benefited from the generously calculated recognition bonds" [Queisser, Monika : 1999]

Page 86   "Job interruptions have strong effects on pension benefit adequacy" [Barrientos, Armando: 1996]

Page 86   "which in practice will mean extreme poverty" [Borzutsky, Silvia: 1998]

Page 86   " the personal pension funds of 45% of women and 34% of men will generate benefits below the minimum pension level" [Barrientos, Armando: 1996]

Page 86   "only between 45% and 35% of the average male pension after they leave the labour market" [Arenas de Mesa, Alberto: 1994]

Page 87   "Studies have shown conclusively that, as a result, the Chilean reform of the pension system has increased income inequality among pensioners" [Sinha, Tapen: 2000]

Page 87   "would have to contribute 15 or 20% of their insured wages, instead of the 10% amount needed by the average male worker to get the same replacement" [Gillion, Colin and Alejandro Bonilla: 1992]

Page 87   "salary replacement rates are 80-86% for men and 52-57% for women" [CIEDESS: 1992]

Page 88   "unless substantial numbers of people – particularly higher earners – have been weaned away from reliance on state benefits" [Johnson, Paul: 1996]

Page 88   "social security benefits were always subject to political risk because governments often failed to index benefits against inflation, or did not pay what they legally owed" [Kay, Stephen J.: 1997]

Page 89   "The armed forces did not join the new system – an option not available to any other group in the country" [Edwards, Sebastian: 1998]

Page 89   "the idea that corrupt and inefficient governments provide a rationale for individual accounts" [Orszag, Peter R. and Joseph E, Stiglitz: 1999]

Page 89   "would-be privatizers in the United States cannot substantiate rhetoric about government inefficiency ruining Social Security" [Kay, Stephen J.: 1997]

Page 90   "the huge sums of money invested will require adequate regulation and will therefore be subject to both political and market risk" [Kay, Stephen J.: 1997]

Page 91   "Chile's experience provides a useful bench-mark against which policy initiatives in Canada can be evaluated." [Pesando, James: 1997)]

Page 92   "indicate that widely decentralized systems – such as Canada's RRSP system is– are much more costly and more difficult to regulate" [Murthi, Mamta, Orszag, J. Michael, and Orszag, Peter: 1999]

Page 94   "the existing RRSP and Registered Pension Plan system, with its tax-deductible contribu-tions and tax-deferred compounding of inter-est, cost approximately $15 billion a year in lost tax revenues" [Government of Canada: 1994b]

Page 94   "the total amount contributed to RRSPs in 1994 was less than 17% of the amount Canadians were entitled to contribute" [Statistics Canada: 1995]

Page 96   "there is evidence that many people also cash in their savings plans when they fall on hard times, such as during recession or job loss" [Frenken, Hubert and Linda Standish: 1994]

Page 98   " The worker also runs the risk of mismanage-ment or bankruptcy of the pension fund that manages his or her savings" [Gillion, Colin and Alejandro Bonilla: 1992]

Page 99   "yet the scheme deprives all wage and salary earners of the right to determine how to dispose of 10 per cent of their earnings" [Gillion, Colin and Alejandro Bonilla: 1992]

Notes to Chapter 4

Page 101   "even though the pensions they will receive at retirement will be less than they would have received under the public pension plan" [Hutton, Will: 1996]

Page 102   "increasingly transferring the burden of providing pensions to the funded private sector, principally on a defined contribution basis" [Blake, David: 2000]

Page 103   "are unlikely to build up to a fund value which would generate a pension big enough to live on" [Tonks, Ian: 1999]

Page 103   "had dropped to about 7.5 million by 1996, representing only 35% of all individuals with some kind of pension coverage" [Tonks, Ian: 1999]

Page 104   "current pensioners in the UK get the largest share of their income from basic state pension" [Government of the United Kingdom: 1998a]

Page 105   "There is a complex array of options available in these third pillar arrangements" - description based on [Tonks, Ian: 1999]

Page 106   "who is covered by what type of arrangement in the UK retirement income system" estimates from [Tonks, Ian: 1999]

Page 108   " the official view now was that state provi-
              sion should be minimal and that people
              should make provision for
              themselves"[Hutton, Will: 1996]

Page 108   "It was estimated that the combined effect of
              these cuts was to reduce the value of SERPS
              benefits by about two-thirds" [Blake, David:
              2000]

Page 109   "Fewer than 50% of them did so" [Blake,
              David: 2000]

Page 109   "leading directly to the personal pensions
              mis-selling scandal that erupted in December
              1993" [Blake, David: 2000]

Page 110   "a 1% age-related National Insurance rebate to
              members of contracted-out personal pension
              schemes aged 30 or more to discourage them
              from recontracting back into SERPS, which
              technically they were allowed to do" [Blake,
              David: 2000]

Page 111   "the employees' National Insurance contribu-
              tion rebate was paid directly into the pension
              fund by the government" [Government of the
              United Kingdom: 2000]

Page 111   "the regulatory framework governing occupa-
              tional pension schemes was tightened to
              reduce the possibility of fraud and/or mis-
              management" [Government of the United
              Kingdom: 2000]

Page 112   "Sun Life Assurance Co. of Canada's British operation had been fined a record £600,000 (nearly $1.5 million) and was assessed an additional £125,000 for legal fees and other costs associated with the regulators' investigation" [Globe & Mail: 1998]

Page 112   "Sun Life has also recently become involved in Chile's mandatory private savings scheme" [Morton, Peter: 1998]

Page 112   "According to one estimate the majority of those who remain in the public plan earn less than about £10,000 annually" [Murthi, Mamta, Orszag, J. Michael, and Orszag, Peter: 1999]

Page 113   "the options for low and moderate earning workers without access to an occupational pension plan, were very limited" [Government of the United Kingdom: 2000]

Page 113   "Those without stable earnings found personal pensions particularly unsuitable for their needs" [Government of the United Kingdom: 2000]

Page 113   "they are likely to be a further contributor to inequality among pensioners" [Government of the United Kingdom: 2000]

Page 113   "clearly hoping that market forces alone would ensure that personal pension schemes would be competitively provided" " [Blake, David: 2000]

Page 115   "A 1998 survey of fund management fees conducted by benefits consulting firm Towers Perrin" [Towers Perrin: 1998]

Page 115   "A 1997 report from the Office of Fair Trading"[Office of Fair Trading: 1997]

Page 116   "In comparison with most occupational schemes, said the report, the level of employer's contributions may be inadequate or non-existent"[Office of Fair Trading: 1997]

Page 116   "the introduction in 1995 of disclosure requirements designed to bring down charges by promoting competition, had only been to reduced average charges from 26% to 24%" [Consumers' Association: 1997] cited in [Tonks, Ian : 1999]

Page 116   "on average, between 40 and 45% of the value of individual accounts in the UK is consumed by various fees and costs" [Murthi, Mamta, Orszag, J. Michael, and Orszag, Peter: 1999]

Page 120   "with current contribution rates, the amounts of money going into individual personal pension funds are unlikely to generate sufficient funds to produce a reasonable pension at age 65" [Tonks, Ian: 1999]

Page 120   "contributions to personal pension schemes are between 1% and 5% of average earnings" [Tonks, Ian: 1999]

Page 120   "will be "shocked" to discover that there are insufficient accumulated funds to generate an income that will maintain the individual's standard of living" [Consumers' Association: 1997]

Page 120   "typically has low maturity values because the plan provider continues to extract the same annual charges as with an active plan" [Tonks, Ian: 1999]

Page 120   "only 57% to 68% of people who started a personal pension scheme were still contributing four years after they began the scheme" [Personal Investment Authority: 1998]

Page 121   "proved to be too radical for the traditional Old Labour wing of the party and was soon replaced" [Blake, David: 2000]

Page 121   "committed to produce a Green Paper which would aim to meet those challenges and ensure proper regulation of pension investments, striking a balance between public and private funding" [Government of the United Kingdom :1998a]

Page 123   "once these new pensions are introduced, personal pensions will become uncompetitive, so that anyone opening a new pension would choose a stakeholder over a personal pension" [Tonks, Ian: 1999]

Page 124   "In the long term, he said. state spending on pensions will be reduced from 60% to 40% of the total" [Darling, Alistair: 1998]

Page 126   "Where possible and appropriate, individuals and employers should be given the flexibility to design equivalent or better benefits." [Day, Stockwell: 1998]

Notes to Chapter 5

Page 129   "its clout came from the millions of voters from all walks of life who received cheques every month without fail" [Zuckerman, Diana: 2000]

Page 129   "Almost everyone acknowledges that Social Security has been an enormous success in providing the elderly, the disabled, and survivors with a modest basic income" [Aaron, Henry J. and Robert D. Reischauer: 1998]

Page 129   "because of Social Security, only 11% of American seniors live in poverty" [Social Security Administration: 1999]

Page 129   "the relentless campaign has reinforced the conviction in the political centre that Social Security needs major overhaul rather than minor surgery" [Kuttner, Robert: 1998]

Page 130   "opponents of Social Security have been waging a kind of holy war for decade now, designed to "wake up" the American public to the supposed dangers of an aging population" [Schultz, James H.: 1999]

Page 130   "should be seen in the context of ever-changing employment needs and the chronic unemployment characterizing market economies" [Schultz, James H.: 1999]

Page 130   "move away from "an emphasis on entitlement and dependence towards greater individual responsibility and self-sufficiency" [Association of Canadian Pension Management: 2000]

Page 130   "workers should be given a "free choice"
             [Piñera, José: no date]

Page 131   "According to Kuttner, the State Street Bank
             has spent millions of dollars promoting priva-
             tization" [Kuttner, Robert: 1998]

Page 131   "the National Center for Policy Analysis has
             been promoting privatization of Social
             Security for the past 10 years, while also lob-
             bying for school vouchers, massive tax cuts for
             the wealthy, privatized prison labour, and
             paycheck deception legislation, as well as
             funding bills opposing patients' rights" [AFL-
             CIO: 2000]

Page 132   "Observers believe that 25% of the funding for
             Cato's privatization project comes from Wall
             Street firms, with banks and other major cor-
             porations also contributing [AFL-CIO: 2000]

Page 132   "the Investment Company Institute, the lobby-
             ing arm of the mutual fund industry, has
             made revising Social Security a top legislative
             priority" [AFL-CIO: 2000]

Page 132   "84% of participants in a survey on ABC's
             website favoured some sort of privatization"
             [Zuckerman, Diana: 2000]

Page 133   "Frank Luntz, who was censured by the
             American Association for Public Opinion
             Research for his failure to disclose his tech-
             niques in his Contract With America polling
             for the Republican Party" [Henwood, Doug:
             1999]

Page 135   "the earnings base on which CPP contributions are collected represents about 67% of
total wage earnings, while the earnings base
from which U.S. Social Security taxes are collected covers approximately 86% of total wage
earnings" Information from the Office of the
Chief Actuary, September 11, 2000.

Page 135   "But poor economic performance prevented
these reserves from accumulating" [Aaron,
Henry J. and Robert D. Reischauer: 1998]

Page 135   "a more important consideration was the fear
that political pressures might lead the trust
fund managers to interfere with private business decisions" [Aaron, Henry J. and Robert
D. Reischauer: 1998]

Page 136   "Board president cautioned that such a spectacular return could not be expected again
because the Board intended to broaden its
asset allocation base, thus decreasing the
volatility of its investment portfolio" [Canada
Pension Plan Investment Board: 2000]

Page 136   "if there are recurring shortfalls, the availability of trust fund assets allows time for the
enactment and implementation of legislation
to restore financial stability to the program"
[Social Security Administration: 2000a]

Page 138   "According to one estimate, replacement rates
ranged from 80% for low wage earners to 25%
to high wage earners" [Leone, Richard C. and
Greg Anrig, Jr. Editors: 1999]

Page 138   "apocalyptic predictions about Social Security
                now represent the accepted opinion of the
                bulk of the American population" [Schultz,
                James H.: 1999]

Page 139   "The surplus, which currently stands at about
                $124 billion, has been accumulating since 1983,
                when the payroll tax was increased. And it
                will help finance the baby boomers' retire-
                ment, which is why the program will not have
                any trouble meeting its obligations when the
                boomers are retiring [Baker, Dean and Mark
                Weisbrot: 1999]

Page 139   "And even then, it will have more than $1 tril-
                lion in the Social Security Trust Fund left from
                previous years" [Zuckerman, Diana: 2000]

Page 139   "the Trustees expect there will be Social
                Security payroll taxes to pay 72% of the
                planned benefits on a pay-as-you-go basis"
                [Social Security Administration: 2000b]

Page 140   "Actuaries for the fund are projecting an eco-
                nomic growth rate over the next 75 years of
                1.4% a year, which is less than half the average
                of the past 75 years, and below the average of
                the 1930s" [Henwood, Doug: 1999]

Page 140   "a violation of all historical precedent"
                [Henwood, Doug: 1999]

Page 141   "the strong economy of the past four years has
                weakened the argument that Social Security
                must be radically changed because it is
                absolutely unaffordable." [Social Security
                Administration: 1999]

Page 141   "These reforms included" description that follows is based on [Leone, Richard C. and Greg
Anrig, Jr. Editors: 1999]

Page 142   "investing up to 40% of the reserves in equities by 2015 would close roughly half of the
projected long-term deficit" [Aaron, Henry J.
and Robert D. Reischauer: 1998]

Page 143   "it would probably not permanently solve the
Social Security fiscal imbalance because it pro-
posed only modest changes" " [Aaron, Henry
J. and Robert D. Reischauer: 1998]

Page 144   "that would be designed to reflect changes
that have occurred in the labour force and in
life expectancy since the program was enacted." [Aaron, Henry J. and Robert D.
Reischauer: 1998]

Page 144   "Workers would be authorized to set up voluntary individual retirement savings
accounts" description based on [Aaron, Henry
J. and Robert D. Reischauer : 1998]

Page 145   "The plan would erode benefits steeply and in
ways that could hurt vulnerable groups the
most" [Aaron, Henry J. and Robert D.
Reischauer: 1998]

Page 145   "This plan, proposed by Democratic Senator
John Breaux" description based on [Aaron,
Henry J. and Robert D. Reischauer: 1998]

Page 146   "The Feldstein-Samwick plan for 2%
accounts" description based on [Aaron,
Henry J. and Robert D. Reischauer: 1998]

Page 146   "when these surpluses begin to shrink, taxes dedicated to retirement pensions will have to be raised, other spending cut, or deficits incurred for several decades" [Aaron, Henry J. and Robert D. Reischauer: 1998]

Page 147   "creating a new tax credit and diverting the surpluses to private accounts would increase the government's long-term obligations and interest costs" [Leone, Richard C. and Greg Anrig, Jr. Editors: 1999]

Page 147   "In effect, Social Security would gradually be replaced with two other benefits: a guaranteed minimum benefit and an additional amount that reflected the returns individuals earned on their PSAs" description based on [Leone, Richard C. and Greg Anrig, Jr. Editors: 1999]

Page 148   "it was estimated that the new system would run a deficit for the first few decades, forcing the government to borrow approximately $2 trillion (in 1998 dollars)" [Aaron, Henry J. and Robert D. Reischauer: 1998]

Page 148   "privatization of Social Security in this way would relieve the government of the obligation to raise taxes to provide the promised benefits" [Leone, Richard C. and Greg Anrig, Jr. Editors: 1999]

Page 149   "if five percentage points of the 12.4% Social Security payroll tax were diverted to private investment, as advocated in the PSA proposal put forwards by the five-member group, it would come to an average US$100" [Eisner, Robert: 1998]

Page 149   "the fear of raising taxes – even by a small amount - currently pervades the political debate in Washington" [Rasell, Edith and Jeff Faux: 1999]

Page 151   "USA accounts, separate from Social Security, will mean hundreds of dollars in targeted tax cuts for working Americans who choose to save more for retirement, with more help for lower-income workers." [Apfel, Kenneth: 1999]

Page 151   "Allowing the government to invest the trust fund in private capital markets would amount to the socialization of a large portion of the U.S. economy" [Tanner, Michael: no date]

Page 151   "Dean Baker of The Century Foundation lists several "thorny issues" raised by Clinton's proposal" [Baker, Dean: 1999]

Page 152   "other pressing public needs will continue to be ignored and that discretionary domestic spending will be insufficient to provide an adequate level of services" [Rasell, Edith and Jeff Faux: 1999]

Page 153   "Bush's privatization plan would cost something like US$900 billion over the first ten years" [Orszag, Peter: 2000]

Page 153   "Four economists looked at how large those cuts would have to be and whether the proceeds of investments in individual accounts could compensate for them" [Aaron, Henry J., Alan S. Blinder, Alicia H. Munnell, and Peter R. Orszag: 2000]

Page 154   "they raise questions about the viability of protecting benefits for current retirees, older workers, disabled workers, and survivors while diverting payroll taxes to individual accounts" [Aaron, Henry J., Alan S. Blinder, Alicia H. Munnell, and Peter R. Orszag: 2000]

Page 154   "The Bush plan would cripple Social Security, expose workers to increased risk and reduce their pension income." [Aaron, Henry J. and Alan S. Blinder: 2000]

Page 155   "privatization of Social Security has more to do with ideological and economic interests than with the solvency of Social Security [Mashaw, Jerry L. and Theodore R. Marmor: 1996]

Page 155   "economist Dean Baker set out a detailed blueprint" [Baker, Dean: 1998]

Page 156   "there is simply no liberal counterpart to the right's multi-pronged campaign." [Kuttner, Robert: 1998]

Page 156   "the liberal side lacks the drama and excitement of what appears to be a big new ideas consonant with the pro-market sentiment of the age" [Kuttner, Robert: 1998]

Notes to Chapter 6

Page 160   "the blueprint for guerilla warfare against U.S. Social Security" see Chapter 1, page 31.

Page 161   "all of the CPP actuarial reports, including those before its inception, projected increasing contribution rates in the future" [MacDonald, J. Bruce: 1995]

Page 161   "all future generations will receive in current dollar benefits over five times what they and their employer contributed, contrary to the belief that they will receive less in benefits than the amount contributed" [MacDonald, J. Bruce: 1995]

Page 162   "Current estimates indicate that is about 1.5% a year" see Chapter 2, page 64.

Page 162   "contribution rates would have to be increased at a faster rate than he had projected in his last report" [Government of Canada: 1995]

Page 163   "it is all but impossible to find a simple relationship between taxes on labour and employment" [Organization for Economic Co-operation and Development: 1994]

Page 164   "the long-run disincentive effects of required contributions to mandatory RRSPs would be small or non-existent, unlike similar contributions to a reformed CPP" [Pesando, James: 1997]

Page 166   "It is quite clear everyone surveyed favours some type of privatization" [Fraser Institute: 2000]

Page 167   "he said Canadians should contemplate winding it up in favour of an expanded private pension system, which would include mandatory RRSP contributions" [Robson, William B.P.: 1996a]

Page 167   "a more secure system based on individual responsibility and control" [Robson William B.P.: 1996a]

Page 167   "According to Day, who issued a press release accompanying the paper" Government of Alberta: 1998a]

Page 170   an assessment of "the merits of turning the retirement component of the CPP into mandatory, individual RRSP style accounts." [Government of Alberta: 1998a]

Page 170   "is it possible or desirable to set up individual accounts for future retirement benefit accruals?" [Government of Alberta: 1998b]

Page 172   if the economic benefits that could be achieved with an Alberta-only plan could also be implemented across the entire plan, Alberta would not need to opt out all Canadians would benefit." [Government of Alberta: 1999]

Page 173   "the province would have to assume an approximately $50 billion share of the CPP's accrued liabilities" [Brown, Robert L.: 1999]

Page 173   "it makes sense to examine further reforms that combine a move toward pre-funded individually controlled retirement accounts with a shift to some other tax base to finance current obligations" [Robson, William B.P.: 1999]

Page 174   "Another paper presented at the conference suggested that a separate pension plan for Alberta might be more costly than for the province to remain within the CPP" [Emery, J.C. Herbert and Kenneth J. McKenzie: 1999]

Page 174   "The only logical model Alberta could have in mind, Brown said, would be replacing the present defined benefit CPP model with a defined contribution system of mandatory retirement savings plans" [Brown, Robert L.: 1999]

Page 175   "The Canadian Alliance policy platform" [Canadian Alliance: 2000]

Page 181   "In 1994, for example, 40% of women's jobs and 27% of men's jobs were non-standard jobs, compared with 35% and 22% respectively in 1989" [Townson, Monica: 1997b]

Page 182   "Many individuals therefore use the services of an "independent expert" who provides advice, recommends the choice of an insurance company and negotiates on their behalf"[Barrientos, Armando :1996]

Page 183   "poor people, who have relatively short life expectancies, will earn a lower return than the wealthy unless some adjustment is made when they purchase annuities [Willmore, Larry: 1998]

Page 185   "the personal pension scheme in Chile has required a great deal of intervention" [Barrientos, Armando: 1996]

Page 185   "the World Bank report lists a number of areas where government regulation is still necessary" [World Bank: 1994]

Page 186   "They rely very heavily on tax subsidies to make them attractive" [Baldwin, Bob: 1998]

Page 186   "administrative costs of the Chilean system to date are "relatively large" [Pesando, James: 1997]

Page 186   "in the Netherlands, which also has a partially privatized system, administrative costs for individual pensions are estimated to be 24% of contributions" [Davis, E Philip: 1997]

Page 186   "the cost of running the CPP is 1.3% of contribution revenue" [Brown, Robert L.: 1999]

Page 187   "the payout of previously accrued retirement benefits would be financed either through a payroll tax (as at present) or through general tax revenues" [Pesando, James: 1997]

Page 188   "the Canadian Institute of Actuaries Task Force on the future of the CPP" [Canadian Institute of Actuaries: 1996b]

Page 188   "An increase in CPP contribution rates with an unchanged (or reduced) level of CPP retirement benefits, should increase personal savings." [Pesando, James : 1997]

Page 189   "a person without preconceptions will find a bewildering diversity of answer in economic theory about whether social security is more likely to raise or lower consumption or labor supply"[Aaron, Henry J.: 1982]

Page 190   "a person can save less in a tax-sheltered private savings arrangement and still attain his or her savings target" [Willmore, Larry: 1998]

Page 190   "there is an abundant literature on the impact of pre-funding of social security on gross national savings, "but no clear conclusion" [Brown, Robert L.: 1997]

Page 192   "Recent Canadian studies indicate the important contribution made by the public pension programs' see [Myles, John: 2000]

Page 192   "would likely lead to an increase in rates of poverty and income inequality among future generations of Canadian seniors" [Prus, Steven G.: 1999]

Notes to Chapter 7

Page 195   "most Canadians believe in the CPP and want it preserved" [Government of Canada: 1997]

Page 195   "a massive majority of Canadians which wants the CPP to continue" and that "this desire cuts across all age groups and all income levels."[Government of Canada: 1996b]

Page 195   "expressed concern about the impact of the CPP on younger generations and suggested that the government offer people under 30 a chance to opt out" [Government of Canada: 1997]

Page 196   "the choice to increase funding to finance the current program came to the top the agenda" [Myles, John and Paul Pierson: 1999]

Page 198   "the Board is actually more like an investment management company than the full-service plan sponsor" [MacNaughton, John A.: 2000b]

Page 198   "our ultimate goal is to increase the value of assets available to the Plan to pay future pensions." [MacNaughton, John A.: 2000b]

Page 199   "as the fund broadened its asset allocation base, the volatility of the portfolio would decline as will the likelihood of achieving such outstanding annual results again." [Canada Pension Plan Investment Board: 2000]

Page 199   "managing these assets "will inevitably involve exploring a full arsenal of investment strategies" [MacNaughton, John A.: 2000b]

Page 200   "The better Canadian firms perform financially over the long term, the better off Canadians will be in their retirement years" [MacNaughton, John A.: 2000a]

Page 201   "Under the new funding formula, assets will eventually reach 20% of liabilities [MacNaughton, John A.: 2000a]

Page 201 "   Bay Street is in line for a big financial windfall" [Globe & Mail: 1997]

Page 201   "running a passive portfolio is not nearly as lucrative as actively picking stocks" [Globe & Mail :1999]

Page 202   "it is impossible to do both" [Baldwin, Bob: 1998]

Page 202   "one of the many factors that makes it impossible for these plans to make a reasonably certain promise of the benefit that will be provided to retirees." [Baldwin, Bob: 1998]

Page 203   "an increasing number of Canadians will surely feel that the CPP is still too unsustainable to rely on."[Slater, David W. and William B.P.Robson: 1999]

Page 204   "improve employer compliance and would decrease the contribution rate [Government of Canada: 1996c]

Page 204   "financial responsibility for redistributive transfers can be shifted from payroll taxes to general revenues" [Myles, John and Paul Pierson: 1999]

Page 205   "According to Maarten Camps of the Netherlands Ministry of Finance," interview with the author in The Hague, July 1999.

Page 205   "it has been a significant success in accommodating various social and economic interests in the context of outstanding economic growth" [Clark, Gordon L. and Paul Bennett: 2000]

Page 205   "the economic virtues of social solidarity are significant and deeply implicated with national politics" [Clark, Gordon L. and Paul Bennett: 2000]

Page 205   "in which old age public pension systems were designed for universal coverage and the entitlement to a retirement income according to citizenship (or legal residence) and prior earnings" [Clark, Gordon L. and Paul Bennett: 2000]

Page 207   "the possibility has not been ruled out, once government finances reach a surplus position in about four years' time" - Maarten Camps, Netherlands Ministry of Finance, interview with the author in The Hague, July 1999.

Page 207   " this approach effectively will require seniors to contribute to the cost of their own pensions" - Maarten Camps, Netherlands Ministry of Finance, interview with the author in The Hague, July 1999.

Page 208   "For a worker whose final salary is about US$20,000, the Netherlands public pension replaces about 66% of final salary" [Davis, E. Philip: 1996]

Page 209   "private sector business opinion has been led by the financial sector and has swung in the direction of supporting full funding" [Baldwin, Bob: 1998]

Page 209   "the path of entitlement and state dependence which is the orientation of much of today's retirement income system" [Association of Canadian Pension Management: 2000]

Page 209   "Individuals aged 25 to 34 are the most likely age group to believe they will not receive anything from public pensions" [Government of Canada: 2000c

Page 211   "In a study of the maturation of this country's retirement income system" [Myles, John: 2000]

Page 213   "low-income workers may never accumulate enough in their pension accounts to support themselves in old age" [World Bank: 1994]

Page 213   "it can change markedly the distribution of income and wealth" [Willmore, Larry: 1998]

Page 213   "By moving from defined benefit to defined contribution, reformers hope to reduce the amount of redistribution that occurs within pension systems" [Willmore, Larry: 1998]

Page 214   "will jeopardize the ability of the state to reshape income inequalities in later life" [Prus, Steven G.: 1999]

Page 214   "would likely lead to an increase in rates of poverty and income inequality among future generations of Canadian seniors" [Prus, Steven G.: 1999]

Page 214   "a well-managed public CPP can effectively deal with all the concerns of those favouring privatization" [James, Steven: 1997]

Page 216   "there are significant risks limitations and complications associated with reliance upon mandatory defined contribution, fully funded schemes as the dominant public pension pillar" [Heller, Peter S.: 1998]

Bibliography

AFL-CIO (2000) *Who's Behind the Private Accounts Scheme?*
Washington: AFL-CIO
http://www.aflcio.org/socialsecurity/private.htm

Apfel, Kenneth (1999) Testimony on February 23, 1999
before *The House Committee on Ways and Means (Archer) on the
President's plan for Social Security.* Washington: Social Security
Administration.
http://www.ssa.gov/policy/congcomm/testimo-
ny_022399.html.

Arenas de Mesa, Alberto (1994) *Seguridad social y mercado del
trabajo: Inequidades de género en Chile, 1980-1984.* University of
Pittsburgh. Manuscript.

Aaron, Henry J. (1982) "Economic Effects of Social Security"
in *Studies of Government Finance.* Washington: The Brookings
Institution.

Aaron, Henry J. and Robert D. Reischauer (1998) *Countdown
to Reform: The Great Social Security Debate.* New York: The
Century Foundation Press.

**Aaron, Henry J., Alan S. Blinder, Alicia H. Munnell, and
Peter R. Orszag (2000)** *Bush's Individual Account Proposal:
Implications for Retirement Benefits.* The Social Security
Network Issue Brief Series; Issue Brief No. 11. New York: The
Century Foundation.

Aaron, Henry J. and Alan S. Blinder (2000) "Bush's Shaky
Retirement Plan," *Washington Post,* Thursday August 24,
2000: A25.

Association of Canadian Pension Management (2000) *A Retirement Income Strategy for Canada.* Toronto: Association of Canadian Pension Management.

Baker, Dean   (1998) *Saving Social Security in Three Steps.* Washington: Economic Policy Institute. Briefing paper, November 1998.

_____. **(1999)** "Two Cheers for Clinton's Social Security Plan" in *The American Prospect Online.* May-June 1999. http://www.prospect.org/archives/44/44baker.html

Baker, Dean and Mark Weisbrot (1999) *Social Security: The Phony Crisis.* Chicago: The University of Chicago Press.

Baldwin, Bob (1997) *Boomers, X'ers, Other Generations and the Canada Pension Plan.* Ottawa: Canadian Labour Congress, Research Paper #5

_____. **(1998)** *Funding Public Pension Plans More Fully: What is (and is not) at Stake.* Research Paper # 10. Ottawa: Canadian Labour Congress.

Barr, Nicholas (1987) *The Economics of the Welfare State.* Stanford, California: Stanford University Press.

Barrientos, Armando (1996) "Ageing and Personal Pensions in Chile," in *Ageing and Social Policy*, Edited by Peter Lloyd-Sherlock and Paul Johnson. London: Suntory and Toyota International Centres for Economics and Related Disciplines, London School of Economics.

Blake, David (2000) *Two Decades of Pension Reform in the UK: What are theImplications for Occupational Pension Schemes?* London: The Pensions Institute, Birkbeck College, University of London. Discussion Paper PI-2004, March 2000.

Borzutsky, Silvia (1998) "Chile: The Politics of Privatization," in *Do Options Exist? Reform of Pension and Health Care Systems in Latin America.* Edited by Maria Amparo Cruz-Saco and Carmelo Mesa-Lago. Pittsburgh: University of Pittsburgh Press.

Brown, Robert L. (1997) *In Defense of Pay-as-you-go Financing of Social Security.* Waterloo, Ontario: University of Waterloo.

———. **(1999)** *Alberta Opting Out of the Canada Pension Plan: Can it be Dine? Should it be Done?* Waterloo, Ontario: University of Waterloo, Institute of Insurance and Pension Research. Canada Pension Plan Investment Board (2000) "CPP Investment Board Cautions that 40% Investment Return is Unlikely Again." Media Release, June 27, 2000. Toronto: CPP Investment Board. http://www.cppib.ca/media/062700_MR.htm

Canadian Alliance (2000) *Policy Declaration.* Ottawa: Canadian Alliance. http://www.canadianalliance.ca

Canadian Institute of Actuaries (1995) *Troubled Tomorrows – The Report of the Canadian Institute of Actuaries Task Force on Retirement Savings.* Ottawa: Canadian Institute of Actuaries.

———. **(1996a)** *Report on Canadian Economic Statistics 1924-1995.* Ottawa: Canadian Institute of Actuaries.

_____. **(1996b)** *Report of the Task Force on the Future of Canada/Quebec Pension Plans.* Ottawa: Canadian Institute of Actuaries May 1996.

Clark, Gordon L. and Paul Bennett (2000) *The Dutch Model of Sector-wide Supplementary Pensions: Fund Governance, Finance and European Competition Policy.* Oxford: University of Oxford, School of Geography.

Consumers' Association (1997) *A Blueprint for Better Pensions.* London, England: The Consumers' Association.

Corporación de Investigación, Estudio y Desarrollo de la Seguridad Social (CIEDESS) (1992) *12 años de modernización de la seguridad social en Chile: Evaluación crítica y proyecciones.* Santiago: CIEDESS.

Coyne, Andrew (1994) "Let's create a nation of savers." *Globe and Mail,* August 17,1994.

Dahlby, Bev (1993) "Payroll Taxes," in *Business Taxation in Ontario,* Edited By Allan M. Maslove. Toronto: Fair Tax Commission and University of Toronto Press.

Darling, Alistair (1998) "Darling pledges a decent and secure income in retirement for all." London: Department of Social Security, Media Centre, Press Release, December 15, 1998.

Davis, E. Philip (1996) *International Experiences of Pension Fund Reform and its Applicability to the Netherlands.* The Pensions Institute Discussion Paper PI-9611. London: Birkbeck College, University of London.

_____. **(1997)** *The reform of retirement income provision in the EU.* The Pensions Institute Discussion Paper PI-9708. London: Birkbeck College, University of London.

Day, Stockwell (1998) *Next Stops to CPP Reform.* Ottawa: June 15, 1998

Denton, Frank T., Christine H. Feaver and Byron G. Spencer (1998) "The Future Population of Canada, Its Age Distribution and Dependency Relations." *Canadian Journal on Aging.* 17:83-109

Denton, Frank T. and Spencer, Byron G. (1999) *Population Aging and Its Economic Costs: A Survey of the Issues and Evidence.* Program for Research on Social and Economic Dimensions of an Aging Population (SEDAP). Hamilton, Ontario: McMaster University. SEDAP Research Paper No.1.

Desjardins, Bernard (1993) *Population Ageing and the Elderly.* Ottawa: Statistics Canada Demography Division. Catalogue No. 91-533E.

Edwards, Sebastian (1998) "The Chilean Pension reform: A Pioneering Program," in *Privatizing Social Security* Edited by Martin Feldstein. A National Bureau of Economic Research Project Report. Chicago: The University of Chicago Press.

Eisner, Robert (1998) *Social Security: More, Not Less.* New York: The Century Foundation Press

Emery, J.C. Herbert and Kenneth J. McKenzie (1999) *Checking Out of the Hotel California: The Desirability of an Alberta Pension Plan.* Calgary, Alberta: University of Calgary, Department of Economics. January 22, 1999.

Feldstein, Martin (1998) *Privatizing Social Security* Edited by Martin Feldstein. A National Bureau of Economic Research Project Report. Chicago: The University of Chicago Press.

Fraser Institute (2000) *Canadian Investment Managers Lukewarm on the Federal Budget and CPP Reform.* Vancouver: Fraser Institute. http://www.fraserinstitute.ca

Frenken, Hubert and Linda Standish (1994) "RRSP withdrawals," in *Perspectives on Labour and Income*, Spring 1994. Ottawa: Statistics Canada. Catalogue 75-001E.

Gee, Ellen (1998) *Population and Politics: Apocalyptic Demography, Population Aging and Canadian Social Policy*, presented at the 9th annual John K. Friesen Conference, "The Overselling of Population Aging: Apocalyptic Demography and the Intergenerational Challenge," Simon Fraser University, May 1998.

Gillion, Colin and Alejandro Bonilla, (1992) "Analysis of a national private pension scheme: The case of Chile," in *International Labour Review*, Vol. 131, 1992, No. 2.

Globe & Mail (1995) "UI premiums poised to drop," Report on Business, March 7, 1995.

_____. **(1997)** "Stocks to bolster CPP," Report on Business, February 15, 1997.

_____. **(1998)** "Sun Life's boss in Britain leaves amid pension sales problems." Report on Business, August 20, 1998.

_____. **(1999)** "Barclays, TD chosen to invest CPP fund," Report on Business, February 18, 1999.

Government of Alberta (1998a) *Alberta Reminds Federal-Provincial Finance Ministers CPP Reform is Unfinished Business.* Edmonton, Alberta: Alberta Treasury.
http://www.gov.ab.ca/acn/199806/6405.html

_____. **(1998b)** *Next Steps to CPP Reform.* Edmonton, Alberta: Alberta Treasury, June 15,1998.
http://www.treas.gov.ab.ca

_____. **(1999)** *Progress made on CPP reform but an Alberta solution is still possible.* Edmonton, Alberta: Alberta Treasury, December 10, 1999.
http://www.gov.ab.ca/can/199912/8541.html

Government of Canada (1979) *The Retirement Income System in Canada: Problems and Alternative Policies for Reform.* Task Force on Retirement Income Policy. Ottawa: Minister of Supply and Services Canada.

_____. **(1994a)** *Budget Speech.* Minister of Finance. Ottawa: Department of Finance, Canada.

_____. **(1994b)** *Agenda: Jobs and Growth - Creating a Healthy Fiscal Climate,* Ottawa: Department of Finance.

_____. **(1995)** *Canada Pension Plan Fifteenth Actuarial Report as at December 31, 1993.* Ottawa: Office of the Superintendent of Financial.

_____ . **(1996a)** *Budget Speech.* Minister of Finance. Ottawa: Department of Finance, Canada.

_____. **(1996b)** *A Report to the Department of Finance of Quantitative Research on Pension Issues.* Earnscliffe Research & Communications (1996) *Ottawa:* Department of Finance.

_____. **(1996c)** *An Information Paper for Consultations on the Canada Pension Plan.* Ottawa: Department of Finance. February 1996.

_____. **(1997)** *Securing the Canada Pension Plan: Agreement on Proposed Changes to the CPP.* Ottawa: Department of Finance. February 1997.

_____. **(2000a)** *The Budget in Brief.* Minister of Finance. Ottawa: Department of Finance Canada.

_____. **(2000b)** *Canada Pension Plan: Old Age Security: Statistical Bulletin.* March 2000. Ottawa: Human Resources Development Canada.

_____. **(2000c)** *Canadian Attitudes Toward the Public Pension Plan and Planning.* Submitted by Ekos Associates Inc. Ottawa. Ottawa: Human Resources Development Canada.

Government of the United Kingdom (1998a) *We all need pensions – the prospects for pension provision.* Report by The Pension Provision Group. London: Department of Social Security.

_____. **(1998b)** *A New Contract for Welfare: Partnership in Pensions.* London: Department of Social Security.

_____. **(2000)** *The Changing Welfare State: Pensioner Incomes.* London: Department of Social Security, Paper No. 2.

Hamilton, Malcolm (1999) *Canada's Retirement Income System or How our Safety Net Became a Mattress.* Presentation to the annual meeting of the Canadian Pension and Benefits Institute.

Heller, Peter S. (1998) *Rethinking Public Pension Reform Initiatives.* Washington: International Monetary Fund, Fiscal Affairs Department. Paper presented at the APEC Regional Forum on Pension Fund Reforms, Cancun, Mexico, February 4-6, 1998.

Henwood, Doug (1999) *TV on Social Security: It's Broke, Fix It.* Fairness and Accuracy In Reporting (FAIR) Extra! New York: www.fair.org

Hutton, Will (1996) *The State We're In.* London: Vintage Books.

International Social Security Association (1998) *The Social Security Reform Debate: In Search of a New Consensus."* Geneva.

James, Steven (1997) *A Public versus a Private Canada Pension Plan: A Survey of the Economics.* Ottawa: Department of Finance Canada, Economic Studies and Policy Analysis Division. Working Paper 97-04.

Johnson, Paul (1996) "The Anatomy of the 'Old Age Crisis'," in *Ageing and Social Policy.* Edited by Peter Lloyd-Sherlock and Paul Johnson. London: Suntory and Toyota International Centres for Economics and Related Disciplines, London School of Economics.

Kay, Stephen J. (1997) "The Chile Con: Privatizing Social Security in America." In *The American Prospect Online, July-Aug, 1997. www.prospect.org/archives/33/33kayfs.html*

Kotlikoff, Lawrence J. (1993) *Generational Accounting: Knowing Who Pays, and When, For What We Spend.* New York: Free Press.

KPMG (1999) *18th Annual Canadian Survey of Economic Expectations.* Toronto: KPMG Actuarial, Benefits & Compensation Inc.

Kuttner, Robert (1998) "Rampant Bull" in *The American Prospect.* July-August 1998. At http://www.prospect.org/archives/39/39kuttfs.html

Leone, Richard C. and Greg Anrig, Jr. Editors. (1999) *Social Security Reform: Beyond the Basics.* New York: The Century Foundation Press.

Leone, Richard C. (1999) "Why Boomers Don't Spell Bust," in *Social Security Reform.* Edited by Richard C. Leone and Greg Anrig, Jr. New York: The Century Foundation Press.

Lloyd-Sherlock, Peter (1996) "The Roles of the Public and Private Sectors in Providing Economic Support for the Elderly," in *Ageing and Social Policy.* Edited by Peter Lloyd-Sherlock and Paul Johnson. London: Suntory and Toyota International Centres for Economics and Related Disciplines, London School of Economics.

Lloyd-Sherlock, Peter and Paul Johnson, Editors. (1996) *Ageing and Social Policy.* London: Suntory and Toyota International Centres for Economics and Related Disciplines, London School of Economics.

MacDonald, J. Bruce (1995) *An Actuarial Monograph on the Canada Pension Plan.* Halifax: J. Bruce MacDonald, Consulting Actuary. (Prepared for the Minister of Human Resources Development Canada.)

MacNaughton, John A. (2000a) *Building the CPP Investment Board.* Remarks to the Rotary Club of Windsor, April 10, 2000.

_____. **(2000b)** *Remarks to the Pension Investment Association of Canada Conference,* May 4, 2000. Toronto: Canada Pension Plan Investment Board.

Mashaw, Jerry L. and Theodore R. Marmor (1996) "The Great Social Security Scare" in the *American Prospect,* Nov-Dec, 1996. http://www.prospect.org/archives/29/29mash.html

Mesa-Lago, Carmelo and Alberto Arenas de Mesa (1998) "The Chilean Pension System – Evaluation, Lessons and Challenges," in *Do Options Exist? Reform of Pension and Health Care Systems in Latin America.* Edited by Maria Amparo Cruz-Saco and Carmelo Mesa-Lago. Pittsburgh: University of Pittsburgh Press.

Messinger, Hans and Brian J. Powell (1987) "The Implications of Canada's Aging Society on Social Expenditures," in *Aging in Canada: Social Perspectives.* Edited by Victor W. Marshall. Second Edition. Toronto: Fitzhenry & Whiteside.

Morton, Peter (1998) "Private pensions give Sun Life springboard into Chilean market," *Financial Post,* October 22, 1998, p. 24.

Mullan, Phil (2000) *The Imaginary Time Bomb: Why an Ageing Population is not a Social Problem.* London: I.B.Tauris Publishers.

Murphy, Brian (1998) "The Impacts of Changing Tax/Transfer Systems on the 'Lifetime" Distribution of Net Taxes: 1984 to 1995," in *Government Finances and Generational Equity.* Edited by Miles Corak. Ottawa: Statistics Canada Catalogue no. 68-513-XIB.

Murthi, Mamta, Orszag, J. Michael, and Orszag, Peter (1999) *The Charge Ratio on Individual Accounts: Lessons from the U.K. Experience.* London: Birkbeck College, University of London, Department of Economics.

Myles, John and Paul Pierson (1999) "The Comparative Political Economy of Pension Reform," forthcoming in *The New Politics of the Welfare State.* Edited by Paul Pierson. Oxford; Oxford University Press.

Myles, John (2000) *The Maturation of Canada's Retirement Income System: Income Levels, Income Inequality and Low-Income among the Elderly.* Ottawa: Statistics Canada.

Office of Fair Trading (1997) *Report of the Director General's Inquiry into Pensions.* London, England: July 1997.

Office of the Superintendent of Financial Institutions (1998) *Canada Pension Plan Seventeenth Actuarial Report as at December 31, 1997.* Ottawa: Finance Canada.

Organization for Economic Co-operation and Development (1994) *The OECD Jobs Study: Taxation, Employment and Unemployment.* Paris.

Orszag, Peter R. and Joseph E, Stiglitz, (1999) *Rethinking Pension Reform: Ten Myths About Social Security Systems.* Presentation to the conference on "New Ideas About Old Age Security," September 14-15, 1999. Washington: The World Bank.

Orszag, Peter (2000) *Impact of 2 Percent Individual Accounts on Social Security Solvency.* Washington: Center on Budget and Policy Priorities. May 15, 2000.

Osberg, Lars (1998) "Meaning and Measurement in Intregenerational Equity," in Statistics Canada (1998) *Government Finances and Generational Equity.* Edited by Miles Corak. Ottawa: Statistics Canada Catalogue no. 68-513-XIB.

Personal Investment Authority (1998) *Survey of Persistency of Life and Pension Policies.* London: October 1998.

Pesando, James (1997) *From Tax Grab to Retirement Saving: Privatizing the CPP Premium Hike.* Toronto: C.D.Howe Institute Commentary No. 93, June 1997.

Piñera, José (no date) "Give Workers a Free Choice." Washington: The Cato Institute. http://www.cato.org

Prus, Steven G. (1999) *Income Inequality as a Canadian Cohort Ages: An Analysis of the Later Life Course.* Hamilton, Ontario: McMaster University Program for Research on Social and Economic Dimensions of an Aging Population. SEDAP Research Paper No. 10.

Queisser, Monika (1999) *Pension Reform: Lessons from Latin America.* Paris: OECD Policy Brief No. 15.

Rasell, Edith and Jeff Faux (1999) *Fixing Social Security: The Clinton Plan and Its Alternatives.* Washington: Economic Policy Institute. Briefing Paper. April 1999.

Reform Party (1995*) Renewing CPP.* Ottawa: October 1995.

_____. **(1998)** *Can Your Pension Be Saved? Should you have the choice to take control of your own retirement?* Ottawa: Reform Party and at www.reform.ca.

Ritter, Archibald R.M. (1992) *Development strategy and structural adjustment in Chile: From the Unidad Popular to the Concertacion, 1970-92.* Ottawa: The North South Institute.

Robson, William B.P. (1996a) *Putting Some Gold in the Golden Years: Fixing the Canada Pension Plan.* Toronto: C.D.Howe Institute. Commentary No. 76, January 1996.

_____. **(1996b)** "Ponzi's Pawns: Young Canadians and the Canada Pension Plan," *When We're 65: Reforming Canada's Retirement Income System.* Toronto: C.D.Howe Institute.

_____. **(1999)** *Precarious Pyramid: the Economics and Politics of the CPP.* Toronto: C.D.Howe Institute. Paper presented at the Institute for Public Economics Conference "A Separate Pension plan for Alberta?" Edmonton, 22 January1999

Samuelson, Paul (1958) "An Exact Consumption-Loan Model of Interest with or without the Social Contrivance of Money," *Journal of Political Economy*, December 1958.

Schultz, James H. (1999) "Saving, Growth, and Social Security: Fighting Our Children Over Shares of the Future Economic Pie?" in *Social Security Reform.* Edited by Richard C. Leone and Greg Anrig, Jr. New York: The Century Foundation Press.

Sinha, Tapen (2000) *Rich man's solution to a Poor man's Problem: A View from the South.* Mexico City: Instituto Tecnologico Autonomo de Mexico (ITAM), Department of Actuarial Studies.

Slater, David W. and William B.P.Robson (1999) *Building a Stronger Pillar: The Changing Shape of the Canada Pension Plan.* Toronto: C.D.Howe Institute.

Social Security Administration (1999) *Will Social Security Be There For You?* Washington: Social Security Administration Publication No. 05-10055. February 1999.

_____. **(2000a)** *The 2000 Annual Report of the Board of Trustees of the Federal Old-Age and Survivors Insurance and Disability Insurance Trust Funds.* Washington, D.C. Social Security Administration.

_____. **(2000b)** *Status of the Social Security and Medicare Programs – A Summary of the 2000 Annual Reports.* Washington, D.C. Social Security and Medicare Boards of Trustees. April 2000.

Statistics Canada (1995) *The Daily,* Ottawa: October 24, 1995.

_____. **(1998)** *Government Finances and Generational Equity.* Edited by Miles Corak. Ottawa: Statistics Canada Catalogue no. 68-513-XIB.

_____. **(1999a)** *Income Distributions by Size in Canada, 1997.* Catalogue 13-207-XPB.

_____. **(1999b)** *A Portrait of Seniors in Canada, Third Edition.* Catalogue 89-519-XPE.

Tanner, Michael (no date) "Tom Daschle's Very Bad Idea" from the Chicago Tribune. Washington: The Cato Institute.

Tonks, Ian (1999) *Pensions Policy in the UK.* Bristol: University of Bristol, Centre for Market and Public Organisation.

Towers Perrin (1998) *European Active Investment Management Charges.* London, England: Towers Perrin, August 1997.

Townson, Monica (1997a) *Protecting Public Pensions.* Ottawa: Canadian Centre for Policy Alternatives.

_____. **(1997b)** *Non-standard work: The implications for pension policy and retirement readiness.* Ottawa: Women's Bureau, Human Resources Development Canada. Unpublished.

Willmore, Larry (1998) *Social Security and the Provision of Retirement Income.* Discussion Paper PI 9805. London: The Pensions Institute, Birkbeck College University of London.

Wolfson, Michael and Brian Murphy (1997) "Aging and Canada's Public Sector: Retrospect and Prospect," in Keith Banting and Robin Boadway (Eds.) *Reform of Retirement Income Policy: International and Canadian Perspectives,* Kingston, Ontario: Queen's University, School of Policy Studies.

Wolfson, M.C., Rowe, G., Lin, X., and Gribble, S.F. (1998) "Historical Generational Accounting with Heterogeneous Populations," in *Government Finances and Generational Equity.* Edited by Miles Corak. Ottawa: Statistics Canada Catalogue no. 68-513-XIB.

World Bank (1994) *Averting the Old Age Crisis.* A World Bank Policy Research Report. New York: Oxford University Press.

Zuckerman, Diana (2000) *The Derailing of Social Security: How Cato and Heritage paved the way for privatization.* Fairness and Accuracy in reporting (FAIR) New York: www.fair.org

Index